Your Career
in the
Comics

Your Career in the Comics

by Lee Nordling
for the Newspaper Features Council

ANDREWS AND MCMEEL
A Universal Press Syndicate Company
Kansas City

03 04 05 06 EDB 7 6 5 4

Library of Congress Cataloging-in-Publication Data

Nordling, Lee.
   Your career in the comics / by Lee Nordling for the Newspaper
Features Council
      p. cm.
   Appendices include cartoonist, syndicate and newspaper biographies and a
list of cartoonist organizations, schools, and museums.
   Includes bibliographical references.
   ISBN: 0-8362-0748-3 (pbk.)
   1. Cartooning—Vocational guidance—United States.   I. Newspaper
Features Council (U.S.)   II. Title.
NC1320.N62   1995   95-19026
741.5'023'73—dc20   CIP

Attention: Schools and Businesses
Andrews and McMeel books are available at quantity discounts with bulk purchase for educational, business, or sales promotional use. For information, please write to Special Sales Department, Andrews and McMeel, 4520 Main Street, Kansas City, Missouri 64111.

Credits
BABY BLUES © Baby Blues Partnership. Distributed by King Features Syndicate. Reprinted with permission.
BEETLE BAILEY © King Features Syndicate Inc. Reprinted with permission.
B.C. © Creators Syndicate Inc. Reprinted with permission.
CALVIN AND HOBBES © Watterson. Reprinted with permission of Universal Press Syndicate. All rights reserved.
CATHY © Cathy Guisewite. Reprinted with permission of Universal Press Syndicate. All rights reserved.
DENNIS THE MENACE © 1995 North America Syndicate. Reprinted with permission of Hank Ketcham and NAS.
FOR BETTER OR FOR WORSE © Lynn Johnston Productions Inc. Reprinted with permission of Universal Press Syndicate. All rights reserved.
FOXTROT © Bill Amend. Reprinted with permission of Universal Press Syndicate. All rights reserved.
HERB & JAMAAL © 1995 Tribune Media Services Inc. Reprinted with permission.
MOTHER GOOSE & GRIMM © 1995 Grimmy Inc. Distributed by Tribune Media Services. Reprinted with permission.
NON SEQUITUR © 1995 Washington Post Writers Group. Reprinted with permission.
PEANUTS © United Feature Syndicate Inc. Reprinted with special permission of United Feature Syndicate Inc.
PLUGGERS © 1995 Pluggers Inc. Distributed by Tribune Media Services. Reprinted with permission.
SHOE © 1995 Tribune Media Services Inc. Reprinted with permission.
SINGLE SLICES © 1995 Peter Kohlsaat. Distributed by Los Angeles Times Syndicate.
SYLVIA © 1995 Nicole Hollander. Reprinted with permission.

Contents

FOREWORD

Founded in 1955 as the Newspaper Comics Council, the group expanded in 1986 to include columnists and changed its name to the Newspaper Features Council, Inc. This professional, nonprofit organization contains a membership roster of syndicated cartoonists and columnists, newspaper editors and syndicate executives.

The Newspaper Features Council provides a unique forum to discuss mutual concerns, exchange information, identify trends and formulate projects to support syndicated features. It also strives to create better published products for the newspaper readership.

It accomplishes this through annual meetings, exhibits, studies, seminars, scholarships, awards, charity and community projects and by publishing artwork and material related to the field of syndication.

This book is part of the council's dedication to providing information about syndication to aspiring cartoonists.

Catherine Walker

ACKNOWLEDGMENTS

All good stories have a beginning, a middle, and an end. At the beginning of this story . . . I'm deeply indebted to Steve Christensen for prompting and promoting me, and for helping to shape the structure of this book. However, without the additional support of Rick Newcombe, Ron Patel and the Newspaper Features Council, the journey of writing this book would have remained just another bar conversation.

In the middle of this story . . . I owe a special thanks to my wife, Cheri, for taking time out from her writing schedule to transcribe thirty-nine interviews, many at such low recording levels that I don't know another human being with enough stubbornness and stamina to listen over and over again to a section of tape while trying to understand each word.

To continue the second act . . . I must acknowledge Robert Reed, Catherine Walker, Bill Janocha, Charles Solomon, Marv Wolfman, David Seidman, Corinta N.C. Kotula, editor Jake Morrissey, and the forty cartoonists, representatives, syndicate executives and newspaper editors who gave honestly and sincerely of themselves to contribute to this book. Without them, there wouldn't be a book.

At the end of this story . . . Gordon Kent has been the fastest back-seat driver of a rough draft anyone could ask for. He showed me where I was coherent, but only coherent; he showed me where I could make my points even better; and he showed where I was speaking in tongues.

I also owe a sincere appreciation to Lee Falk, who has helped me with his insight and supported me with his understanding.

Lastly, thanks to all my friends and relatives who've ridden shotgun for me over the years, and most recently the Everetts, who probably still don't believe we now live on the same coast.

I dedicate this book to my parents, Stan and Virginia, my brother, Dennis, and most of all to my life partner, Cheri. I love you all.

INTRODUCTION

Shangri-La. Camelot. Utopia. Just because you want to go there doesn't mean you can find a flight.

I know. I tried.Want to be a brain surgeon or rocket scientist without being told how to do it? It's tricky.

I know. I tried.

("No no no! Put that squishy part back where it belongs and do the lobotomy right!")

Cartooning may not be brain surgery, but don't let that fool you, because brain surgery's not cartooning, either. Still, they have one thing in common. You can jump into brain surgery and syndicated cartooning without any talent (aptitude), education and training, but I wouldn't recommend it. The results—in both cases—can be really sloppy, especially in the area of cartooning. That isn't to say you couldn't be a success in either field, but two successful lobotomies (or well-executed dailies) in a row are very unlikely.

TALENT IS WHAT YOU CAN USE, ABUSE OR OVERCOME.

At fifteen, I wanted to be a cartoonist. I made a couple bucks copying Big Daddy Roth drawings onto T-shirts, and a girl in biology class giggled at the cartoons I passed to her. Did that mean I had talent, or *enough* talent to "make it"?

There's no yardstick to hold up and determine whether cartoonists "have what it takes to make it" or whether they're "wasting their time." It doesn't exist—at least not on a pass/fail basis.

I suspect "the fulfillment of talent" has something to do with Edison's 1 percent inspiration/99 percent perspiration quotient. However, I don't believe anyone can point to somebody and say, "You do (or do not) have *enough* talent to catch the big brass ring of syndication's success, fame and fortune."

That's because the big brass ring is a slippery and unpredictable little sucker.

EDUCATION IS THE BRIDGE BETWEEN HOW THINGS WENT LAST TIME AND HOW THINGS SHOULD GO NEXT TIME.

Once upon a time, in a world I never knew, many young cartoonists learned the craft of cartooning while working on the staffs of newspapers and magazines. Others began by freelancing their cartoons to ravenous publications. Fledgling strips and panels were cultivated and sometimes given years to develop.

◆ ◆ ◆

When I started, it was a whole different story. It's a story that could take place today.

1967—I took a drawing class in the tenth grade and creative writing in eleventh (and got a "C" I'd still like to discuss with the teacher). Education of a sort, granted, but I had a tough time turning it toward my ambitions as a cartoonist.

In the twelfth grade, something wonderful happened. A respected English teacher—whose advanced-placement classes were far beyond my reach (or interest)—liked the strips I wrote and drew for the high school paper. Other kids said they wished *they* could draw cartoons.

I was a hit. A star!

So when my journalism teacher wouldn't let me sign my name to a series of cartoon ads I created for the local gas station, I was stunned.

"Schulz signs his ads," I whined.

"And you can sign yours," Mrs. Byan snapped, "when *you're* as famous as Charles Schulz."

Now *that* was an education! If my name had been a drawing card, she'd have *begged* me to sign my cartoons. If she needed me more than I needed her, I'd have gotten my way through a sheer battle of wills. If I had a contract, this wouldn't have been an issue. If I hadn't been such a pouty, self-absorbed little putz, I might have been able to get her to do me a favor. But I didn't realize any of this, because it wasn't printed between the covers of a book called *Cartooning—Lee Nordling's Personal Guide to Getting What He Wants.*

(By the way, if you see that book, pick it up for me.)

It was a long time before I realized the different forms education can take.

◆ ◆ ◆

I went to San Jose State University and ended up in the advertising department. The program blended concept, writing, art and design. For a career in cartooning, this combination of skills was the closest thing I could find to education or training. There were no other avenues open to me, nothing that said, "This is what you need to learn to be a cartoonist."

I read books on the history of comic strips, and that gave me some perspective.

I read every cartoon collection I could lay my hands on, trying to figure out where they went right.

I read the comic page every day, analyzing why a strip worked, why a strip didn't work and what a strip that didn't work could've done to work. (I took this exercise very seriously and still recommend it as a daily ritual.)

I developed all sorts of theories about a new type of strip that would pop on a comics page (editorially and visually), the merits of the four-panel gag versus the three-panel gag, the visual pacing of the stage-bound strip versus the "cinematic" strip and the appeal factor of characters with big round eyes (this was pre-*Garfield*).

However, the disadvantage of being an entirely self-taught cartoonist is that education and its practical application may or may not have something to do with one another. Without guidelines, self-teaching is very much like trying to find your way with an unlabeled street map. If you're fortunate enough to get somewhere, it doesn't mean if you really knew where you were going.

While in college, I was fortunate enough to meet Charles Schulz; then, a few years out of college, Mell Lazarus. I can't say I understood their advice but, in hindsight, it was the right advice. I simply didn't understand the craft or business of being a syndicated cartoonist well enough to follow it. I was certainly less savvy than some (most?), but how could I apply professional advice when I didn't really know what it meant to be a professional?

Schulz and Lazarus gave me on-the-nose insights that are covered extensively throughout this book, but how do you apply advice like "write what you know," when no one taught you *how* to tap into your own observations on the way people behave toward each other?

When the man says, "Your humor needs to come from your characters," what's he talking about? Aren't the word balloons pointing to the characters? Don't the punch lines twist? What's wrong with puns? I *like* puns.

It took years to discover that humor needs to rise out of the personal idiosyncrasies a cartoonist creates in his characters (and if you haven't created them, create them). Characters need to be put in situations that stimulate what is unique to their personalities. Ideally, those unique responses will be humorous.

For example, which is a funnier situation: Calvin promises to tell the truth for a whole day, or Snoopy promises to tell the truth for a whole day?

When you know your characters, you'll know what kind of roadblocks to stick in front of them.

◆ ◆ ◆

The newspaper syndicate was (and still is) a very mysterious place. It's where you send your strip samples, then pray for something other than a printed reply.

In the early years, I knew my work was improving when editors started writing personalized rejection slips.

Once, a syndicate held onto my strip for ten months, and I was encouraged. I thought that meant they couldn't bring themselves to say "no." Actually, it meant the sample had been shoved twenty thousand leagues under somebody's submission pile, and I'd been foolish enough to call politely only once every two months to ask about it. Finally, I told the editor how long I'd been waiting. Two weeks later, I received a call and a very sincere apology, along with the rejection. That's when I knew I was making real progress. I'd made personal contact with a syndicate editor, and he was giving me feedback.

I had a relationship!

I expected the editor-I-have-a-relationship-with to pick out twenty-five or thirty of the forty-two strips in my sample and say, "Keep these in, write some more, and you're on your way." If that didn't happen (and surprise, surprise, it didn't), at least he could say: "Oh, bad luck, sport! Cat strips are out of fashion this year. Why don't you try something with a fish?"

I was convinced syndicate editors knew exactly what type of strip they wanted and were just waiting for me to figure it out.

"We have a winner! Nordling's surveyed our list, pinpointed our editorial Achilles' heel and given us a gag strip in a historical period that someone hasn't done yet." Or "Hey, look, guys! Just what we need—a Gary Larson knockoff!"

I had one other hope: Let the syndicate team me up with an artist or a writer. Yup, I know it sounds like a quote from Segar's Wimpy ("Let's you and him be partners"), but it made sense to me. The editor-I-have-a-relationship-with receives a submission from another cartoonist and says: "Eureka! If we combine this strip with Nordling's writing (or art), we'll have a winner."

Was I naive to think any of this might happen? Of course. Mind-numbingly naive? Absolutely. But remember, I didn't have any other measure for success or failure, short of syndication or no syndication.

I wasn't a single-panel cartoonist who could submit gags to the decreasing magazine market.

I wasn't (at that time) a comic book writer or cartoonist who could sell to the major comic book companies or the (then-burgeoning) underground comics market.

I was an unsold syndicated cartoonist in one of the most highly competitive markets of all. For years, I created strip sample after strip sample, polishing my ability to create and package forty-two well-balanced strips, daily and Sunday, convinced that all I needed was the opportunity to show more.

Once, early on, I received a syndication contract from a small eastern syndicate.

My wife, Cheri, and I celebrated and went out for an expensive dinner.

Sure, the contract had some problems. My lawyer said the syndicate wanted my first-born male child and, yes, I could conceivably owe it money at the end of the contract period.

But I was too nervous to call. What if I offended the editors by mentioning the problems in the contract and blew the deal? Afraid of a face-to-face (or even phone-to-phone) encounter/confrontation, I sent back the contract with lines crossed out, notes scribbled on the margins, all the changes initialed and a letter explaining everything I wanted and how much I was looking forward to working with them.

The syndicate responded with a letter, saying how sorry it was that the contract had been unacceptable.

And that was it.

I didn't call to find out what went wrong, because I figured I'd already irreparably blown it. Maybe I had. But hindsight says I'd have been better off establishing a personal relationship with someone there in the first place, discussing the points of contention in the contract and finding out where the syndicate was flexible. Then, if there were still any deal-breakers, we could have parted ways in a more professional manner.

So what did I learn from this heartbreaking experience? Next time, do your celebrating at McDonald's.

◆ ◆ ◆

I didn't work on a syndicated strip for another six or seven years.

By then, I'd published cartoons in a few weekly papers and magazines, spent several years on the board of C.A.P.S. (The Comic Art Professional Society, a Los Angeles–based group), worked as a comic art packager for Mattel Toys and the art director of the Los Angeles Times Syndicate.

Finally, I became a staff comic strip writer at the Walt Disney Company.

So here I was, part of a team of six cartoonists, writing gags for several different strips, learning to write for fifty gazillion different characters, learning to structure my week, learning to explore the potential of a comic strip universe and learning to be self-critical (before the other staff writers got their shot at me).

In short, like most cartoonists today, I started publishing strips without any extended experience as a professional. It was like being handed a scalpel, a book called *How to Perform a Lobotomy,* and a patient stretched out on an operating table.

And the patient was expected to live.

REAL TRAINING IS HAVING THE OPPORTUNITY TO BOUNCE BACK FROM MISTAKES. (ON-THE-JOB TRAINING IS HOPING YOU DON'T GET BOUNCED OUT THE DOOR.)

In that land of long ago, assistants spent years learning their craft, taking direction from cartoonists and art directors, lettering, filling in blacks, inking, contributing in gag sessions, whatever was needed, until finally they sold a strip of their own.

For others, magazine cartooning became the stepping-off point into syndication, and by then, most of them were seasoned pros. They'd already established their daily regimens of creating new material. They knew how to cull the stronger work from the weaker work, make a deadline, then move on to the next deadline.

Today, most newly syndicated cartoonists face a tough combination of challenges that all strike at once. They need to be consistently brilliant (but not "too weird"), flexible (without sending the lamb to slaughter) and on time (without incurring a lot of extra FedEx charges). They also have to know what's expected of them as professionals (without a *Syndicated Cartoonist's Introductory Handbook*), open lines of communication with their editors (so they can be allies, rather than antagonists) and grow as writers and artists (without losing touch with their strips).

In short, most training for the syndicated cartoonist is on-the-job training, and the introductory experience can be quite like a birth, where the cartoonist is brought kicking and screaming into a world that slaps him on the fanny and says, "We love ya, but get a job, ya bum!"

That's a lot to go through, and it all happens *after* the multiyear contract is signed.

There are other fields that can lay the groundwork for a prospective syndicated cartoonist, but many of these fields are just as difficult to enter, most notably editorial cartooning. Other fields include: self-syndication (where you get to learn even *more* all at once), magazine cartooning (a continually shrinking market), greeting cards, comic books, animation and storyboarding.

Ultimately, the contemporary syndicated cartoonist may just learn to do things the hard way . . . with one mistake after another.

WHY WILLIAM GOLDMAN IS RIGHT.

Taking talent, education, experience and effort into account, it may be easier for some than others to achieve the goal of syndication. Still, there are few instances where absolute success or failure can be certifiably predicted.

William Goldman once wrote, "Nobody knows anything." He said that about film industry professionals being able to predict box-office success, but I think it's also true in the business of newspaper syndication.

Tomorrow (and I guarantee it . . . I *know* it), some wonderful, truly inspired strip won't click with a large enough audience, some truly average strip will hit the merchandising mother lode, and some truly amateurish strip will tickle somebody's cerebral cortex and get syndicated. Then the day after tomorrow, the reverse will also be true.

So, if nobody knows anything, why listen to what anybody says about your work? The answer to this one's up to you.

Personally, I'd rather build on my education than coast on my naïveté or my opinion. With labels on a map, I have a better chance of finding the destination I'm aiming for, whether it be Shangri-La or Miami Beach.

This book is intended to be *your* street map. Yes, one with labels. I can't promise *all* the streets will be labeled, or that having this map assures your arrival at your chosen destination.

But it's the map I wish I'd had with me.

Lee Nordling
Stamford, Conn.
May 1995

Part 1—The Players

> *You can't tell the players without a program.*
> —*Unknown ballpark vendor*

On the face of it, newspaper syndication has three completely different casts of characters—from role players to stars—with completely separate functions. Underlying these functions are the needs for the symbiotic relationship that keeps them tied together.

On the face of it, cartoonists produce comic strips and comic panels. Underlying them are the abilities and drive required to produce these features.

On the face of it, syndicates distribute comic strips and panels, as well as other material. Underlying this are the challenges they face in launching new features and retaining old features.

On the face of it, newspapers purchase comic strips and panels. Underlying this are the realities of publishing material in a shrinking industry.

Somewhere, the efforts of the cartoonist, the syndicate, the newspaper, and occasionally the literary representative—each with their own separate set of agendas—cross paths. When they do, millions of people read the product of these efforts every day.

The purpose of this section is to explore the mingling of art and commerce required by the three principal players of newspaper comic syndication. As you're squished between sensibililties, in much the same way Charlie Chaplin was run between the cogs in *Modern Times,* please remember these discussions are not intended to teach the process of being a cartoonist, syndicate employee or newspaper features editor. They are intended to view this process.

So keep your distance.

Do not accommodate other people's sensibilies. Understand them, then absorb them.

Do not overanalyze. Look in the mirror and fix what you see.

And never, never, never, never, never rationalize why the "good stuff" we discuss about professional cartoonists applies to you, but the "bad stuff" we discuss about beginning cartoonists doesn't.

THE SYNDICATED CARTOONIST

If we go back to the beginning days of cartooning, we find that most of the men came out of newspaper jobs. Then, just before World War II and right after, almost all of the cartoonists—Hank Ketcham, Mort Walker, Johnny Hart and others—came out of magazine cartooning. There were fewer jobs on newspapers, so we all got our start selling to magazines. Where people are coming from these days, I don't know. In fact, I think they are coming out of nowhere.

—CHARLES SCHULZ, *PEANUTS*

I think a lot of people have aspirations or dreams of being a writer or a photographer or a cartoonist or an actor, and a lot of them get scared about ever doing anything about it. They don't pursue it, because these aspirations they've had all their lives have been in the vacuum of fantasy. Once you start taking steps toward making it a reality, it gets really scary, mainly because reality will never, ever live up to fantasy.

When you're young and you're reading the comics, and you say, "Oh, God, wouldn't it be great to be a cartoonist," all you see is that cartoon sitting there. It's already done. You don't realize what it took to get that cartoon done and put there every day.

It looks easy, but that's one of the things a cartoonist is trying to do. It's supposed to look easy. When you see Barry Bonds at bat, knocking the ball out of the ballpark, it looks easy.

"Well, shit—I can do that." Well, no, you can't.

It's the same thing with cartooning. It's just silly little drawings. What's the big deal? Well, here's a piece of paper. Show me how damned easy it is. You did one cartoon. Okay, do another, and another, and another, and another.

There are realities that have to be made clear. Cartooning is a business. There are deadlines. You can't just do the cartoons when you feel like it, or wait for inspiration. You make the inspiration.

Charles Schulz had a very good line, many years ago, when he was asked about writer's block. He said that writer's block is for amateurs. If you're a professional, you don't get writer's block, especially if you can't afford to.

WILEY MILLER, *NON SEQUITUR*

The challenge of an artist is to put stuff down on paper on a regular basis. People like me, who had some interest in cartooning all along, were never suited to be cartoonists, because I simply didn't have the drive to want to put it down on paper every day. And you can't sit back and think about it. You have to actually do it.

—JAY KENNEDY, KING FEATURES

Really, what makes the job interesting are the creative challenges.

—BILL AMEND, *FOXTROT*

THE ANATOMY OF THE CARTOONIST

The many-headed Hydra and the cartoonist have a lot in common, but Hercules never killed a cartoonist.

—SMART-ASS AUTHOR OF THIS BOOK

It's often been said that the cartoonist needs to be the writer, director, director of photography, cameraman, script supervisor, property master, casting agent and actors, all rolled into one. This takes a multitude of talent and abilities, but saves a bundle on catering truck service.

There are three essential skills a cartoonist must have: strong drawing skills—the art in a comic has to be high quality; very strong writing skills; the ability to be funny.

—ANITA TOBIAS, CREATORS SYNDICATE

The most important skill and talent for a cartoonist is a sense of humor and/or a better-than-average ability to draw. I'm saying "and/or" because obviously, in some cases, one can carry the other. I think the writing carries the drawing, because what do you have if you don't have an idea? You just draw pictures. This is the Sun and that's the house.

—JOHNNY HART, *B.C.* AND *THE WIZARD OF ID*

When kids study art, they should study design, they should study drama, they should participate in theater, they should learn to take good photographs. These aspects all come into play when you sit down to fill up a space. It's so important, and very few people have done it.

—HANK KETCHAM, DENNIS THE MENACE

It's awfully important to be able to communicate your thoughts well in words, and also convey them in pictures.

I think also it is helpful for a cartoonist to have some sort of acting ability. I don't mean necessarily any stage experience, but I think it is fairly important to be able to throw yourself into the shoes of the characters and think as they would think, in terms of the words they would say and the body language they would send.

I think it is also helpful for a cartoonist to have a broad range of interests. I'm always telling young cartoonists, don't just study art. Take math class. Take history. Study foreign language. When you have the responsibility of doing a strip day after day after day after day, the bigger the pool of information that's in your head to draw upon, the better off you are.

I'm not sure how the humor process works in the brain, but I think part of being creative is the ability to link not obviously connected elements together and forge them with the random chunks of data you've got floating around in your skull. Some combinations work, some combinations don't. So the more combinations there are—like Tinkertoys—the better your chances are that it will be interesting.

—BILL AMEND, FOXTROT

THE ANATOMY OF THE CARTOONIST

TALENT

The cliché: Talent—either you got it or you don't.

The reality: Talent—if you got it, great, but if it can't be seen, that doesn't mean it can't be cultivated. On the other hand, it doesn't mean it will be cultivated, either.

The talent to be a syndicated cartoonist is multifaceted. It may burst out so strongly in one area—such as writing—that it compensates for other areas as they struggle to develop and catch up.

The important thing to remember is that talent is a rough, uncut diamond that needs to be polished with years and years of hard work.

I think that talent actually has to speak for itself. People can't give you a job because they owe you a favor. There's just too much at stake.
—LYNN JOHNSTON, FOR BETTER OR FOR WORSE

<u>THE ANATOMY OF THE CARTOONIST</u>

ORIGINALITY

Originality is a double-edged sword. Just because editors and readers listen for a new voice crying out from the masses doesn't mean they're willing to listen to someone speaking in tongues.

If you discover you're "too original" for the medium of newspaper comics, rather than trying to adjust or compromise your originality, you may be better off trying another medium.

However, if you're comfortable swimming in the waters of newspaper syndication, don't do the same old backstroke, butterfly or breaststroke. Find a way to swim that only you can do, because there are a lot of people out there doing the dog paddle.

I think that the cartoonist who is not imitating and who moves into a fresh direction—even though the water is very deep—has a much better chance of success.
—TONI MENDEZ, LITERARY REPRESENTATIVE

Presuming you had ten submissions that were all professionally drawn and all well written, I think the ones that would tend to get the most interest at a syndicate and among newspaper editors are the ones that are different, the ones that are unusual.
—STEVE CHRISTENSEN, LOS ANGELES TIMES SYNDICATE

I keep the material fresh and individual. I fully believe that a cartoonist/writer, a guy who writes his own material, needs to do an individual job. He needs to do what he does best. He shouldn't try to fashion his feature for what he thinks the market needs or what the traffic will allow. He has to make his material his own. If he knows a particular subject, he should do his strip about that subject, and if he has a certain type of humor that is natural to him, do that. Don't pattern yourself after the current front-runners among cartoonists. So many young people do.

However, I fully believe there is nobody in the business who has not started out imitating somebody else. I know I did. I taught myself to draw by imitating the cartoonists in the New Yorker. *I even tried imitating Al Capp. He was so good. His drawing was so crisp and neat. George Lichty* (Grin and Bear It) *was, to me, the ultimate cartoonist.*

There are always your idols, but that doesn't say that you won't develop your own individuality, a combination of the art style and the humor and the presentation.

Most importantly, it has to be you yourself. It has to reflect your own personality and what you can do best.

—BIL KEANE, THE FAMILY CIRCUS

To make it nowadays, you need true originality. An editor at a newspaper has to decide whether or not to kill a comic strip to put a new comic strip in. Each time an editor takes a strip out, you get five hundred phone calls, and a new strip has to be really good to listen to five hundred phone calls. Even a bad strip that gets pulled gets phone calls. Somewhere, somebody thought it was the best thing in the world.

—JANE AMARI, THE KANSAS CITY STAR

THE ANATOMY OF THE CARTOONIST

THE POINT OF VIEW—LOOKING IN

If you say what you think, and not what you think you should say, then your work will be honest, and honesty's really the best policy. The alternative is having to live with a point of view and cast of characters you don't believe in, and this would be the equivolent of getting married to someone you don't care about and may grow to hate.

The point of view of a strip has to be honest. By that, I mean it has to flow from the cartoonist's personal experience.

—RICHARD NEWCOMBE, CREATORS SYNDICATE

I think whatever you do in your strip reflects your innermost soul, you might say. And if you are a lousy person, it is going to come out in the strip, some way or another. While you are in show business, and people do like the erratic, I think most people eventually respond to a good person, a person who is interested in them, a person who is interested in life.

—MORT WALKER, BEETLE BAILEY

You can't force it. I have said this to all kinds of young guys. You cannot mechanically produce a comic strip.

I honestly do believe—not for it to be depressing to young people who want to get into the business—that a cartoonist who has made it is analogous to the people who become superstars in the motion picture business. There is only one Paul Newman or one Robert Redford. One Clark Gable. But for every one of those, there's got to be twenty thousand or more who have aspired to be a Paul Newman or Robert Redford. So the odds are incredible.

By reason of that, unless it comes from within—and that doesn't mean it comes easy—the important thing is that it comes out, and you have the strength, and the perseverance, and the wherewithal—you know some people have to support a family—to continue to try and try and try and try.

—JOSEPH D'ANGELO, KING FEATURES

I don't think it's just artistic talent, although I think that's important. And I don't think it's simply understanding the marketplace, which is how I think syndicates often go wrong, because they try too hard to do that. I think it's having a certain kind of human insight, and then, of course, the ability to somehow convey that with humor.

—JAY AMBROSE, ROCKY MOUNTAIN NEWS

Cartooning is a point of view, a personal point of view. It's very autobiographical. It's your perspective that has to go on the page, and that is what ultimately makes a comic strip successful.

Greg Evans did a terrific piece for Cartoonist Profiles. He was talking about that very topic—a brilliant analogy—that when you're reading Calvin and Hobbes, *you're not reading* Calvin and Hobbes. *You're reading Bill Watterson. When you're reading* Peanuts, *you're not reading Charlie Brown. You're reading Charles Schulz. Their perspective, their ideas, are going to filter through their characters. That's what you have to develop, and that's what's going to be a success, not trying to do another version of* Blondie. Blondie *for the nineties.* Blondie *is already there.*

—WILEY MILLER, NON SEQUITUR

The Anatomy of the Cartoonist

THE POINT OF VIEW—LOOKING OUT

Try watching *Johnny Got His Gun* and you'll see what happens to a cognizant quadriplegic man who can't see, can't hear, can't speak and can't move. Johnny exists in a world of complete and utter darkness and comes to live for the sensation of sunlight on his skin. It is the most horrifying film I've ever seen in my life.

Try creating a feature that does not reflect the world you see and the world you hear, and that feature will live in the same darkness Johnny lives in. However, readers will not wait around for the sensation of sunlight on their skin.

The cartoonist has to pay attention. It's similar to what you do as an editorial cartoonist. You have to be reading, and keeping up with the news and with the changes of venue out there in the mirror of your life. A comic is really just an extension of yourself, your perspective, your point of view, and it's your take on today's world.

—WILEY MILLER, NON SEQUITUR

I think comic strip artists need to look at the front half of the paper, to see what's bothering us and what we're thinking about, to see that we're all talking about on-line systems or that the country has taken a conservative bent, and the smart artist will incorporate it.

As an artist you need to know that, because you need to know the milieu in which you work. It is not done in a vacuum, and if you don't change as the population changes and their interests change, then you don't look like you have any relevance.

—JANE AMARI, THE KANSAS CITY STAR

I think when you deal with political and cultural ideas, you need to be able to synthesize what you're reading and hearing into the strip format. You have to be able to edit and to absorb things quickly, and to hope that what you're interested in and talking about will stay around for the weeks that it takes the strip to reach the newspaper.

—NICOLE HOLLANDER, SYLVIA

The cartoonists' challenge is to find humor in the things around them in life. And in terms of where that comes from, I think their challenge is to not become so ghettoized that they only look at other cartoonists' work. If they can't experience life in many different ways, they should at least read about it and view it in other mediums.

—JAY KENNEDY, KING FEATURES

I think that the creator needs to be aware of what's going on in the world—even if the strip is not reflecting the current hard news events—and to be aware of pop culture. If he or she is aware, the strip takes on the sense of knowing contemporary topics.

—SUE SMITH, DALLAS MORNING NEWS

Cartoonists have to know what's happening in the world and inject that into their work.

If you're going to create in a small limited world, you're work will be repeating itself.

—TONI MENDEZ, LITERARY REPRESENTATIVE

You need to look current, both with problems and the way life is lived today. At the same time, you need to be entertaining.

—JANE AMARI, THE KANSAS CITY STAR

It is really important that cartoonists read and watch TV and talk to people.

The common mistake I see is that people decide to be a cartoonist pretty early on in life, and as a general rule a lot of them have an incestuous relationship with the art form. They know what they want by the time they're eight, so they just read other cartoons. And then all cartoons become derivative of other cartoons, and the whole art form spirals downward.

The better cartoonists are the ones who are getting inspiration from outside of other cartoons. It is wise to look at other cartoons to see the craft of it, but the inspiration should come from outside other cartoons.

—JAY KENNEDY, KING FEATURES

THE ANATOMY OF THE CARTOONIST

WRITING

In newspaper comics, writing is the process in which ideas are expressed, whether it be with a manuscript, notes jotted on a napkin or single or sequential images with or without captions and balloons.

The important thing is to determine the elements—the choice of images and the choice of words—that will communicate an idea. Making these determinations is the writing.

Cartoonists have always been thought of as artists first. I think the opposite is actually true. I think that great cartoonists are writers first.

They have the ability to store an idea or picture or pictures in maybe twenty-six syllables. That's really tough to do. Even if it's a pantomime, the writing's there. The idea is just everything. There're great comic strips that are beautifully drawn, and there are great comic strips that aren't so beautifully drawn, too.

—JERRY SCOTT, BABY BLUES AND NANCY

That's the funny part. I got into this just because I loved to draw. Then I found out that most of it is really writing, which terrifies me. I never thought of myself as a writer, but I kind of turned into one, over the years. Bill Maulden once said—specifically about political cartoons—"a really great idea doesn't necessarily need great art to make it a great cartoon." A great statement. You could be Toulouse-Lautrec, and if you had a crappy idea it would still be a crappy idea, no matter how beautiful it looked.

So I think coming up with the good idea is pretty key.

—JEFF MACNELLY, SHOE AND PLUGGERS

The challenge is trying to be funny every day, trying to say something that is original.

I am appalled at the number of cartoonists who seem to think there is nothing in the world except television or dieting. Either they are talking about something they saw on TV or else they're talking about somebody trying to lose weight. There is more in the world than that, and you have to draw upon your own experience, your own lifestyle and the things that you know.

—CHARLES SCHULZ, *PEANUTS*

My challenge is to say it in the fewest possible words, to take my original thought and boil it down, sometimes just ending up with one word instead of twenty.

—MORT WALKER, *BEETLE BAILEY*

When I am thinking of ideas, I am constantly telling myself I've got to pick ideas that I physically laugh at. I can't say about an idea, "Now, they'll like this. There's humor in this. They'll think this is funny." No, they won't think this is funny unless I think it's funny. If I laugh at it, even if it's standing right on the precipice of good taste, I'll do it. Then, when the syndicate calls and says, "Oh, God, we can't," I'll say, "Look, I'll take the hits. Let the papers drop. This is funny."

You have to be pleasing yourself. If I were going to talk to a group of people who were about to start a comic strip or start writing, that would be the first thing I'd say.

—MIKE PETERS, *MOTHER GOOSE & GRIMM*

I am very much in tune with the way things are worded and how a situation is set up, with the fewest words possible and with a cadence that is enjoyable. and that to me is a real art form in itself, the writing and timing of comics.

—LYNN JOHNSTON, *FOR BETTER OR FOR WORSE*

You have to develop characters. You have to know how to plot. You have to have a certain sense of timing and rhythm.

They say you should use as little dialogue as possible. Well, that's normally true, except that there are people in this business who write so well you can read a lot of it and not have any problem with it.

—MELL LAZARUS, *MISS PEACH* AND *MOMMA*

I think the most beautifully drawn strip isn't going to work if it doesn't have a good sense of humor. I mention humor first because I think it is no accident that people still call their comics, well, "comic." It's humor. And a lot of people still call them funny papers.

—JOSEPH "CHIP" VISCI, *DETROIT FREE PRESS*

My biggest challenge is to try and do things in a way that always seems fresh and new, even when the underlying subject matter may be something that I have explored before. And part of what helps is that I subtly adjust the strip with the changing trappings of society. Five years ago, I may have had more Star Wars *references. Now, it's "X Files." That helps a little bit.*

I used to always say the writing was the easy part and the art was the hard part. I'm not so sure anymore. Also, when you have the same characters in a comic strip format, a lot of the dialogue that would naturally come out of their mouths in a certain situation is dialogue you have already used, and you start having to think of second-tier and third-tier dialogue that works equally well, that's not been tried before.

—BILL AMEND, *FOXTROT*

You have to find out what you want to say. If you have nothing to say, then don't bother.

—WILEY MILLER, *NON SEQUITUR*

Cartoonists need to write with a consistently funny and a consistently unique voice.

—DAVID HENDIN, LITERARY AGENT

I want each gag to be the funniest. Everything we do has to be better than anything we ever did before. It's like trying to climb a mountain that doesn't have a top, which is better than falling into a pit that doesn't have a bottom. [laugh]

—JOHNNY HART, *B.C.* AND *THE WIZARD OF ID*

Obviously there are space limitations. When my wife read Mell Lazarus's *novel,* The Neighborhood Watch, *she said, "I had no idea Mell was such a tight, efficient writer."*

Mell told me, "The best training for a writer is to write those three balloons each day. You have to be tight."

—RICHARD NEWCOMBE, CREATORS SYNDICATE

At present, I think the hardest part is working in the defined area and developing an idea pretty much in one full panel—say a third or a fourth of the strip—and dedicating that space just to stating the situation, before I can start working on the joke.

—SCOTT ADAMS, *DILBERT*

I have always felt that it was a fifty/fifty division between the ideas and the artwork. I still think that's true, though it's not reflected in the work appearing in newspapers today. I hear from some news-paper people that new features are sold strictly on the humor or gag.

—Bil Keane, *The Family Circus*

My challenge as a writer is trying to keep a sameness about the strip and the characters, and yet trying to stay abreast of contemporary thinking.

—Mell Lazarus, *Miss Peach* and *Momma*

It's a question of the author being in touch with the world, what's going on with it. I think that a lot of the energy that goes into a strip comes from daily life, his daily life. It calls for terrific honesty.

—Stuart Dodds, Chronicle Features

First and foremost, I write for myself. The strip helps me muse about things and helps me process my own life. The strip is very per-sonal that way. The audience is a complete abstraction for me, and if I really thought about so many people reading my work every day, I'd probably be too intimidated to publish it. Still, I do regard the strip as a communicative effort, and through my work, I'm trying to talk to readers who are interested in the same things that I am. Oddly, the more personal something is, the more universal it is as well. Cartoonists don't often write very honestly—the need for a punchline and a tidy story encourages glib writing—but when we dig deeper to truthful ex-periences, that's the work that really touches people and connects us all.

—Bill Watterson, *Calvin and Hobbes*

My main daily challenge is to recover my sense of humor from the heap of stuff around me. I have never been able to write the strip think-ing that somebody else was going to read it. I can only write the strip if I really, really get back to how the strip started—which is sitting back and reflecting on the disasters of the day or week and writing it out almost like therapy. Obviously, I draw a point where the character ends and I begin, but I think my strip is always best if it is honest and pretty connected to real experience. And so, in my type of strip, I don't have the option—I can't, it doesn't work for me—to say, "Oh, what do I think readers might respond to?" Mine only works on what am I really really tortured about this week, and where I can find a sense of humor about it.

—Cathy Guisewite, *Cathy*

The Anatomy of the Cartoonist

ART

In newspaper comics, whether it be composition, drawing, letter-ing or color, the art is the physical, two-dimensionalized interpretation of the writing.

Proficiencies aside, it is vitally important that the imagery be filtered through a single vision or consistent sensibility. Contrasting sensibilities—such as three-dimensionally rendered characters in a two-dimensionally rendered world, different rendering styles of characters next to one another, a character's hands that hang at the same place below the waist as when his elbows are bent—show weaknesses in the visual interpretation of a cartoon world, and they destroy the illusion of that world.

The drawing is the fun part. Basically, I learned to write so that I could draw for a living. The writing is very difficult for me. I enjoy getting my thoughts down on paper, but trying to do that on a daily deadline varies from challenging to hellish. Failures are very public, and successes are short-lived. It's the pleasure of drawing funny pictures that makes up for it.

—Bill Watterson, *Calvin and Hobbes*

I think our challenge is to elevate the integrity of art and humor in the industry.

There is a certain thing that has been established throughout the years. Each artist copies the last artist and improves on the style, and it gets better and better and better. At least, I think that's what the challenge should be, to try to uphold what has already been done and to improve on it, lend to it, add to it, refine it.

—Johnny Hart, *B.C.* and *The Wizard of Id*

If you don't know how to draw, you need a style.

—Anonymous

We had an interesting story, relating to the combination of text and graphics.

Sally Forth *is done by Greg Howard, who used to be an attorney. And Greg taught himself how to draw, and obviously he hones in on the text to a great extent. He is very successful today. He is one of our more powerful strips at King. At one point, he wanted to devote more time to the text, so he went out and got a collaborator to do the artwork. Well, when the man's work started to appear in the newspapers, all hell broke loose, because people said that doesn't look like* Sally Forth. *And here, where he thought he wasn't a strong cartoonist, evidently he had a style that was very appealing.*

—Joseph D'Angelo, King Features

I never pick up any gauntlet. I have no illusions about my drawing. I have no idols, nobody I'm trying to emulate. I just draw pictures.

—Mell Lazarus, *Miss Peach* and *Momma*

I've gotten to the point where you just go ahead and do it, and you can't be too critical of yourself.

It's a lot like writers and musicians. If you're confident about what you're doing, and you just say, "This is what I do, this is the way I do it, this is the way it's going to be, and I feel good about it," that confidence comes out in the art. You can say this guy is a terrible artist, but at some point, if he has good material, you start to appreciate the art from another angle.

—PETER KOHLSAAT, *SINGLE SLICES* AND *THE NOOZ*

I'm trying to draw the strip in such a way that it enhances the joke, rather than distracts from it or just leaves things flat.

I suspect my writing talents are a little bit stronger than my drawing talents, so part of my challenge is to try to improve my art. There's been a good deal of evolution in the art.

Another challenge has been trying to render the strip in an interesting way, day after day, because so much of the strip takes place within the home, and the camera angles tend to be rather boring. The problem is that I have designed my characters in such a way that it is not very easy to move the camera around, but I'm getting there. I think I've been more experimental on my Sunday strips over the last year or two.

—BILL AMEND, *FOXTROT*

You keep refining and refining. Not to say you continue to develop more minimalist approaches, but you refine your artwork so that it becomes easier to read, works in the space as well as it can, creates excitement. Like working with design elements and space elements, it's really the basic craft of the art form.

—JERRY VAN AMERONGEN, *BALLARD STREET*

I try to make the thing as readable as possible. I have a goal called see-ability. I want them to be able to see what's going on, without them having to work at it. People aren't going to give you more than seven seconds to read that strip, and if you occupy them longer, or if they just look at it, and it looks like it is difficult, or there's too many words or something, they're just going to pass you by.

—MORT WALKER, *BEETLE BAILEY*

I strive to keep it fresh and do it fast.

—NICOLE HOLLANDER, *SYLVIA*

I think drawing is infinitely more important than people realize. As the reader glances down through an array of strips, the ones he or she will read are the ones that are fun to look at. The drawing should be appealing. The cartooning style or the caricaturing should be mild. I'm a great believer in mild caricature, not extreme cartooning. If you look back on all of the great strips in times past, they were all rather mild in their approach to drawing.

—CHARLES SCHULZ, *PEANUTS*

Whatever approach one takes to the art, I think it should complement the style of writing and the characters. I think that probably is the key.

Sometimes, comic strip artists are criticized for not having "artist" skills, but I think those who are charged with that—those who have nevertheless been successful—have managed to have art that complements what the characters are about.

—LEE SALEM, UNIVERSAL PRESS SYNDICATE

Human beings are visual animals. We interpret every piece of information visually. When a writer writes visually, he forms a picture that is in his head and has it develop in your head. He does that through his words. So, where the writer tries to paint a picture with his words, we write words with our pictures. We're just in a different venue.

I've always felt cartoonists serve exactly the same function as columnists. We just work in a different format. However, the visual is far more powerful than the written word. Reading is similar to taking a Polaroid picture. The image gradually appears, and then it's there. It's kind of a filtering process, whereas with a cartoon or a photograph, the picture is there. The picture has a direct pipeline into some emotional center in the back of your brain that gets this emotional visual reaction. It's just a very powerful tool.

If a cartoonist can hone those skills—first of all, to be a writer, get the idea of what he wants and then produce it visually—that's the most powerful impact that you can have.

—WILEY MILLER, *NON SEQUITUR*

Drawing the strip (Nancy) *is like trying to do somebody else's homework. There's a special responsibility I feel toward it that needs a consistency with the former* Nancy. *But it's also got to be my own stuff, or I couldn't draw it. I couldn't just sit down and trace his work or light box it.*

It took me years to learn how to draw the Nancy *character. Look at the first five, six, even seven years of the strip that I worked on. It's not very good. It's not very consistent.*

It wasn't like I didn't try, because when I started this thing I was working fourteen/fifteen hours a day, six or seven days a week, just trying to make it look right.

Now I think I can be comfortable with almost any strip I've done in the last three years and say, "Yeah, that looks like today's drawing." It's taken me that long to learn how to draw her. It could be that I'm just slow. I'm certainly no animator.

—Jerry Scott, *Baby Blues* and *Nancy*

The text is so, so very important. But another factor that has to be considered—once having graphically designed a character that for whatever reason you find appealing—you simply find the character humorous to look at. You don't even have to look at the text. You look at the character, you smile, and then you look for the gag. It's not true of everything, but it's true of those unique graphic characters.

—Joseph D'Angelo, King Features

I think the ability to draw is sadly lacking in today's market. The ability to employ good design into the graphics is something that would be appreciated by everyone.

—Hank Ketcham, *Dennis the Menace*

It's a challenge to take that little space and somehow make it so appealing that it stands out from all the other clutter on the page. All you see across the page now is a blur from the same sort of drawing.

—Ron Patel, *The Philadelphia Inquirer*

I like to make it visually interesting, mostly so I won't get bored to death drawing it.

Over the years, the cartoons that tend to bore me have been the New Yorker–type cartoon where two people are saying something witty to each other about something. I always feel that is a waste of space for us, as cartoonists, because we can draw anything. We can draw animals talking to each other or have ridiculous things going on, dinosaurs flying through the air. We really are unlimited as to what we can do visually, so I tend to look for ideas that are going to jump out at the reader, something unusual that they've never thought about before, or seen before.

You are shortchanging the medium if you are just drawing guys sitting there. Sometimes you need to do that, and it's fun to do, but I like to make it visual.

—Jeff MacNelly, *Shoe* and *Pluggers*

I go back to the old Mack Sennett theories, "Keep it moving, keep it moving."

People are attracted by action, and they are attracted by funny pictures. Something to look at. I really don't like talking-head strips— even when I draw them myself—or what I call wallpaper gags where the scene is the same. I just don't like to do them. Mack Sennett was pretty successful with his theory, and I think that's what I look for visually.

—Mort Walker, *Beetle Bailey*

CHARACTERS AND WORLDS

Your characters are your props, the universe they live in is your stage, and they are the conduit for your ideas. While neither will be brought into existence fully realized, developed with a polish that comes only from age, you hope they will be brought into existence with the facilities to grow and not wither.

One of the things that always strikes me—and this is among the beginners—is how many think that drawing a comic strip is simply coming up with a gag and drawing around it, and that's not a comic strip at all.

If you are going to sit down to do a comic strip or panel, I feel that you have to think about what you want to say, the same way that a novelist might. I have often told people who have come in to see me, if Joe is one of your characters, then you need to write a whole personality for Joe. Before you ever start on the comic strip, you have to know what Joe is like. You have to know in your mind who your characters are, and then you begin to put them in a strip and see how they react.

Even if your strip does not have running characters, the work is still processed through a particular point of view.

*—*SUE SMITH, *DALLAS MORNING NEWS*

As a strip progresses, the most important thing is the development of character. Very few of us can remember anything that was said in past comic strips, except for a few phrases. But we can all remember the great characters like Popeye, L'il Abner and Skippy. We may remember a few phrases that cartoonists have coined, but mainly we remember the personalities of the characters and the way they looked. I think that's very important.

*—*CHARLES SCHULZ, *PEANUTS*

I'm thankful that when I created the strip, I created strong, interesting and flexible characters, or what I think are strong, interesting and flexible characters. It makes the challenge of writing dialogue that

---

much easier. I'm at a point where I can throw Jason and Paige into a situation, and nine times out of ten, words will start popping out of their mouths immediately by themselves. They don't always deal with the very funny important panel, but at least I'm not having to start from scratch every time.

I don't know how Gary Larson can do what he does. The whole thing every day. It's very nice and comforting having a cast of characters that I know very well. I can rely on them to help me out.

—BILL AMEND, FOXTROT

If you develop a world, a universe—within your strip, in your mind, in your creativity—that is flexible enough and ingenious enough, it should never die, because it should take on its own life. Characters take on a life of their own.

—DAVID HENDIN, LITERARY AGENT

It's important to have an intense interest in doing the work. The comic will reflect the level of interest that the cartoonist has in the work, so if he isn't in love with the characters himself, there is a good chance the readers won't care about the characters either.

—JAY KENNEDY, KING FEATURES

Not too long ago, a very famous producer, the recipient of many Oscars, said to me, "I get excited when the characters are alive. There don't have to be too many of them in a film for situations to ring true." That goes for a comic strip as well. The cartoonist must make the characters live.

—TONI MENDEZ, LITERARY REPRESENTATIVE

THE ANATOMY OF THE CARTOONIST

CONSISTENCY

Can you jump rope?

I could probably get that sucker over my head and under my feet once. Twice? Well, maybe if I practiced, but I wouldn't bet my paycheck on it. Little girls and prizefighters spin those ropes around their bodies in such a way that their synchronous movements are dazzling.

Still, I could probably get that rope over my head and under my feet once, so does that mean I can jump rope? 'Fraid not.

If you can manage only one good cartoon—even if it's a shining star that rises out of the mire and makes people want to sing—does that mean you can sustain the quality required for a daily comic feature? 'Fraid not.

In syndicated comics, sustained quality is infinitely more important than occasional quality.

Consistency in syndication is awfully important, if not the most important thing. It is a little bit like baseball, where your great valuable players can hit consistently and stay around the .300 mark or so, not where you have to hit a home run every time.
—JERRY SCOTT, *BABY BLUES* AND *NANCY*

In baseball, the .300 mark will get you into the Hall of Fame. In comics, the .300 mark will get you a seat in the bleachers.

Cartoonists have to be fresh and original every day, without letup.
—ALAN SHEARER, WASHINGTON POST WRITERS GROUP

You need to have a lot of staying power. A lot of times, when you get into this strip business, you are going to be around for five, ten, twenty years, so you need to be consistent over a long period of time.
—BRUCE BEATTIE, *BEATTIE BLVD.*

It comes down to, "Can they consistently connect with a sense of humor?" That doesn't mean that everybody has to "get it" every time. It just means that the strip has to be consistent, so that those people who appreciate it get a kick out of it 90 percent of the time.
—JOSEPH "CHIP" VISCI, *DETROIT FREE PRESS*

I think the most important aspect of cartooning is clearly the writing, as opposed to the drawing.

The drawing has to be professional enough, so that at a glance you can tell you are dealing with somebody who knows how to illustrate, but the writing is what's going to drive it in the long term. It's what's going to keep bringing readers back day after day.

That ties into the ability to continue to put out a consistent level of work over a very extended period of time. You have to produce these things week in and week out. They have to be consistent in the quality of work. They can't be really high, then have burnout periods where the level dips substantially, because the editors will only tolerate that for a certain period of time.
—STEVE CHRISTENSEN, LOS ANGELES TIMES SYNDICATE

One of the things that the syndicate is always looking for is that you're not a flash in the pan, that you have consistency, and that you can keep this thing going. We're not talking about six weeks or six months. Hopefully we're talking an extended period of years. Do you have the ideas firmly in your head so you can keep producing?

—SUE SMITH, *DALLAS MORNING NEWS*

Something I always strive for in my work is consistency. I think that is the most important aspect to a comic strip. I'm talking about a daily feature. It's not good enough to have one or two or three good cartoons a week, and have three, four or five okay cartoons. Those are low standards. I have very high standards for my work. If I'm not producing my best, then why bother?

I approach Non Sequitur *exactly the same way I did my editorial cartoons, one cartoon at a time. I pick a topic, find out how I feel about it, then figure out how to approach it and get as much impact out of it.*

It takes a long time and a lot of hard work, but the end result pays off. You have a much better cartoon or consistent cartoon, and also you'll be more successful. That reputation will eventually get out there, as opposed to doing average work, and that reputation is going to get out there, too.

—WILEY MILLER, *NON SEQUITUR*

THE ANATOMY OF THE CARTOONIST

CRAFT AND DISCIPLINE

Craft in comics is understanding the many different techniques of the form that make it work, and applying them to your own work.

Discipline is working. It's not talking about working or thinking about working. It's knowing what you need to do to get a job done, then getting it done.

I think discipline is an entirely important characteristic that a cartoonist must have. You must have the ability to work, day in and day out, turning out a product, which, I am the first to admit, is very diffi-

cult. You sit down in the morning with a blank piece of paper, and you're expected not only to create incredible text and humorous text, but also to draw.

I honestly do believe that there is no way anyone can be a cartoonist, unless he has the basic latent genius for it.

But I want to go one step further, and it's got nothing to do with craft. It's got more to do with character. It's discipline, perseverance, and talent. Don't give up. Do you know how many of the great cartoonists that are being recognized today as great had three, four, five failures before they hit on the strip that made them famous? Chic Young did several strips before he struck it on Blondie.

—JOSEPH D'ANGELO, KING FEATURES

I find that when a lot of people come to us, they're full of themselves. Some of their ideas are quite good, but they don't have an understanding of the marketplace. They've not read newspapers, and they should. I should say that it is a requirement. Something between the raw talent and the medium itself, that's craft.

—STUART DODDS, CHRONICLE FEATURES

There are a number of professional cartoonists who work as professional cartoonists in places like Mad or the New Yorker who try comic strips, and they are near misses. Those people have earned the right to ask me or to ask the editor or head of any syndicate to look at their material by virtue of being professional cartoonists.

They may make it or not make it on any particular strip, but basically they are already at the professional level. The same thing holds true for editorial cartoonists. Editorial cartoonists are not going to send you a comic strip that sucks wind. They may send you one that doesn't work, for one reason or another, but they're not going to send you something drawn on tissue paper that's the wrong size, that's drawn in magic marker and bleeding all over the place with a little note that says, "I need somebody to edit these." And that's not an exaggeration. I get that kind of stuff.

—DAVID HENDIN, LITERARY AGENT

When the first six weeks of sample packages look good, we look at the pedigree of the cartoonists to see what kind of stability they have in their background. We look for evidence that they might have the ability to keep something going. A couple of times, I have been led astray by the idea that someone who works in the greeting card industry can really keep something going.

—RON PATEL, *THE PHILADELPHIA INQUIRER*

THE SOLO ACT AND THE COLLABORATORS

A man's got to know his limitations.

—DIRTY HARRY, *MAGNUM FORCE*

Determining the need for a collaborator is an extremely personal choice.

If you are considering working with a collaborator, you need to make an evaluation of your own abilities, an evaluation of your prospective partner's abilities, then make a judgment on whether or not each of your strengths and weaknesses complement one another.

An alternative is to meet someone for the first time and say, "Do you want to work together?"

The reality will probably be somewhere between these two extremes of a cold calculation and love at first sight.

Having a partner is a little bit like being married. I don't think we've had a major disagreement about the strip yet.

So far, egos haven't gotten in the way, where I say, "Look, this is a funny gag! Draw it, jerk, or else!" We don't do that. If Rick feels really strongly that a gag isn't funny, or it isn't timed right for the development in the strip, or it's not factual, I generally take it back.

I'll say, "All right. Okay." I'll put it away for a while, then I'll bring it back, and I'll resubmit it to him. I'll change a couple of words and say, "You're on." I have one Sunday page I've been trying to sell him for . . . it must be three years. It's still just about having a new baby. Now that Wanda's pregnant again, it's valid again. I'll still try to get him to draw it, because I think it's funny. But there's no shortage of material, so I don't live and die by it, if he doesn't draw it.

Conversely, if Rick draws something that doesn't work, I have the ability to say, "I think this is timed all wrong," or "the characters are in the wrong position," and he'll respect my opinion.

—JERRY SCOTT, *BABY BLUES* AND *NANCY*

Collaboration would give some different perspective, and interject some new ideas, and kind of be a sounding board for you.

The disadvantages would be that as soon as you have anybody else's opinion involved, you're tampering with your sensibilities. I fantasize sometimes that I would write the strip with somebody, or that somebody would come along that would help me, but deep down I know that my complete, crippling insecurity about my own work is what fuels the work, and I really am better left here alone, floundering around in my own creative vat. That pain of creation, the insecurity of it, and the loneliness of it are part of my process, and I would sacrifice that as soon as I had a collaborator.

—CATHY GUISEWITE, *CATHY*

I think the strip reflects the attitude of one person. That's what makes it unique. The individual. And I think when you get a committee working on it, it tends to lose some of its life. While I worked with collaborators over the years, I have primarily used their collaboration as suggestion, then put it in my own words and my own thoughts.

—MORT WALKER, *BEETLE BAILEY*

I think collaboration works very well for a lot of people. It depends on your style; If you have a flexible style it's easy to work with other people's material.

—MELL LAZARUS, *MISS PEACH* AND *MOMMA*

I think it's entirely up to the cartoonist/creator. If he feels that he either needs help in drawing or he needs help in gag writing, what's the difference? The important thing is to come up with a product which, let's face it, is initially his creation, and a product that's going to be attractive to the public and the readership. If there's a certain way that's accomplished, I don't think it's anything cartoonists should be ashamed of.

My concern is that the quality of the strip is maintained, and that it's on time so that we can service the newspaper clients.

—JOSEPH D'ANGELO, KING FEATURES

I think the difficulty with a collaborator is usually the writer. A lot of times, the guy writing for a cartoonist needs a little education in the visual. It's not talking heads. On the other hand, I do have kind of a budget. You're talking about a panel that a lot of newspapers are shrinking down to the size of an airmail stamp, so you can't exactly draw six people sitting around a kitchen table dissecting a frog. It's not going to translate.

—JEFF MACNELLY, *SHOE* AND *PLUGGERS*

The only time I would encourage collaboration would be when the cartoonist had one of the two skills so clearly mastered that you hate to see that talent go to waste, for example, when you've got somebody who can draw extremely well but isn't a very good writer or isn't a very

funny writer. Or you have a writer who has really great characters, a really good setting, a good story to tell, but the drawing is so unprofessional that it is off-putting.

If somebody were really top-notch as a writer or an artist, I might suggest that it would be worthwhile to find somebody who could provide the other element. But generally, I'm not too optimistic about that process working out.

—STEVE CHRISTENSEN, LOS ANGELES TIMES SYNDICATE

If you're doing the strip by yourself, it is certainly an uncompromising and singular solution. It's your voice, period.

If you're working with a collaborator, you may have a goal you are both working toward. I think the positives to working with a collaborator would be that the combination of two talents—a writer and a good artist, let's say—makes a better whole.

If a single individual can't take it all the way, then maybe two people can take it all the way.

I think the other positive to two contributing is that each contributor might push the other one beyond where they have normally gone themselves.

There is a downside, too—I don't know that this happens all the time—and that's if the strip gets to be one of those mechanical efforts, where one partner is less committed than the other.

—JERRY VAN AMERONGEN, *BALLARD STREET*

The advantages of collaboration are that you have two different heads, so you have two different ideas, two sources for gags. and you have someone who backs you off from going down some narrow avenue of your humor—that is so idiosyncratic to you—that no one else is going to follow it.

The drawbacks, of course, are it's a collaboration, which means that there is always room for disagreement. and also, there is a time constraint. It takes more time to do work for someone else than it does to do it yourself.

—JAY KENNEDY, KING FEATURES

The disadvantages of collaboration might be just not agreeing on principle of the quality or the direction you're going. Someone has to be the leader. Someone has to determine to make the final judgment, and there might be an ego problem there of who is in charge. It's just a matter of personalities. Of course, they wouldn't be together if they didn't get along in the first place, but like a marriage, sometimes they get a divorce. And sometimes, the cash flow is minimized when you have a collaborator.

—HANK KETCHAM, DENNIS THE MENACE

In general, the best strips and panels come out of one mind. I always say that when you create a fiction, whether it is a comic strip or a novel, there's really only one place that it is totally alive, and that's in the mind of the creator. If there are two creators, it makes it very much more difficult.

In previous years, when story strips, adventure strips, continuity strips were more of a factor, that was different. Those demanded the skills of almost a novelist or short story writer to write the story, and the stories could easily be illustrated by a cartoonist or an illustrator.

With the type of strips that are popular today, it's really a situation where the characters have to be alive in the mind of the creator, otherwise I think there are strikes against it.

—DAVID HENDIN, LITERARY AGENT

If the partnership is a really good partnership, there would be the camaraderie of coming up with lines together and working on something together. Playing house with a friend is so much more fun than playing by yourself. Remember being down on your knees, playing cars or something with another kid? One says pretend this and pretend that, and you're both in such a fantasy world that the day goes by before you know it. This is the same sort of fantasy world. So if you find someone whose fantasies work with yours, I think its a superb and enviable thing. But when it doesn't work, it is sheer hell.

—LYNN JOHNSTON, FOR BETTER OR FOR WORSE

It's like a marriage. It's fine when everybody is in love.

—TONI MENDEZ, LITERARY REPRESENTATIVE

It depends on whether the collaborator can draw or not. I think a comic strip cannot be written at a typewriter. Some of the story strips might work, but I think that the strip will suffer because the comic strip is still an art medium. If you can't draw, you cannot think of drawing ideas. It's important that the person doing the creating can also draw because out of your ability to draw comes your ability to think of funny pictures. So, I think there is a handicap there in collaboration. Person-

ally, I couldn't stand having to argue with somebody over whether or not something is funny.

—Charles Schulz, *Peanuts*

If the people are really in sync with each other—on the same wavelength, as it were—collaboration could be a really positive experience. There's an energy out of two people exchanging ideas, and the creative process may be greater than either of them can do on their own.

On the other hand, if the messages they're trying to deliver are not in sync, it could be a pretty uncomfortable process—generally one doomed to a pretty short life.

—Steve Christensen, Los Angeles Times Syndicate

I don't think that someone should say, "I can't draw very well," and then just give up, because you can teach people to draw, if they have a strong enough desire. So I don't think people should give up on themselves quickly.

I think cartoonists need to seriously listen to feedback that they get. They should consider getting a collaborator when they have reason to believe by virtue of a consensus in the feedback that it is time for them to do that.

Or if they simply know from the start that they have no interest in doing the other half of the strip, then it's time to get a collaborator.

—Jay Kennedy, King Features

THE EDITOR INSIDE YOU

There is a saying that cannot be repeated too often: writing is rewriting.

Many years ago, I knew an extremely talented syndicated cartoonist. His strip had occasional moments of brilliance and too many moments of dysfunction, unfortunate material that weighed him down like a pair of cement galoshes.

I asked him if he couldn't try to upgrade the overall quality of his material, perhaps rate them one to ten and only go with his sevens to tens.

Quite seriously, he said, "But all my gags are tens."

All creative people, whether they're a cartoonist, writer, artist, or musician, need a personal thermometer to tell them when their work is done. The integrity of their work is ultimately tied to the effectiveness of their thermometer.

There are two clear editors in my life. One is the FedEx truck. So at some point you have to be done and say, "This is the best I can think of."

—Cathy Guisewite, *Cathy*

I have absolutely no ego in my work. I have been writing novels for years, and I have no problem being able to cut whole pieces, whole runs or passages out of a book. When you've worked so hard to put them in, and only because you love them, they mean something to you—but they don't enhance the book. I find that a week later, I can go back over the book, just as brutally as if I were another person, and cut stuff. I think I'm a pretty good self-editor.

I've drawn complete strips. I might have thought they worked in the writing and the penciling, and then I inked them completely, and they don't work, and I throw them away. And I do it readily. In fact, I'm kind of pleased when I come to that conclusion, because it reassures me that I'm paying attention.

—MELL LAZARUS, MISS PEACH AND MOMMA

This is one of the things I look for in submissions that I get. I'm looking to see that someone is a fairly good self-editor. If someone sends me thirty-six gags, and he has one in there that's too gross, well, maybe that's just an accident. But if he has thirty-six strips, thirty of them are great and six are just over-the-line gross, it tells me there are problems with this person, and that he doesn't have the ability to be a self-editor. And that it is going to be a high-maintenance strip. Then I have to go straight to that issue and see very quickly whether this is something he can learn, or whether this is something he just doesn't have the ability for.

—JAY KENNEDY, KING FEATURES

I don't trust myself, because I usually look at an idea and think, "That's the greatest idea I've ever gotten," and I'm sure somebody else thinks, "I don't get it." So you realize you have to have a sounding board. You have to have other people looking at it. I don't trust people that just set down whatever they think, without consulting their wife or son or their assistant or editor or somebody.

—MORT WALKER, BEETLE BAILEY

To make sure that the voice is authentic, to make sure that the conversation flows naturally, I speak it out loud. If it sounds natural when I speak the words, then I know the feeling's there that I've tried to convey.

—STEPHEN BENTLEY, HERB & JAMAAL

There is a flaw in our thinking which occurs every now and then. A cartoonist hits a slump—not where he or she can't think of anything, but where, for a certain period of time, he or she is no longer able to judge whether what they have thought of is funny.

I've often wanted to clip out a sample of comic strips that I call "nongags." They simply weren't funny because the cartoonist didn't know they weren't funny. I look at something and I think, "That's not funny. That's not even a joke." You see, on the day the cartoonist drew it, he didn't know that. And those are the little slumps that I worry about.

While I was having lunch today, I was thinking of something and I thought, "I don't know if that's funny or not. I have no idea." But I'm continuing to think about it, and I'll work it out. I just use my own judgment. I never show them to anybody else. I never test them on anybody else. I just send them in.

—CHARLES SCHULZ, *PEANUTS*

I've never had a cartoon rejected by a syndicate. Of course, my real editor is in the kitchen cooking dinner. Thel looks at everything before it leaves here, and she will occasionally put her finger on something and say, "Now wait a minute," and, when she points something out to me, I go back to the drawing board.

I am a stickler for detail, and I will check and recheck. I go to the dictionary. I make sure everything is spelled right. Every drawing has five fingers on the hands, the car has the kids' seat belts fastened.

Occasionally there is a word or something that slips through, and I will get a call from Paul [Hendricks at King Features].

For the most part, when you are syndicated you are the editor, when submitting the work. Occasionally a syndicate will have somebody work with you—at the beginning anyway—to oversee what you are doing, but sometimes that kills creativity.

—BIL KEANE, *THE FAMILY CIRCUS*

I write it first, I put it into the strip, and then it always changes. So there is a process that's going on from the writing.

I write on a Powerbook, and then I write it by hand, and then I send it to a friend who is an editor. She corrects that, and she also will say, "You know this would be clearer if you said it this way," and we discuss it. It might be that I don't agree with her, and of course I'm the final say. That's what's interesting about syndicating yourself, because I do have the final say. Certainly a newspaper can decide not to print me, but usu-

ally they just decide that or don't decide that. No one calls me and says, "Maybe you shouldn't have put this in."

—NICOLE HOLLANDER, SYLVIA

We're always our hardest editors. I'm talking about the cartoonists who are good. The ones who are bad are going to constantly be saying, "Oh, this is humorous, and I'm sure they're going to think this is funny." But the great ones, the ones who always rise to the top, those are the ones who make it look so easy when they do them, but it's real hard. It's real hard.

When I saw The Unknown Chaplin, *I realized that here was one of the greatest comedic geniuses of any time, and he sweated bullets coming up with those things. Yet when you saw the finished pieces, it was like water over a rock. It was seamless. And yet, for him to get to that, he would go home and act like he was sick for five days and not come to work because he couldn't get over a certain hump or a certain problem. I learned a ton from that.*

When I look out and I see The Far Side *or I see* Calvin and Hobbes *or I see* Shoe *or things that I think are really great, things I really laugh at myself, my first inclination is to say, "Oh, see, those guys are just very natural, and it comes very easy for them." What I've learned is it doesn't come easy. It comes really hard. What they are are great editors. They do not allow themselves to be mediocre. They force themselves to be great, and that's just the act of editing and everything coming together. A lot of it is the editing. A lot of it is saying no to fifty ideas before you get to the one that actually works.*

—MIKE PETERS, MOTHER GOOSE & GRIMM

Cartoonists who are syndicated understand the editorial process. But in my opinion, every cartoonist, just like every writer, needs a good editor. Beyond themselves.

—DAVID HENDIN, LITERARY AGENT

It's an alarm that goes off. I think the key in any creative sort of endeavor is to look back on the stuff you did a year ago—if you have the guts—and hate it. Then you're getting somewhere. Ask yourself how you would do it differently today than you did it last year. It's useful to look back on your stuff, but I try not to. I try to take each one as a new deal.

—JEFF MACNELLY, SHOE AND PLUGGERS

One of the little tricks that I've had over the years is I thumbnail sketch an idea out—I have a sketchbook I work with—and when I think of an idea, I let it sit there in the sketchbook or I draw it in an actual thumbnail rough form. Within three to four days, a number of things start to happen, one of which is you get to know in a real hurry whether the cartoon is good or bad. You get a little distance from the cartoon, and it is a very effective way of being objective about your own work. The second thing, when you look at the work you did three to four days ago, sometimes there is a new angle there, and a fresh approach comes into it. A lot of times, I'll look at stuff for the second time, and all of a sudden I find a much better solution to the puzzle.

I think being your own editor is ultimately a process of being very honest with yourself about your own work. Most cartoonists, if they are at all successful, have a very highly tuned antenna about what is good in their work and what is bad. I don't think there is really any cartoonist out there who doesn't know when they're doing crummy work. We all know when it is good and when it's not. There is a certain amount of self-criticism and honesty that you inherit in the whole creative process.

In my particular case, when I do my roughs for Beattie Blvd., *I send them to my editors in New York, and they take a look. If there is anything that they think is in bad taste or they don't think is funny, then we talk about it and throw out the ideas that aren't working. But by and large, I'm my own worst critic.*

It's an inherent part of the whole creative process, and until you really have that ability, I think you are really handicapped. It is all part and parcel of the whole process of learning as a cartoonist who you are as a person and what it is about that feature that allows you to get yourself out on paper for other people to understand.

—Bruce Beattie, *Beattie Blvd.*

You constantly make decisions. In writing, you reread, then juggle the words around and eliminate the duplicities and add more interesting words and phrases. As far as humor is concerned, you look for clarity, for impact, and an element of surprise. Does it fit your character? Did we do it before? Is it current? A lot of these little things are judgment factors that are sitting in your head, that come into play when you're making these evaluations. You must have a very, very low acceptance ratio, because you are a tough, tough editor.

—Hank Ketcham, *Dennis the Menace*

I want myself to send out the best work that I can possibly send out, despite the fact that the deadlines are relentless.

As time went by, I thought it would be easier, that I would become so used to this that it would just happen, and I would take a lot of time off. But it has happened in reverse, and I am more demanding of myself, more self-critical, more determined to do the best work I have ever done. I'm not in competition with anybody else but me, and so that's taking more time now than ever before.

—Lynn Johnston, *For Better or For Worse*

I think it runs the full gamut. Some people are marvelous self-editors, or they have a network of friends and family members who can serve in that role, so a syndicate editor doesn't really need to do much for them. All they require is somebody to make sure the words are spelled right. Others feel they need input from the syndicate on the best delivery of a gag or the development of a character, and they seek it out. So some people don't need it, and others really benefit from it.

—ANITA TOBIAS, CREATORS SYNDICATE

I think a cartoonist learning to function as his own editor is a natural part of the evolution of any strip.

We work very close to the artist for the first two to three years. We work very hard to make sure we all have a common understanding as to what's going on, and the artist pretty quickly picks up on what we mean by a common understanding. Then I think that whole role of editor also falls on the cartoonist's shoulders as well. Most cartoonists we work with are willing to take on that role, as well as just presenting stuff to let somebody else make the judgments. By then the artist has a better sense of the market, what the syndicate's looking for, and most important, what the readers are looking for.

—LEE SALEM, UNIVERSAL PRESS SYNDICATE

The quality of a strip is probably determined by the quantity of ideas in the wastebasket. Every cartoonist writes a lot of bad strips, and the never-ending pressure to meet deadlines encourages cartoonists to publish virtually everything they think up. The only way to resist that pressure is to stay far enough ahead of the deadlines that you can throw away mediocre material and write something better. Of course, every idea you throw away doubles your workload, because you have to write one idea to make up for it, and another idea to get ahead. It's very frustrating to do, but if you're right up against the deadline, there's no quality control. It's just garbage in, garbage out. I've been in that situation, and it's miserable.

Normally, I stay far enough ahead that I can edit my strips many times. I write a month's worth of strips before I ink any of them, so I can focus solely on the writing problems. I reread the ideas over several days, and see how well they hold up to fresh scrutiny. I rework anything that seems awkward, and weed out the weak ones. After I've written a number of strips, I show the roughs to my wife, whose critical judgment I trust. Then, when I go to ink the strips up, I usually refine the writing once more. Sometimes the prospect of spending an hour or two inking will reveal a lukewarm enthusiasm for the idea, and I'll abandon it. I try to weed out as many unexciting ideas as possible, and I wish I could weed out even more.

—BILL WATTERSON, *CALVIN AND HOBBES*

In the beginning, cartoonists very clearly need editing and a bit more coaching than they do later on. In time, they become more aware of who they are writing for—of who they are addressing—and they become more self-aware and able to criticize their work. But I've found at the beginning, they're not their own best editors. They always need editors.

—STUART DODDS, CHRONICLE FEATURES

THE BUSINESS OF BEING A PROFESSIONAL CARTOONIST

Being a creative artist for a living, whether it be a cartoonist, writer, artist or musician, has a thrilling upside. You do what you do, and someone gives you money.

There's also a great big reality check involved. That "someone," whether he works for a syndicate, publisher, production company, film studio, gallery, night club, recording studio or label, expects to get something for his money, and if the work doesn't meet the standards he needs to turn a profit, you won't be working together for long.

That's the marriage of art and commerce. That's business.

Cartoonists need to realize that they should try to fit their approach to cartooning to the business of cartooning. I find some people who do some really nice submissions that I can't sell, and I find myself writing, "Try to sell this as a comic book."

These days, if you're interested in telling stories and don't care much about humor, then you should be thinking about comic books.

If you're interested in—something I'll say quite derisively—testosterone adventures, then superhero comics.

It might be that you are a very sentimental writer, in which case you might end up doing greeting cards.

So you should be aware that there is more than one outlet for cartooning.

—JAY KENNEDY, KING FEATURES

You've got to know the business you're trying to get in. You just don't create in a vacuum.

—ALAN SHEARER, WASHINGTON POST WRITERS GROUP

Years ago, I remember hearing beginning cartoonists and others who were just in the business refer to syndication as "this crazy business of slinging ink." Well, that's a stupid phrase, and this isn't a crazy business of slinging ink. It's a very serious business, and we are like actors in the theater. We are like the ballplayers. We are at the mercy of the guy who owns the team. We are like the writers who are at the mercy of the person who owns the publishing company. I think this is true of all phases of entertainment. We all have to go through our first editor, and then kind of work our way up. But we have to protect ourselves, and it takes a long time to learn that. That's the business part of it.

—CHARLES SCHULZ, PEANUTS

The cartoonist has got to understand that even though he is a creative person, that this—in the final analysis—is a hard business. It's a business, and it's a difficult business. It's a very, very competitive business.

Today we have some very strong syndicates out there. So once having recognized that he has been given an opportunity by a syndicate to have his strip launched, he needs to understand there is a very substantial investment in launching that strip. It could be anywhere conservatively from $100,000 to $150,000. Not that I think that they wouldn't consider it seriously, but it is a very serious business.

You're dealing with humor, so you may take things a little lightly. But once you're in the pipeline and you have a contract with a newspaper and they expect to get Beetle every day, you better be damn sure you got it out there every day.

—JOSEPH D'ANGELO, KING FEATURES

You make a lifetime commitment, producing one drawing every day of your life, whether you like it or not, whether you feel up to it, whether you're ill or healthy or on vacation or what. The sword of Damocles hangs over your drawing board, and you are under this stress of deadline pressure. Sometimes it gets a little old after a few years and you kind of remember the good old days of freelancing when you could just take off. This doesn't happen in syndication, so I caution the youngsters several times before they rush off to the syndicate with a brilliant idea that they'll be saddled with for the rest of their lives. It's a marriage is what it is.

—HANK KETCHAM, DENNIS THE MENACE

Your name is out there. Your picture is on an editor's desk, and this may lead to other things, but it is no ending of itself. It is only a beginning. The work really begins once you become syndicated. Once you are syndicated, the deadlines are relentless and unforgiving.

—ALAN SHEARER, WASHINGTON POST WRITERS GROUP

I think when you sign up to do the job, there are certain things you understand. The definition of the job, I think, is to help newspapers sell newspapers, not to please cartoonists or to please yourself. There's a responsibility to the public, and I feel very strongly that you're there to entertain. I feel that you're there to make a connection with people who do want to read on the comic pages about stuff they go through.

—JERRY SCOTT, BABY BLUES AND NANCY

This is speaking as someone who owns his own syndicate—I have a little more freedom here—and that is that I look for cartoonists I think I can work well with, who I think I will like and get along with. I run a hundred miles from anyone I think is going to be a prima donna.

—RICHARD NEWCOMBE, CREATORS SYNDICATE

It certainly is not the glamorous life I imagined it would be, which frankly is fine. I enjoy the anonymity that goes with cartooning. There is a fame attached to the work, but not necessarily the creator. That's just fine, but I did imagine I'd be having lunch with Bill Murray and dinner with Bruce Springsteen. [laugh]

—BILL AMEND, FOXTROT

THE BUSINESS OF BEING A PROFESSIONAL CARTOONIST
WARNING SIGNS TO BEGINNERS

It's perfectly natural to want to be great right away, to see things in your work nobody else sees. It's perfectly natural to love your ideas and protect them like your children. It's perfectly natural to think that because you've done your best, your best is good enough, but that doesn't make it so.

In order to grow into a professional, you need to understand that effort and quality are not necessarily commensurate with one another. With this in mind, it's important to realize that when someone is giving you feedback, he's trying to help you, not hurt you.

It does not matter that you do not agree with his opinion, and it is not important that he understand your opinion. It's completely irrelevant to your purpose of getting feedback and making a judgment as to how that feedback applies to your work.

When you ask someone for feedback, there should be no room for debate. There is only that person's opinion. It does no good to give him your opinion, because he doesn't need it and can't use it. But you can use his opinion, so you should probe further to find the reasons he thinks what he thinks. Since understanding his opinion is the only thing that matters, the probing should not be defensive. There's no reason for you to be defensive, because the other person's not attacking, he's explaining, and it's your job to try to understand him.

It is extremely unprofessional to ask someone for his opinion then argue with him. When someone offers his opinion, he knows he's risking confrontation. However, in order to help, he goes ahead and gives his opinion. If you argue with someone, you're depriving yourself of the insight this person can offer, and, if your response makes this person gun-shy, you may be depriving the next cartoonist of an honest answer, and that would be a crime.

So tuck your ego down deep where it can't be bruised. If your work is good, it will speak for itself. If your work is not good, then you may have an opportunity to find out how to improve it. If you work toward this end, you can only gain, you can't lose.

Y-o-u c-a-n-n-o-t l-o-s-e.

There is something wanna-be cartoonists have to be very realistic about. First, your family and friends are always going to think that your creations are wonderful.

I get letters that say, "Everybody I've showed this to thinks this is better than Garfield.*"*

Then I look at it, and it's less than amateurish. Sometimes I say this is not for me, and other times I am very frank. I say, "Look, if you can't learn to draw a lot better, you shouldn't be wasting your time doing this."

—DAVID HENDIN, LITERARY AGENT

I think you have to be very, very aware of what's out there. and you have to be very aware with how you compare with what's there, which means being your own worst critic or best critic. I don't know whether it's a talent or a sense of maturity that makes you accept and work with criticism.

There are a lot of people who really like their own work. and a lot of their family, friends and colleagues will say, "Oh, that work is wonderful. You should submit it to a syndicate."

That's a wonderful incentive to do so, but when an editor or another cartoonist will say, "This isn't working for this reason or that reason," many people will get angry and throw their stuff down and say, "Well, my mom likes it. What the heck do you know?"

So a lot of cartoonists don't take the time anymore to critique people's work, because it just isn't worth the effort when the results are so rarely favorable.

—LYNN JOHNSTON, *FOR BETTER OR FOR WORSE*

There are these people that have the mistaken belief that their idea is original. They come up to me and say, "I've got this wonderful idea."

Then they show me something that's very similar to a lot of things on the market, or it's just dumb. I'll bet the syndicates get that a lot more than I do, and I certainly get plenty.

—Ron Patel, The Philadelphia Inquirer

I don't think they have a concept of the volume of people who are interested in this, and I think any given cartoonist sitting by himself in his living room thinks, "I'll bet nobody has had this idea before." My guess is there aren't very many ideas somebody hasn't had before.

—Jane Amari, The Kansas City Star

These poor souls send me stuff. They think it's going to be simple, and it's not. I don't know where they get the idea that it's easy. I cannot imagine where that comes from.

—Rosalie Muller Wright, San Francisco Chronicle

It's tough on these people. I have so much sympathy and empathy for them, and the thing I'd tell them is that there is no direct route to syndication.

You've just got to jump in. You do what you've got to do. You send stuff out. You start to get a feel for what people think of your stuff, and if parts of it need work, you're just going to have to work on it.

You're going to have to do cards. You're going to do advertising. You're going to do freelance. You're going to do whatever it takes, and if you're not committed, you're not going to get there.

People just don't realize the commitment you have to make. I gave up a dental practice to do this. I worked my ass off—and this is forty hours a week—and I was making very, very little headway. Of course if I'd have been a great artist, it would have been easier, but this is just something that takes a lot of work, a lot of commitment. If you're not ready to really commit to it, then I'd say it's just not going to work.

—Peter Kohlsaat, Single Slices and The Nooz

The Business of Being a Professional Cartoonist

Inconsistency

No one's going to look for the needle in the haystack. No editor's going to say, "I like this one gag out of the thirty-six. The strip shows great potential."

The editor is much more likely to say, "I like thirty-five of the thirty-six gags. The strip shows great potential." He wants a haystack-size pile of needles.

If the samples can't sustain the humor, then I'm seriously in doubt, unless the executives at the syndicates have them do months and months of work.

I recently had one panel pitched to me as a Far Side *replacement, and I said, "Well, I got about five here that are good, but they're all right here at the front end. What's going to happen in a week or two? All of a sudden it's dropping off."*

He said, "Oh, no, you got to understand."

And I said, "I think I understand."

I could just tell by the way that he responded to me that he had a loser.

—JOSEPH "CHIP" VISCI, *DETROIT FREE PRESS*

GOING BACK TO THE DRAWING BOARD

It is very painful to say, "I have made this thing as well as I can make it, and now I need to say good-bye and move on to the next thing."

If you can say this, you have the makings of a professional.

A comic strip or comic characters tend to be almost like a love affair for people. You fall in love with these characters to the point where giving them up is like breaking up a love affair.

If somebody has developed a set of characters and constantly submits to the syndicate, and year after year gets rejected—they'll have sent me the stuff—and I'll advise them, "Put these characters away and develop some new ones, because they're not working, then send me some work in six months."

In six months, I guarantee they'll send me the same characters with the same captions and a letter saying, "Well, what do you think of this?" and you want to tear your hair out and say, "Divorce this thing! Put it aside! Put it away and start a new relationship!" But they can't. It's literally like divorcing a loved one.

To put it aside, I think they have to be able to start again, to understand that they are not killing something off.

When you think of a comic strip that is syndicated—the amount of material that you need over the years—no matter what you do, you're not losing anything by putting it aside. You can always use it later, and I'm willing to bet that if you did do a syndicated strip based on something else, and you did go back to your old work for material, you'd say, "Thank God! I didn't submit this, because I can do so much better now."

Once you are in the industry, once you've reached a level where you do get a contract, you do get into it. If you can sustain it, and you do improve as years go by, you're overwhelmed by how far you've gone. and people don't know that. They don't perceive that, and they're not prepared for that.

All they can see is what they're doing now and what's not happening for them now, and they'll blame everybody but themselves. They'll blame the editors, other cartoonists and circumstances, and they'll get angry with everybody. They won't be objective, and they won't say, "Well, if everybody has turned it down, and other cartoonists have said it's not working, maybe I should put it aside." That's what they have to do.

—LYNN JOHNSTON, *FOR BETTER OR FOR WORSE*

THE BUSINESS OF BEING A PROFESSIONAL CARTOONIST

INCOME TRUTH VS. INCOME FICTION

No one knows how much money you will make in syndication. They can guess. They can be optimistic. They can be cautious. They can be earth-shatteringly depressing.

With this in mind, be prepared for the long haul. Be prepared to hold two jobs for several years. Know how long it will take you to produce a week's worth of strips, and figure out how to wrap that time around a full-time job.

If you prepare for only the best-case scenario, you may not survive the harsh realities of newspaper syndication.

If you are prepared for the worst, you have a better chance to survive the first two years, which is arguably the most tumultuous time for a new feature.

As any editor, I get phone calls and letters from people who think they are going to be syndicated, and they seem to think it is a relatively simple matter. They don't seem to understand that there are very, very few people who make a good living through having their stuff syndicated.

You know, there are more successful lawyers in the city of Denver than there are successful cartoonists in the whole country. It's fairly select company, and it's just—it's tough! Very, very difficult. I don't think people understand that.

—JAY AMBROSE, *ROCKY MOUNTAIN NEWS*

I have been with a couple of syndicates, and they really do promise to make you famous, and they promise to make you wealthy.

Now who could resist that? Only it doesn't happen, you know. It turns out to be true for a very small portion of cartoonists.

—NICOLE HOLLANDER, *SYLVIA*

With Nancy, I was hired for a settlement, specific guaranteed amounts. It was more money than I was making before, and it allowed me to work full-time as a cartoonist, and I thought it was great.

Baby Blues, taught me how little you could make the first couple of years.

—JERRY SCOTT, *BABY BLUES* AND *NANCY*

There are so few people who really make a good living at syndication. It is such a wonderful way to make a living, and it's a shame that so few people can, because there are just a very limited number of spots in the paper. When I started, I definitely didn't know that every time a new strip starts in a paper an old strip has to end, and pretty much that's the way it still is. The canceled strip always has a loyal following, and it makes it very hard for the new strip to get a foothold, because the old strip has a following that will miss it.

—CATHY GUISEWITE, *CATHY*

The first notion that probably needs to be dispelled is that you can make a ton of money at a syndicate. Because, unless there is a lot of merchandising involved in it, it is a fairly unlikely prospect.

—STEVE CHRISTENSEN, LOS ANGELES TIMES SYNDICATE

In the market today, unless you have a unique piece of material, your chances are not going to be high for a major success. I would go into it with an attitude that says, "I'm going to make a specific amount of low-end dollars for a given amount of time, until the comic strip begins to take care of itself." As the popularity of your strip grows, so will your income.

—STEPHEN BENTLEY, *HERB & JAMAAL*

I tell anyone who comes to us with a strip we take on, "If you're employed, stay employed." There are no guarantees. Though we all have

high hopes, those high hopes are not always matched by the constant market.

—Lee Salem, Universal Press Syndicate

Some people say, "Gee, I'd like to be a cartoonist. How much money do you make? I want to be rich. What does it take to be a cartoonist?"

Well, immediately you say, "Don't give up your day job, Jack, because you'll never get into this business. If money is your number one goal, you're not a cartoonist."

—Lynn Johnston, *For Better or For Worse*

Syndication is usually a guarantee that you're not going to get rich. Every syndicate has a few creators that make a ton of money, a ton of creators that make very little money and a bunch of creators that kind of make middle money.

There are many, many comic strip cartoonists that draw daily comic strips in the United States that earn less than $30,000 per year, some that earn even less than that, and probably less than ten that earn over a million dollars a year.

—David Hendin, literary agent

I think there is a whole set of things that apply now that didn't apply years ago. Notably, for all effects and purposes, the day of the thousand-newspaper strip is over. The big papers buy an awful lot of territory. In some cases, they exclude fifteen to twenty daily markets. So I don't think newcomers should really look toward that superstrip classification.

—Mell Lazarus, *Miss Peach* and *Momma*

There is a very small percentage of cartoonists who reach superstar status, just as there is in any field. Yet I think this industry seems to attract more dreamers than most industries. Out of five thousand submissions, there could be three thousand of these individuals who envision themselves making Charles Schulz's income, which is obviously not going to happen.

We always try to explain this. Even if you start with fifty papers, at an average billing of twelve dollars each, that's $600 a week. Let's say the Sunday printing costs $200 a week, so that's $600 less $200, which means you've got $400 a week to split with the syndicate. So you'll be getting $200 a week—less than $10,000 a year—and that's if you have fifty papers.

—RICHARD NEWCOMBE, CREATORS SYNDICATE

It's only the very best that make a whole lot of money, and of course, licensing is the way they really get rich.

—JAY AMBROSE, ROCKY MOUNTAIN NEWS

I think the first preconception that needs to be dispelled about syndication is that it is a way to get rich. But that is a preconception that usually the people with little talent or hope of succeeding need to be divested of.

Those people, who have a lot of talent and the real potential, rarely are the ones who think they are going to get into this because they have the potential of making a lot of money. But I think they believe in themselves enough—they have to—to believe that they can earn a living at it.

—JAY KENNEDY, KING FEATURES

I just finished a conversation last Thursday with a friend of a friend of a friend. His questions were all about launching a column, and then he asked me how much he would make. I started sketching out how much I thought he might end up making, if he was very, very successful with a column of that sort and he said, "That's all?"

I said, "Yeah. If you're going to make a lot of money, you're going to have to be one of these super-successful columnists or cartoonists and get your feature in a thousand papers."

—RON PATEL, THE PHILADELPHIA INQUIRER

There's a really wide range of income levels—from "don't quit your day job" to "as much money as anybody could reasonably want or expect to have."

I think someone has to go into cartooning with the attitude that: "I'm doing it because I love it. I'm doing it because I'm passionate about it. It's my life's work, and it may or may not produce the income that I would necessarily hope for."

—ANITA TOBIAS, CREATORS SYNDICATE

It's surprising to me the number of people who think they are going to make their fortune in comics or panels. They haven't got a clue.

—SUE SMITH, DALLAS MORNING NEWS

However, if it turns out you are showered with gold and silver the first day your strip is launched, pinch yourself. It's time to wake up and go to work.

TOOLS OF THE TRADE

Since cartooning is such a personal form of expression, the choice of tools is just as personal.

Pads of paper, sheets of paper, nonphoto blue pencils, graphite pencils, mechanical pencils, pencil sharpeners, erasers, pens, markers, Rapidographs, pen tips, brushes, ink, white out, lettering guides, rulers, T squares, Glide-liners, drawing boards, drawing tables, photocopiers and computers all contribute to the process. However, all of these may not be necessary for your process.

The key to determining what you need for your process is simple.

If it works for you, use it.

If it doesn't work for you, but you want it to work for you, practice with it.

If you have no use for it, don't worry about it.

The reproduction of your comic feature is the yardstick that you should use to measure your tools.

I have my dailies printed up on smooth surface Strathmore in two different forms—some with one long, unbroken panel, and others in three equal panels.

I use a #2 soft pencil, and I use a C-5 chisel-point Speedball pen for lettering. I've used that same pen point for fifty years, from when I did comic magazine lettering. And my drawing pen is actually a writing pen. When I worked at the Art Instruction Writers Correspondence School, every now and then they would send up a couple of diplomas, and all the instructors would sign them. One day, they sent these pens up. It was thought they would be good for signing the diplomas. I tried drawing with it. I find it is the most perfect drawing pen there is because it will hold its point. It is a very strong pen, but it will also give a very fine line if you draw from the side, and when you bring it down, the point will broaden without double-crossing you. So, I've been using the same pen point for over forty-five years. There's no ink splatter, and you can go up against the grain of it too. It's the only pen that I've used.

Back at the correspondence school, I experimented with other pens for a while. I was drawing with a brush, but you need more room when you're drawing with a brush. The style that I've developed has become a very tight style, and so I only use a brush for filling in Lucy's hair and backgrounds and things like that.

—CHARLES SCHULZ, *PEANUTS*

I'm not an experimenter, but I'm always getting tired of whatever I'm using, so I go out and I buy a different kind of felt-tip pen. I haven't cracked a bottle of India ink in twenty years. I miss the smell. Great smell. I thought maybe I should just buy a bottle and just open it every morning. and I'd take a whiff and then close it up again.

On Miss Peach *I use a blue pencil. On* Momma *I use graphite, because it's a little harder to pencil, and I work a little harder on the faces. I find I can't do that with a pen. I can draw the* Peach *characters almost cold, just sort of indicate places for them, and I ink them. On* Momma *I'm a little more concerned with expression.*

—MELL LAZARUS, *MISS PEACH* AND *MOMMA*

I use a Rapidograph pen. I draw on high-surface bristol board. I use the light box method. I don't ever draw in pencil. I do the roughs on tracing paper, and then when I get them to look like I pretty much want them to look on tracing paper, I use a light box to trace them onto bristol board.

—CATHY GUISEWITE, *CATHY*

I draw everything up in HB pencil first. I don't do thumbnail sketches or doodles or anything, which is too bad because the people who do have the most wonderful notebooks you've ever seen. I don't have any of those, which is too bad because they're heirlooms.

I draw everything up on Strathmore bond paper, smooth surface #2 weight, so it's heavy enough. It's not a really heavy weight. I use the good old high school HB pencils with a kneaded eraser to take away the mistakes, and then I use C-6 Speedball pen to do almost all the drawing. It gives me the feel, the right pressure, for bringing that character to life. I like the weight of it.

I use a waterproof ink made by Pelican, and I use a brush for backgrounds and all kinds of things.

With Mike Peters's help, I'm going to try to use a brush for some lettering. He uses a brush for lettering the big emphasis words. He showed me how he does it, and it's very quick. of course he's got a practiced hand there, and I'm going to be all thumbs, but it's such a beautiful result that I'm going to give it a shot.

—LYNN JOHNSTON, *FOR BETTER OR FOR WORSE*

My strip is very low-tech. I don't get excited by pens and papers: They're just tools. I use a small sable brush and waterproof black ink to draw. I letter with a Rapidograph pen, and I use a crow-quill pen for assorted odds and ends. For years I worked on any cheap bristol board that came in a pad, but sometimes the quality was poor and it didn't take the ink well, so I switched to Strathmore bristol. Anything that's comfortable to work with is fine. You can do a great strip with lousy tools, and a lousy strip with great tools.

—BILL WATTERSON, *CALVIN AND HOBBES*

I have even given up using a drawing board. I draw on my desk or the dining room table, wherever there's a surface.

Really, all I need is a good piece of paper and a pencil. I use three-ply Strathmore, so you don't feel the rough surface below. If the paper is too thin, every crack in the table throws your pencil off. I use whatever pencil I can pick up. I have about six kinds right here. They appear after a golf game. I like a softer pencil. I don't like a real hard pencil. It bites into the paper, and it's hard to erase. I like a two-and-a-fourth pencil, but I don't know what these are I have now. Let's see—this pencil says: "Boca Raton Resort Club."

—MORT WALKER, *BEETLE BAILEY*

I've pretty much settled down into the cheapest paper I can use that works. Right now, I'm working on the back of my stationery. That works really well. It's good paper, and I have a couple thousand sheets of it laying around, so that works well, and I just use a felt pen.

There's no secret. You just find what works for you. I have a simple style, it works on simple paper.

—PETER KOHLSAAT, *SINGLE SLICES* AND *THE NOOZ*

You know what I've come to do? I'm just terrible about this, but it works for me. I go three, four, five months with the same pen point. I just seem to go with it, as the point begins to wear out or blunt or do whatever it does. It's just the style I'm using to draw in. I sort of do these herky-jerky little things.

I used to always have this fresh pen point. I'd go through one a week, or one every two or three days. Now it's almost laughable. I've got this old beat-up thing. The one that's in here now, I bet it's been in here for three months.

—JERRY VAN AMERONGEN, *BALLARD STREET*

TOOLS OF THE TRADE

EXPERIMENTING WITH NEW TOOLS

Many artists continue to experiment with new tools and new techniques, constantly challenging the way they've done things in the past.

Early on, I experimented with new tools. Not now. Early, very early, I thought maybe I was going to use a mechanical pen to work with. I was a little leery of a dip pen, but I soon got to that. I felt comfortable with that. I couldn't keep the mechanical stuff cleaned out enough. Way too sensitive, way too putzy.

—JERRY VAN AMERONGEN, *BALLARD STREET*

It's so easy to use the same old pen and brushes and never to try anything new.

I recently visited with Mike Peters, and it was wonderful to watch him use a brush and the different lettering equipment he had, and to talk to him about what worked for him. I have purchased a set of Windsor-Newton brushes, and I'm using the same sort of stuff that he's using, not that I would copy Mike. I just want the challenge of learning something new. Even if it's a false step, it still alters the look of my work a little bit.

—LYNN JOHNSTON, *FOR BETTER OR FOR WORSE*

I think that a lot of the cartoonists now—with the advent of Xerox machines—do their original art and keep their original art at home. They Xerox it and send in the copy, which we reproduce and use to service the newspapers. In the production process, we found that works very well, as long as it is a good Xerox machine.

JOSEPH D'ANGELO, KING FEATURES

A growing number of cartoonists are creating cartoons on a brand-new type of drawing table: the computer screen.

For some cartoonists, the computer offers the opportunity to expand the possibilities of what they can do with their strip or panel: A cartoonist can stretch a character, for example, or devise unusual effects with shading. For others, it may be a time- or money-saver: Typing the text into balloons instead of inking a week's worth of dialogue, or sending a week's worth of panels to a syndicate's bulletin board might push an artist's deadlines forward or save on overnight delivery charges. Soon, like the pen, pencil and brush, the computer may simply become another tool of choice.

Cartoonists' interest in using a computer as a drawing board has gone hand in hand with newspapers' changing needs. Some newpapers are beginning to demand that syndicates make all comic strips available as electronic files. In addition, syndicates are creating "bulletin boards" on which they make available some or all of their comic strips and panels. Newspapers can download, or retrieve, the features as they need them.

I'm not convinced the days of simple pen, brush and ink are numbered, but it won't be long before they're joined by the scanner, the computer and the modem as the necessary tools of the profession.

THREE VIEWS OF THE CARTOONIST

I'm going to paraphrase an old story, and if I don't get it right at least I'll have made my point.

Three blind men held onto an elephant and tried to explain what an elephant was like.

The first blind man held onto the tusks and said, "An elephant is smooth and hard with a sharp point on one end."

The second blind man held onto an ear and said, "An elephant is flat and thin."

The third blind man held onto the tail and said, "An elephant is like a snake with a hairy tip."

The following are three industry perspectives of cartoonists and their role in the process of syndication. Perhaps somewhere in this, we shall discover more than a flat, thin, sharp-pointed, hairy-tipped snake.

THREE VIEWS OF THE CARTOONIST

HOW THE CARTOONIST VIEWS HIMSELF

Well, they're essential.

—JERRY SCOTT, *BABY BLUES* AND *NANCY*

The cartoonist is what makes the newspaper a daily friend, instead of a messenger of bad tidings.

—JOHNNY HART, *B.C.* AND *THE WIZARD OF ID*

It's an odd thing, but as a cartoonist you sit in your room and do your work on a daily basis. Unlike a stand-up comedian who gets immediate feedback by applause—or lack of it—the syndicated cartoonist is really working in a vacuum. The newspaper's applause of the comedian isn't really there.

—ANONYMOUS

I think that one of the charms of cartoonists' work is that they are still doing things they liked to do when they were a kid. They reflect that innocence, the childish enthusiasm, wonder and awe that you have as a child.

I think if you get cynical, your strip is not going to make a good impression, so cartoonists have to be treated in a special way, because they are special.

—MORT WALKER, *BEETLE BAILEY*

If people haven't got what it takes, then it doesn't matter how many classes they go to, or how many studios they get in.

Some people think that simply knowing you by osmosis they will be successful. They think, "If I come to your studio, and I sit, and I watch you work, maybe I will get a job," but it's not like that. You have to be born with it. Wombed with it. You have to have those genetic mutant genes. In order to have what it takes, you have to be a writer, a director, an artist, a performer, a comedian, a musician. You have to have all kinds of little elements in there that all come together to produce the phenomenon that is a cartoonist.

I never knew I was different. I thought anybody could do it, and it's not until you get into the business that you realize not everybody can do this. Not everybody can be an Olympic skater. Not everybody can get a novel published that hits number one. The people that do achieve those things have talent, and they have drive. And it's those two things, more than luck. Luck happens when the talent and the drive are evident. Luck happens through other people who open doors for you—and with you—for the sheer joy of saying: "I did it. I helped. I was there when she needed an open door."

I've had lots of open doors.

—LYNN JOHNSTON, *FOR BETTER OR FOR WORSE*

I have always said, the greatest thing about being a cartoonist is we can't be promoted, so we don't have to worry about working up the corporate ladder.

—JEFF MACNELLY, *SHOE* AND *PLUGGERS*

There is tremendous genuine affection and support within the community of cartoon artists.

Once I became involved with these people—and it's Hollywood that made it feel this way—I thought there'd be a lot of insincere air kissing and congratulations, and behind your back they'd be hoping I'd fail. It's nothing like that. It absolutely isn't.

I could tell you stories that would make you weep. How fond, how supportive, how caring cartoonists are of each other, and how far out of their way they will go to help. Financially, personally, any way they can.

I can't tell you stories, because it would be naming names, but there have been some absolutely overwhelming cases of just generosity and help and care that you wouldn't get in any other field where we're in competition with each other—and we are. But we tend to let the syndicates compete for us.

I think that we are also very honest with each other, and I think that is where we run into trouble when we're working with brand-new cartoonists who want our advice. We're also very honest with people that come to us. I think that honesty is such a gift to the person on the receiving end, because, considering the type of people most of us are, we're not out to wound anyone. We give them an opportunity by helping them out, and I think they perceive this as being negative stuff. If we do criticize their work, it comes from a real sense of wanting to encourage and help, not from a sense of wanting to stifle the other person's abilities.

—Lynn Johnston, *For Better or For Worse*

Three Views of the Cartoonist

How the Syndicate Views the Cartoonist

Obviously, the cartoonist is the creative force, the one who generates the product. Without the cartoonist, none of us would have a job.

The flip side of that coin, though, is that without the syndicates, the salespeople, and all of the businesspeople, the cartoonist would have a wonderful product, but no market value.

—Anita Tobias, Creators Syndicate

I think the key element is the cartoonist. He or she is a prime player. Syndicates wouldn't exist without talent. Talent could exist without syndicates, so we try to build a company built on that understanding and appreciation. A number of the things we've done—giving people leaves and establishing vacation policy—have been criticized by newspaper editors, but I think those who appreciate features and the effort it takes to produce them are supportive of us.

—Lee Salem, Universal Press Syndicate

The cartoonist is the major creator whose work is a significant part of the daily newspaper's major readership builder.

We take on a cartoonist, and no one can represent a feature better than the creator of that feature. We have cartoonists, and we have writers who love to call editors on occasion or visit them when they're traveling in town, and that all helps. We encourage it, and we love it, but it's not necessary. Our role is to help the cartoonist produce the best possible strip to the best of our ability—and then to do the best of our ability to sell it, and to represent them in the best possible light. Anything the cartoonist does to help that along is only going to help in the success of the strip.

—ALAN SHEARER, WASHINGTON POST WRITERS GROUP

Historically syndicates haven't given cartoonists as much trust or confidence as they should. For the most part, the cartoonist, the one who has created the work, really should have control over the final output. Obviously, it's a business decision. The syndicate knows things about libel law or invasion of privacy or whatever that the cartoonist does not know about, so it's up to the syndicate to explain the risks to the cartoonist.

In a lot of ways, the cartoonist is the boss. The cartoonist is the asset. When a syndicate is sold, what they're selling are the contracts they have with the cartoonists. Those are the assets of the corporation.

—RICHARD NEWCOMBE, CREATORS SYNDICATE

THREE VIEWS OF THE CARTOONIST

HOW THE NEWSPAPER EDITOR VIEWS THE CARTOONIST

I would say that the cartoonist is the communicator. Like a bridge, like a pipeline, like a lightbulb, like a bloodstream, they have to create the bond with the reader. And the good ones really do that well. They create such a bond that the reader simply can't do without them.

—RON PATEL, THE PHILADELPHIA INQUIRER

I like to draw the distinction between humorist and comedian. I think of humorists as people like Garrison Keillor and Will Rogers and Mark Twain. Comedians we could list forever. I think there is a deep humanity to one, while the other kind of delves on the surface, and I think the best cartoonists are probably those who somehow have this deep humanity, who are humorists and are able to convey it.

I suspect if you look at those cartoon strips that have been most successful, have most affected us, have made us stop and think, they have a depth to them. They have a great humanity to them.

—JAY AMBROSE, ROCKY MOUNTAIN NEWS

Some people are what we call high-maintenance employees. Sometimes they're worth it.

The really creative people like Dan O'Neill, like Berkley Breathed, even Gary Larson, are a little bit off the mark. I mean, they're not guys in business suits and ties. They've got a creative spark, and they are a little bit off-center. Maybe that's what gives them their point of view.

—Rosalie Muller Wright, *San Francisco Chronicle*

THE INDEPENDENT REPRESENTATIVE

Representatives. Agents. Developers. Packagers. In the world of syndicated cartooning, these people may perform vastly different functions even though they all perform within a very narrow focus of the industry.

The independent representative may be a developer or packager who works with you to create or develop a feature for submission to syndicates and also handles the contract negotiation. Traditionally, they work for a percentage of the strip over the lifetime of the feature.

The independent representative may be a literary agent or literary representative who specializes in comics features and takes on completed strip samples, sells them to syndicates, handles the contract negotiation and continues to represent the strip and all its ancillary products. Traditionally, the literary agent and literary representative work for a percentage of your gross income for the length of their contract with you.

Nicole Hollander uses a representative to sell her self-syndicated *Sylvia* to newspapers, which just goes to prove you need to determine your needs.

DETERMINING THE NEED FOR A REPRESENTATIVE

I would say to someone coming to us, if you need guidance, that guidance should be twofold: the guidance that you get editorially, and most important, in your business negotiations. Keep in mind, accepting something because you have waited so long for it may hurt you later on. You need the expertise of an attorney or a businessperson who will interpret legal documents for you and guide you accordingly.

—Toni Mendez, literary representative

Since all syndicates review all over-the-transom submissions, it is very difficult to determine when it might be to your best advantage to get an independent representative.

With a lawyer, you have council. With a representative, you have someone whose battles are your battles.

Ultimately, it may come down to whether you want an adviser you can pay off or a partner you need to share your earnings with.

Once again, only you know your needs.

It depends upon the individual. Some cartoonists will come to us at an early stage of development. Other cartoonists are ready for their work to go to the syndicates, and some people are working alone and they're lost. They want someone to talk to. Some of them are fortunate to have friends who are cartoonists. Today, cartoonists are lucky because there are schools where they can get feedback.

But when the syndicate is ready to offer a contract, then I believe cartoonists need professional advice.

—Toni Mendez, literary representative

Someone outside the syndicate stands to write themselves into your contract and own part of what you're doing, and I see terrible results in that.

—Lynn Johnston, *For Better or For Worse*

I don't really think cartoonists need a rep.

—Anonymous syndicate executive

I think the only time to consider a rep or agent is when you're so bad that nobody wants you.

—Anonymous

By the way, that is less of the pie that you will get, since you already share your money with the syndicate.

—Stephen Bentley, *Herb & Jamaal*

I can just tell you what changed my life, and that was that I got a rep, a woman who had worked for syndicates, who sells my work and who I have never met. She's in Florida, and she works on the phone, and she loves selling, loves the strategy of it, and that was my weakest point.

I couldn't bear to call people and not have them answer my calls or reject my strip. It's very hard. You're trying to be tactful and you really want to say something really rude to them.

I tried many things before I was lucky enough to find her. I hired a friend of mine who was an actor. I thought, "Well, he's used to rejection,

*so he can do this for me," and he said it was the hardest thing he had
ever done. He could only do it for twenty minutes at a time, then he does
a lie-down with a cold compress on his head before he'd start again.
That was very difficult.*

—Nicole Hollander, *Sylvia*

*My guess is that there are few people who, after they have been re-
jected by syndicates, would go to an outside developer or agent and then
get syndicated.*

*I think a syndicate's editorial staff is pretty good at picking what
they pick and why they pick it. That's not to say they get everything, but
I think they are pretty sharp and understand the competitive nature of
the business.*

*I think an outside developer does have the luxury of being able to
take the time, maybe more time than a syndicate has to work on a feature and develop it, and that may be the plus in working with somebody
outside the syndicate.*

—Lee Salem, Universal Press Syndicate

*I don't think cartoonists really need agents. What they do need
and what they should always get, after having reached a position of
consideration by the syndicate, is a lawyer. They should have a lawyer
to help them negotiate either a development deal or the formal contract
with the syndicate.*

*It is well known that within the industry—McMeel, D'Angelo,
Newcombe, United Media—we all say we get five thousand to six thousand submissions a year, and we take a look at every single one of
them. Obviously we discard many. We pick three a year. Three a year
out of five thousand to six thousand submissions. So if you're going to
be picked, it is because you have a special, unique talent. It's not like
you need an agent like an actor or actress, where the agent is going to
get you roles because he knows producers and directors. Oh, sure, if a
Lew [Little] or a David [Henden] comes in, we'll look at it a little closer
than if it had come in over the transom, but only that.*

*You've got to believe in your own talent and believe in the reality
that syndicates do take submissions seriously. They don't take them
lightly.*

—Joseph D'Angelo, King Features

*Cartoonists have to do it all on their own. What's the difference be-
tween me packaging my work and sending it off, or some agent packaging it and sending it off? I love the gag that says an agent is the guy
who hates you for taking 70 percent of his money, because that tends to
be the way it is.*

When some cartoonist writes to me and says, "Oh, I've met this per-

son who thinks I'm really talented, and they're acting as my agent," I want to scream, "Stop! Act as your own agent, because there's nothing an agent can do for you that you can't do for yourself." But so many cartoonists are so insecure they feel they need an agent. Or gullible enough. An agent will tell you that without them you won't survive. Without them you'll never get a job.

I've had an agent. I wouldn't hear from her for six months, and when I was ready to dump her—this was for licensing, so this is different—I would be ready to say to her, "You know, I think it's time for us to part ways," and she would by osmosis know what I was thinking and say, "I have been working so hard for you. I've been trying to get in touch with you. You won't believe what I've been doing. Without me—"

Suddenly I'm thinking, "Oh, my God! How could I have doubted this wonderful, helpful person?" But she wasn't really doing anything for me. and so, an agent will convince you that you cannot survive without them.

You have to ask ahead of time, "What is an agent's role in my life?"
—LYNN JOHNSTON, FOR BETTER OR FOR WORSE

THE AGENT'S ROLE IN THE DEVELOPMENT OF A FEATURE

It is the same as being an editor—guiding and molding talent by asking provocative questions to help the cartoonist bring out characters and situations to their fullest degree.
—TONI MENDEZ, LITERARY REPRESENTATIVE

How many fingers in the creative pie are too many fingers? Two? Three? Four? When does a pie cease to be your pie and turn into finger pie?

In the broad sense, the answer to this is probably connected to the clarity of the creator's vision. If the creator is able to process and interpret the feedback constructively into the feature, then the pie can never cease to be your pie.

Calvin and Hobbes was originally a family strip and focused on the parents. Someone at a syndicate wanted Bill Watterson to focus on the kid and the stuffed tiger. Simply put, someone was perceptive enough to give this advice, and someone else was perceptive enough to take it.

As the creator, you always have choices, and it's up to you to decide whether or not to take them.

I don't ever think a cartoonist needs a developer. I once had someone call me, who I think was a developer, and he suggested I change the name of the strip, that it might make it more acceptable, and I thought, "If that's what a developer is, I'm not interested."
—NICOLE HOLLANDER, SYLVIA

The best source of good development of a strip would be found within a syndicate that has a broad history of successful syndication of cartoonists, as opposed to using an agent or outside consultant.

Although there are some agents that I think are probably pretty good, the syndicates are in the best position to know whether a strip is likely to succeed or not, whether a strip can find a unique place in the market. I think they're good judges as to whether a cartoonist is going to be able to maintain a level of enthusiasm and creativity for a very long period of time and not burn out in six months.

And I think the syndicates tend to react quite quickly to a good submission, so I don't think having an agent brings anything to the table, other than perhaps in negotiating your contract.
—STEVE CHRISTENSEN, LOS ANGELES TIMES SYNDICATE

People send me something and say, "I'm a very good cartoonist. Look at my drawings and help me develop them." That's not what it's all about.

It's all about refining something that is already very, very good. Refining, refining, refining. Helping, helping, helping. Suggesting, suggesting. Saying, "What if? What if this character did this?"

The cartoonist says, "No, no, that wouldn't be true to my idea."

Good! That's good. That's a good interaction. That's development. I say, "Do you think this?"

The cartoonist says, "No, I don't," or "let me think about it."

You mention something, and they stew on it. They think about it, and that's the development process.

The other thing you have to remember is that the agent really is not the editor.

Even though my background is editorial, the agent is not the editor—not of a comic strip, not of a book—so I have to be very careful not to convey that I am editing this and that it's going to be perfect when I'm done.

If I'm successful, what's going to happen is that I'm going to get it in the hands of an editor who is going to want to tinker with it a little bit more. So I really am not a heavy developer. I don't grade gags. I don't give people homework.

Every once in a while, I've dealt with a hugely talented cartoonist who, for whatever reason, hasn't been able to put together a strip that really works. Sometimes they're editorial cartoonists, and they're really pressing, pressing, pressing.

I have had some advice that I've developed, and I think it is probably the best "development advice" I have given people.

First of all, you usually won't create the right idea when you're pressing too hard. So I have given actual assignments and told the cartoonists not to draw anything that has to do with this strip for two or three months.

I've said, "You can think about it all you want. You can champ at the bit all you want, but I don't want you sitting at that drawing board trying to crank things out."

"Well, what am I to do?"

"Here's what I want you to do: I want you to go to the shopping center, to the mall, to the zoo. Go out with your kids. If you don't have kids, go out with your dog. If you don't have a dog, go out and walk. Go do things. Go watch people. Go to the supermarket every day. But don't sit down at your drawing board, and don't set anything in stone."

If you don't let them draw for two or three months, their ideas stay in flux, and an idea that seems great one day modifies a little the next day, and the next, and the next, and sometimes it works.

There's no guarantees, but I think it's good, because a lot of very talented people say: "Okay, let's see, there's a lot of senior citizens, so I think I'll do a senior citizen comic strip." Forget it. Occasionally people have successfully delineated a market need and created a strip to go into it. There have been exceptions, but they invariably don't work when they're manufactured.

—David Hendin, literary agent

The Agent's Role as a Continuing Representative

Inevitably the question becomes, "Great, you helped me sell the comic strip, but now what do you do?"

The representative and the cartoonist must keep communication lines open constantly. As time goes on, it is even more important.

As long as a contract exists between talent and a representative, the representative is responsible for the career of the talent in all aspects and receives compensation accordingly.

—Toni Mendez, literary representative

Three Views by a Representative

Since the role of the independent developer is a tributary of the traditional process of syndication, it's more important at this juncture to get their view looking out than the view of others looking in.

Three Views by a Representative
How the Representative Views Himself

I call myself a representative because we represent more than just negotiations. I hope we guide and I hope we stimulate and I believe those that are in the business trust us. To me that's the most important element.

—TONI MENDEZ, LITERARY REPRESENTATIVE

First of all, there is no doubt about this: When a syndicate takes on a comic strip, it takes on a comic strip because it thinks that comic strip is going to make money. If the standard split is fifty/fifty—which it is—then the syndicate and the cartoonist are going to make money together.

However, the syndicate has all kinds of people there, plus its own lawyers, plus its own staff, and my view is that the cartoonist needs someone of substance and of knowledge in the business to help weigh down his side of the table.

When Pat Brady is in there talking to the syndicate, if Pat says something to someone at the syndicate, they may turn to one of their colleagues and say, "What do you think of that?"

Well, if Pat's in there by himself, and they say something to him, what does he do? Who can he ask, "What do you think?" Well, he can turn to me and he can say, "David, what do you think of that?" It weighs down the table on the side of the cartoonist.

Many cartoonists have made satisfactory deals without having agents or without having representatives, and I think it is going to go more and more toward that.

In the book business, many publishers won't even look at un-agented submissions. Why is that? Well, because agents provide a screen. In two years, I've looked at four hundred cartoon properties. I think I've submitted four to the syndicates, and I sold one of the four.

The one thing I know—and it's absolutely true for anyone that is known in the business—if I send something to United Features or King Features or Universal Press Syndicate, it goes right to the top. It skips a couple of levels, because they know me and they know my track record in the business. That doesn't mean it's not going to be rejected, but it's not something in a slush pile that some secretary is going to read and blow off.

I think the biggest advantage is just having somebody you can look at and say, "Well what do you think of that?" and when they tell you, you can go to the bank with it, because that's your agent, your representative, your person that is working with you.

One of the problems with an attorney is that an attorney may be great at negotiating a contract, but I'm not sure those attorneys are willing or able to analyze those monthly statements and interact with the marketing people on a regular basis. One of the things a good agent can help a cartoonist avoid is getting into a nagging situation with the syndicate. The agent becomes the nagger, but one hopes they aren't actually nagging.

—DAVID HENDIN, LITERARY AGENT

HOW THE REPRESENTATIVE VIEWS THE CARTOONIST

Cartoonists are wonderful people. They are unusual—different from authors, illustrators or creators in other art forms. I have an expression for it. They reduce everything to the commonest denominator. They get rid of all the garbage, and just see "it" in its purest light. They have to in order to do what they are doing. They are really remarkable people. As you can see, I am fond of them. They are very special.

—TONI MENDEZ, LITERARY REPRESENTATIVE

HOW THE REPRESENTATIVE VIEWS THE SYNDICATE

Syndicates really don't make a property happen. The property makes itself happen. The syndicate facilitates it.

The proof of that is, let's say a syndicate has a property it thinks is great, and it decides it is going to have million-dollar sales and promotion for syndication and licensing. There is no guarantee at all that this will make that property happen. In fact, the odds are that it won't make the property happen. The properties that happen are the properties that grow on their readers and explode, because they are what they are.

—DAVID HENDIN, LITERARY AGENT

THE SYNDICATE

As their role pertains to comics features, the syndicates perform a variety of functions for themselves, for cartoonists and for newspapers.

They review feature submissions, work with cartoonists to develop properties, sign contracts with cartoonists to distribute features, promote features to newspapers, sell features to newspapers, print and distribute features to newspapers, bill and collect receipts from newspapers, pay contractually agreed-upon monies to cartoonists and keep cartoonists continually updated with a client list and each paper's pay rate.

Syndicates seem to serve so many masters, it's no wonder they walk a tightrope that sways in a breeze.

Syndicates are not your parents.

I think that cartooning is extremely childlike. It is the only profession—other than being a cowboy—that you can start doing when you're two or three years old and still do when you're fifty. And there's that side of this profession that says, "Let me do my drawings and you take care of me."

Boy, when I first joined the syndicate, I thought they were going to be my parents. Here is this large organization who wants to do nothing but take care of me, and give me money, and make sure I'm happy, and

---

to let me do my thing. Boy, that's a great thing. That's worth the price of admission. And you know, there would be no jumping from syndicate to syndicate, or need for new contracts, or "Okay, let's fight over this," if that one simple thing were true, if they just took care of you. But that's not realistic.

—MIKE PETERS, MOTHER GOOSE & GRIMM

It's not always the best things that are the most popular. Look at literature. Look at art. Look at music. It has nothing to do with how good something is or how intelligent something is. It all boils down to "what can they sell?"

—PETER KOHLSAAT, SINGLE SLICES AND THE NOOZ

THE EDITOR

It's a rare combination of market savvy and editorial savvy that culminates in the traditional syndicate cartoon editors. They have to understand and anticipate their syndicate's needs and the newspaper's needs, as well as have an articulate working knowledge of the comic strip art form.

Because the cartoon editor is the cartoonist's pipeline into the syndicate, the cartoon editor is either the mediator or arbiter between art and commerce.

In general, the editor has a couple of roles.

One role, of course, is in the acquisition and development of cartoons. The second part is in the actual editing of cartoons.

Every writer I know benefits from a good editor, and every cartoonist I know could benefit from a good editor, if they turned in material early enough for the editor to work on it. That doesn't mean an editor is supposed to rewrite a cartoon or make changes in gags, but an editor is the closest person to a strip who is not the cartoonist.

Sometimes your perceptions of your own creations get a little warped or stale. Your editor is a partner who can keep an eye on that and help maintain a certain voice and consistency, if you begin to drift from it in a way that is not productive.

Another important role of an editor is just really being somebody to talk to and somebody to communicate what's going on at the syndicate.

—DAVID HENDIN, LITERARY AGENT

When I started the strip, the editor at the syndicate worked a lot with me to help me clarify who the characters were, and I mean he really worked with me.

I would send him roughs for everything I did. Before I finished them, he would comment, and then we would talk about them. Period-

ically, I would fly there with a sack of roughs. We would go over them.

He would kind of guide me on what worked, what didn't work, and continued to help me keep characters in focus. He really encouraged me to consolidate miscellaneous male characters into one character, Irving, and miscellaneous women characters into one girlfriend with a real personality.

That was real helpful to me in the beginning. After a while—I'm going to say a couple years—I quit sending roughs, but I still would call every two weeks and read strips to him before I drew them. It was like getting an okay on the strips. And at that time, he would say, "This one works. This doesn't work. This works better than this one. Here's why." It was really a lot of attention and really a lot of hand-holding and guiding. It was really valuable to me.

I think when the strip was about five years old, he said, "You really don't have to check anymore. If we get strips in and we have a problem with them, we'll call and we'll talk about it, but you're really on your own." At the time, I really felt it was like getting the training wheels off the bike. At this point, I don't talk to anybody there about it ever. There's no comment good or bad from them. I just sort of keep doing it.

—CATHY GUISEWITE, *CATHY*

A really good editor can work with a cartoonist and significantly contribute to the growth of a strip. While there is certainly a place for that, it is not necessary for all comics. Some are already fully developed, and the only job is to make sure the words are spelled correctly.

—ANITA TOBIAS, CREATORS SYNDICATE

The role they have usually played for me is a taste one, but I think their greatest service is the spell-check service. I always thought I was a great speller, but when you get into the lettering, that messes it all up. I think your creative thing kind of takes over. I really enjoy lettering, and sometimes I get carried away and throw in an extra letter.

—JEFF MACNELLY, *SHOE* AND *PLUGGERS*

They're more in the line of censors than editors. They don't know how to write gags. They don't know what's funny. They don't really know much about cartooning. They're out there just as a watchdog, trying to make sure that nothing offensive goes out that they're going to be in trouble over. They're so afraid of offending anybody—this is generally a problem with editors in newspapers, too—that nothing really gets done.

Cartoonists have to let creativity flow, go with it and not worry about offending anybody. When it comes to satire, somebody is going to be offended. If you try to do satire that pleases everybody, it's going to please nobody. You're going to end up with something very bland. You can't worry about offending anybody. You know where the line is. You know what the readership is out there. You're not going to do in Play-boy what you do in the comic strip. You should have that general assessment of it.

—WILEY MILLER, *NON SEQUITUR*

I think a great cartoon editor knows a feature is the property of the creator, so he can be that silent collaborator.

First, you wouldn't get together if there was nothing there. The syndicate editor spots what is there. It may have to move in this direction, or it may have to move in that direction, or there may be a character who has more force and more potential than the creator realizes.

The editor does this, not by being a sledgehammer, but by being a sounding board, being able to respond as well as to help create, but always in the background. Being a confidante. Being a voice that the creator hopefully respects and can respond to.

A good editor helps form a real partnership with the creator, and when it works it's like a beautiful symphony.

—JOHN MCMEEL, UNIVERSAL PRESS SYNDICATE

Right at the beginning of my work with Universal Press, I desperately needed Lee Salem. I think if you have a very good cartoon editor—and I'm sure they're as scarce as anything—that person can be the difference between your being launched with confidence and flair, as compared to your sort of bumping out of the chute and landing on your backside.

—LYNN JOHNSTON, *FOR BETTER OR FOR WORSE*

I think all cartoonists benefit from a good editor. Not just an editor who can fix the diction or the punctuation, but an editor who can help them develop the concept and the progress of the strip. An editor who can tell them when they're over the line in issues of things like taste. An editor who can keep them pumped up, almost like a coach, and keep them enthusiatic about doing the work.

—STEVE CHRISTENSEN, LOS ANGELES TIMES SYNDICATE

I am much more actively involved during the development period and the initial first year or two of the strip. And then a lot of my functions drop off after the second year or so.

By that point, they will be very versed in syndication and know where the lines are, so I don't guide them as much. So my role changes. I think my real job, early on, is to point out to the cartoonists their strengths and their weaknesses, to say, "This is what you do really well. This is what you don't do well." I think that's the most important thing.

And then I would teach them about concerns that are more business concerns. They should be aware of simple things like: You don't do jokes about illnesses, because somebody out there is suffering from that illness at this moment, or their family members are, and at this point of time in their lives, nothing is ever funny about whatever illness they have.

I don't want to start saying, "Here are a list of things that are really tough to do," because I don't want to fill their heads with the negative before they really figure out what they are doing. And also, there are always exceptions to everything you say, so you don't want to make absolutes.

—JAY KENNEDY, KING FEATURES

In my case, the editors make sure that the continuity and the integrity of the strip are maintained. Their focus is on whether or not I'm staying on the concept and the characters, so they kind of pinpoint any deviation from the norm. Whether or not that deviation is good or bad, I can at least be aware of it. They also take care of my spelling and diction, the line editing.

Also, they stay attuned to the political correctness. Am I offending someone? Is there a reason? I should talk with them to find out whether or not it is something I want to continue to do and accept the responsibility.

—STEPHEN BENTLEY, *HERB & JAMAAL*

By the time one of our cartoonists sends something in, it is usually well developed. We are really the first line of reaction on how it works. Of course, we always check for the obvious things, spelling and things like that, but it is rare that we will question our cartoonist on the way he drew something.

We just feel that he is the artist, and it is his artwork. If there is an image that we don't think is going to reproduce, well, we'll tell him that. But it's a rare day that we'll tell him, "You gotta move a tree. You gotta put a plant here," or anything like that.

The covenant we have—it's in our agreement, but it's also a covenant with all of our writers and cartoonists—is that when it comes here it is as much of a finished product as they can make it. And that's their responsibility. We then try to serve as the first readers, the first eyes of the public, and I think a lot of people count on us for that.

—ALAN SHEARER, WASHINGTON POST WRITERS GROUP

THE CHIEF EXECUTIVE OFFICER

Every company needs a big-picture guy, someone who evaluates the operation, maintains intercompany relationships and plans for the future.

Their names are at the top of the syndicate mastheads, but what do they do?

I can tell you what I do in my workweek. I brought my son to work one day. It was around Christmas. Later at home, we were sitting around the dining room table, and my teenage daughter says, "So, Jack, what does Daddy do all day?"

Jack says, "He talks on the phone."

And she says, "How fun!"

—RICHARD NEWCOMBE, CREATORS SYNDICATE

They've got to look good, have a firm handshake, wear great ties, know where to eat, and—I think it's the old Teddy Roosevelt—speak softly and carry a big stick.

—LYNN JOHNSTON, *FOR BETTER OR FOR WORSE*

The syndicate president is like an orchestra conductor, sort of a combination of producer of the show and conductor of the orchestra. Ultimately, it is the syndicate president's responsibility, but it depends on the syndicate. Some syndicates' presidents are quite removed from the day-to-day operations.

—DAVID HENDIN, LITERARY AGENT

I think there are a lot of CEOs that don't do much.

—ANONYMOUS

I think their role is to set the direction for the kind of syndicate they want to be.

I think syndication in its best form is more than just a collection of junk that you go out and market. I think the president sets the tone for the kind of business they're going to do.

—JANE AMARI, *THE KANSAS CITY STAR*

They're the ones who are the cornerstone of the personality of the syndicate. And the way they approach business, the way they approach talent and the way they approach employees helps develop the

character of the particular operation. They generally have a high profile in the industry, and people in the industry look to them for leadership.
                              —LEE SALEM, UNIVERSAL PRESS SYNDICATE

I guess if you're John McMeel, you figure out a million ways to make more money. A million more mugs and T-shirts, and book publishing. He's just a house afire with his new ideas on how to license and market, and that's where the money is—let's face it—licensing.
                    —ROSALIE MULLER WRIGHT, SAN FRANCISCO CHRONICLE

I think the role of a CEO in this kind of media business is to be focused in terms of "where are we going to be two, three, four, five years from now?"

When those creators invest their confidence in us, and their hopes and their dreams, we give them the best editors and the best salespeople. We attempt to give them all those things. The CEO has got to be thinking in terms of, "Okay, how do we fulfill that dream for the creator?"

Well nowadays, that means we're talking about the information highway. We have to be thinking in terms of, "If we're going to go out there and create a market, how can that market best serve the creator and the company?"

At the same time, that CEO better stay in contact with the people who put him there, and that's his creators. So we get very involved on every level. That's what it's about. That's what it has to be about. It's the CEO's responsibility to also be involved. He better know the pluses and the minuses of his own operation, and sometimes he can only find that out through talking with the creators.
                          —JOHN McMEEL, UNIVERSAL PRESS SYNDICATE

The president's goal is to produce continued growth in their company, and that is harder and harder to do in newspaper syndication, because of the dwindling number of newspapers, the dwindling number of competitive markets, and very tight editorial budgets, which lead to very tight editorial space.

A good CEO is looking for ways to diversify the syndicate into allied businesses, to continue to produce new revenue streams, to take advantage of new opportunities and new technologies, to look for kindred companies that can synergize with what syndicates have traditionally done, to make sure the managers supervising various departments of the syndicate are effective, to maintain good relations with contributors and try to maintain a high profile for the syndicate, in terms of its reputation.
                  —STEVE CHRISTENSEN, LOS ANGELES TIMES SYNDICATE

The Sales Personnel

Whether it's by phone or in person, the syndicate salespeople are the ones who offer comics features to newspapers and ask them to buy, plead with them to buy, convince them to buy, and come back again and again and again.

The salespeople cultivate relationships with newspaper editors, striving for relationships of mutual understanding, trust and reliance. The syndicate salesperson is often the newspaper editor's conduit of topical syndicate information for what's hot and what's not.

In the movie *Hoffa, Danny* DeVito said, "Do not take 'no' for an answer, because if you will not take 'no' for an answer, eventually the answer comes back 'yes.' " Ultimately, this is what syndicate salespeople are asked to do, and they walk a tough line between gaining client trust and having to perform.

I think it's important that the creator and the editor work closely together and then listen to the sounds and the vibes that they get from the people in the field. That input needs to be processed, because if the salesman doesn't sell, he loves to make excuses about why he couldn't sell. Our editors listen to our salespeople very closely, and then they filter what really comes back.

—John McMeel, Universal Press Syndicate

Man, cartoonists think they've got a tough job. Cartoonists should go on some sales calls. These guys are getting told no in their face all the time.

I think that communication between the cartoonist and the salesperson can really be valuable to the sales. Those people are the heroes. They're the workhorses of the whole thing.

—Jerry Scott, *Baby Blues* and *Nancy*

They sell the product of the syndicate, not necessarily your product. Whatever the syndicate has given them to sell.

—Stephen Bentley, *Herb & Jamaal*

They maintain the customer service function. I suppose if the newspapers are unhappy with the drift of the strip, rather than calling me they may call the salespeople. The salespeople would then call Lee Salem, and Lee would call me.

Universal Press has about seven salespeople who drive around the country and have one-on-ones with newspaper editors. It works pretty well. I have been fortunate in getting to know these people pretty well. I get feedback from them, in terms of how editors are reacting to my strip, and also I can let them know what future directions the strip is taking.

—Bill Amend, *FoxTrot*

I don't think cartoonists appreciate how difficult it is to go out there and drive around in your 1991 Dodge and try to sell your work. Salesmen have to see the same editors over and over. If a cartoonist's work isn't getting any better, or if the guy isn't doing anything new, it kind of puts the salesmen on the spot. But when the salesman finally does sell it, I think the cartoonist should be sending the best work that he or she can. That salesman works very hard.

—Charles Schulz, *Peanuts*

The salespeople are key. They're the ones that go out and sell it. It's true that, after a certain point, some strips sort of go out there and sell themselves. But that first couple years is tough, because the strip hasn't built up any kind of body of work.

—Mell Lazarus, *Miss Peach* and *Momma*

It's important that the salesmen have relationships with the clients we serve, and that the newspaper editors be able to trust their judgment.

—Lee Salem, Universal Press Syndicate

There shouldn't be a need for salesmen. If editors were doing their job and took the time to learn about purchases, you wouldn't need salesmen. You know what salesmen do? They go in, they sit down with the editor, hand him the sales brochure and proceed to explain to the editor what he is reading. That's nuts. The editor is supposed to look at it and figure it out for himself.

—Wiley Miller, *Non Sequitur*

In my other life I was in sales and marketing. I never had too much trouble packaging up ideas and concepts, and figuring them out, and organizing them, and getting them to the sales force.

When I'm doing my own stuff, I'm emotionally involved in it—my ego is involved in it—and I am a miserable salesperson for it. All I have to do is have a few people say, "Ah, I don't know about that," and suddenly my self-esteem is crumbling.

So I think when it comes to selling your work directly to people, whether it's in the area of licensing or syndication, the sales rep becomes a pretty critical element.

I think the sales reps in syndication oftentimes don't have direct contact with the cartoonist. I do now. I think it is important for the sales reps to know what you are trying to accomplish. As a cartoonist, it would be good for you to know that your sales reps understand what you're doing in your strip, understand how to read it, and then be able to transfer that into benefits for their customer, the newspaper.

Sometimes there are sales reps who show it to the editors, and they just have to rely on the fact that the editor likes it. If the editor starts to turn up his nose at it, they flee from it. They can't stand in and do a little teaching about it.

If the sales reps have success with it early on, then you are in good shape, because they're going to feel positive about it and they're going to push it. If people turn their noses up, and the sales reps don't themselves have a conviction about it, they are far more reluctant to pull it out of the bag.

—JERRY VAN AMERONGEN, *BALLARD STREET*

I very smugly say, "Oh, yes, I'm in over fifteen hundred papers," but who put me in fifteen hundred papers? Maybe my work is worthy, but I didn't trek it from door to door, shake hands with the editors, and beg for one more look.

—LYNN JOHNSTON, *FOR BETTER OR FOR WORSE*

Selling comics features is a much different proposition than selling text features. A good comics salesperson needs to identify with what the cartoonist is trying to tell the reader, and they need to be able to sit down and enthusiastically and clearly articulate those concepts to a newspaper editor. Not only why a strip is different from other strips that appear in the editor's newspaper, but why this strip deserves to be in the paper and what the benefit to the reader would be.

—STEVE CHRISTENSEN, LOS ANGELES TIMES SYNDICATE

They've really got the toughest job. My impression of the syndicate salesman in the newspaper world is that he is about the lowest man on the totem pole. A lot of times—it depends on the editor and the relationship he has with the editor—he comes into the office, and the editor starts yelling at him for how much he's paying for the features, or for what he's not getting offered. He tends to be the point man between us and the editor. I think it's a tough job.

Also, the thing that all of us don't often realize is that you are competing against people in your own syndicate. When a salesman comes to an editor, he's got two hundred things to show him, so it's a difficult way to get your stuff in front of an editor. But it's really the only way.

—JEFF MACNELLY, *SHOE* AND *PLUGGERS*

It's tough. Foot soldiers. Everything has got to be sold. You have to sit across from the editor, and if you have built a track record, you have to talk about why this company is behind this feature. You have to create a climate in that office the moment you walk in. Hopefully, you have a success record that you are walking in with, but selling our features is not like stocking a supermarket shelf. We're not putting product up there where somebody comes along and takes this and takes that.

Everything we do, we are doing for a reason. We know what is out there. Our job is syndicate "informationship." Newspapers and syndicates are all in this together. The only enemies we have out there right now are time, TV and other competing media that take time away from the readers.

We are developing features that will attract and hold readers. When our people go in to see an editor, he or she has to know why they are selling that feature and what our purpose is behind it.

A good salesman is a person who knows his or her market, knows his or her editor, doesn't waste the editor's time and gets across the points that are necessary.

—JOHN MCMEEL, UNIVERSAL PRESS SYNDICATE

The role of the sales personnel is to get the comic strips sold to the newspaper. The problem is, that ain't easy.

From the beginning, the sales organization includes marketing, promotion, advertising. They create brochures. They try to create a positive selling environment for the feature, then they try to put that positive selling environment into the editor and turn him into a client.

—DAVID HENDIN, LITERARY AGENT

I think that a syndicate is as good as the people you deal with, and the number of salesmen that they have.

One of the things that I always tell people who are looking at this syndicate or that syndicate, there's one real, very easy thing to ask. "How many salesmen do they have? Do they have people who actually go out and glad-hand editors, or do they just have people who call?"

Syndicates that just have call-out people are fine and can be very good syndicates, but I think they always have one hand tied behind their back, because the number of salesmen who are on the road truly helps the number of papers you are going to get, just by the number of people going out and talking to editors.

—MIKE PETERS, MOTHER GOOSE & GRIMM

The role of the sales personnel is to listen to the newspaper editors, to hear what they are looking for, and then to match up what we offer to what they are looking for. Additionally, to highlight the strengths, the high points of the strip.

The most important thing, to start with—because you can't get anywhere until you accomplish this—is to get the editor's attention. Salesmen form personal relationships with the editors and get their attention. That's important, because without it you can't go any further.

Then they get the feedback on what papers want, so I can pass it along or think about that in terms of future things in development.

—JAY KENNEDY, KING FEATURES

Their role is to go out and get as many newspapers excited about the cartoonists as they can.

—ROSALIE MULLER WRIGHT, *SAN FRANCISCO CHRONICLE*

A good salesperson can sell a wretched comic. I think that they are that important, especially in major metros.

A lot of newspapers buy comics they don't put in the paper. They buy them, and they watch them for a while to see if they get better or get worse. If they're not sure, and they can't decide if it's the right thing or not, they'll buy it.

It's a truth of the industry. A lot of good comic art gets bought and left in drawers, and it's left in drawers for two reasons:

1) Rarely—it's a competitive market and you're trying to keep it out of the hands of the competition.

2) In a lot of markets, syndication is a good old boy business. If you're a good syndicate rep and you have a good relationship with editors, they'll buy your stuff. Sometimes they won't put it in their paper, but they'll buy your stuff because they know your livelihood depends on selling.

There are some excellent salespeople in this business and there are some awful ones, and it's real easy to tell them apart.

—JANE AMARI, *THE KANSAS CITY STAR*

A salesman should be selling strictly on the strength of the feature itself. If it's not strong enough for you to be doing that, then you shouldn't be selling it. An editor should realize that.

—WILEY MILLER, *NON SEQUITUR*

I think the best work these people do is to keep the editors aware of the changes in the business. Quite often, an editor is distracted from the comics by all the other sections of the paper. The comics page is just there every day, whereas the rest of the paper has to be thought about hourly.

The syndicate people who call us should be telling us what's happening in the business that we should look for. Sometimes that means telling us a little secret that a certain strip just may be departing from the pages sometime soon, because a certain creator has decided he would much rather make T-shirts for a living. Sometimes it's to say, "Hey, have you thought about the needs of the current society," then bring up the idea that people are time-pressed and offer a comic that makes fun of being time-pressed.

So I see them as being a source of information and delivering the goods at the end.

—RON PATEL, *THE PHILADELPHIA INQUIRER*

I have seen salespeople come in with absolutely ghastly material and try to tell me that it was the greatest thing since sliced bread. I don't appreciate this. I think sales is all about building a trust with somebody.

They should say, "This is a new feature. I have sold it in several places already, and it looks like it's going to take off. However, I have to tell you that personally I don't think it's very good," like a person in a restaurant will say, "Don't go for the beef tonight. It's tough. Try the fish."

I know that may sound like he or she may be shooting themselves in the foot, but I don't think so. The next time this person comes around and says, "Sue, this is great," it probably will be, even if I can't see it.

—SUE SMITH, *DALLAS MORNING NEWS*

There's a difference between a peddler and a true salesman. The peddler could sell shoelaces today and cartoons tomorrow. The sales-man can sell us all an idea—and that's what the strip is, an idea.

We are selling ideas. We are merchants of ideas. When you talk ideas to editors, you are talking their field. They know what they want. And you better know their paper before you go in there, so you don't start talking about a feature, when he's already got five features cover-ing that area.

—JOHN MCMEEL, UNIVERSAL PRESS SYNDICATE

FEATURE DISTRIBUTION

Most comic strips and panels are sold to newspapers as one price for the six daily strips and the same price for the color Sunday.

For billing and bragging purposes, a daily and Sunday sale to one newspaper counts as two papers, and a daily only or Sunday only sale counts as one paper. Consequently, if a strip is listed as running in one thousand papers, it is more likely to actually run in only one-half to two-thirds that number.

Newspapers have very similar reasons for buying features sepa-rately or simply running one and not the other.

We usually buy both, but sometimes we will simply start a cartoon in the dailies, and not move it to Sundays unless it's really proven to be a winner. It's a space consideration.

—ROSALIE MULLER WRIGHT, *SAN FRANCISCO CHRONICLE*

The Sunday is almost always printed out of house. It has a print-ing contract. We're buying the newsprint retail, basically. It's extremely expensive and going up, so when a publisher looks for a place to cut, Sunday comics is the first place they cut. I happen to think that is somewhat shortsighted, because I think comics readership is one of the ways we get our hooks into kids.

—JANE AMARI, *THE KANSAS CITY STAR*

With me, it's just a practical kind of thing. Sometimes you don't want the Sunday because you've already got your Sunday filled with a pretty good package.

You might not want the daily, although that is a whole lot rarer. You would ordinarily at least get the daily, and usually you buy both. The syndicate salesmen are very reluctant—especially in a competitive market—to let you have one without the other.

If you don't want to get both, they'll trot over to see your competitor, and so we almost always end up getting both.

—JAY AMBROSE, *ROCKY MOUNTAIN NEWS*

There is a lot more space in my particular paper for comics daily than Sunday. I think that is probably the case around the country. That's why there are more daily comics than Sunday comics.

Because you do have so many icons in every Sunday section, you have far less flexibility in dropping comics for new ones. Every now and then something drops out like The Far Side *and you can make a change, but it is just difficult to put something new in.*

In terms of buying a new feature, there's also that trust level. You're more willing to experiment with the daily because the space is less a premium. But to make the big jump and say you're going to start with the Sunday as well, that's quite a significant show of faith in a cartoonist. Not only are they going to be able to sustain this wonderful thing six days a week, but they're also going to do it in color in a bigger platform, bigger canvas.

Since the daily is already a pretty significant risk, I think risking both Sunday and daily is expecting too much.

—RON PATEL, *THE PHILADELPHIA INQUIRER*

THREE VIEWS OF THE SYNDICATE

Okay, back to the elephant.

What's the role of the syndicate in the process of newspaper syndication?

THREE VIEWS OF THE SYNDICATE
HOW THE SYNDICATE VIEWS ITSELF

A syndicate is a hybrid between a literary agency and a publishing company.

I've heard cartoonists say that it would be outrageous for an agent to take 50 percent. How do the syndicates get away with it? I think that's wrong, because a syndicate does more than an agent. A literary agent negotiates a deal with a publisher. The publisher is the one who has to collect the money from the bookstore. The publisher is the one who pays the agent and the writer.

In our case, we function like a publisher. We edit the material. We distribute the material. We collect the money from the newspapers, then we pay the cartoonist. But historically, that has not been the syndicate's real function, and they treated the cartoonist as an employee, without having to pay them vacation pay or salary. I thought that was wrong, too.

If creators are independent contractors, then you have to give them their freedom. In that sense, I believe that with our relatively short-term contracts, the syndicate works for the cartoonist. We don't own their work.

So in some ways, that puts us in a competitive disadvantage. In other ways, I think it is more attractive to a lot of the more talented new cartoonists.

—RICHARD NEWCOMBE, CREATORS SYNDICATE

The syndicate is a necessary element in the lives of many cartoonists. Many cartoonists don't want to deal with marketing. Like I said, the talent would exist without the syndicate, but the talent couldn't necessarily appear in all the papers he or she now appears in without some agency that can transform that talent into something that will match with market interests. And I think that is the primary function of the syndicate, to look at all the aspects of a particular comic—and that would include editorial, sales and marketing—and try to be sure that it does the best job it can.

—LEE SALEM, UNIVERSAL PRESS SYNDICATE

We're the people who take the embryo of a product that an artist has developed. He's created it, he loves it, but he doesn't know whether or not it is marketable. Someone at some level of the syndicate says, "I'm going to roll the dice on this one. I believe it can have value." The syndicate does not necessarily create the market, but it presents the product to the marketplace, and the syndicate's promotional and sales effort creates the value for that product.

—ANITA TOBIAS, CREATORS SYNDICATE

THREE VIEWS OF THE SYNDICATE

HOW THE NEWSPAPER VIEWS THE SYNDICATE

The syndicate is like the film distributor, but different from the Hollywood studio system. I don't think the syndicate really works very much in the role of the producer. I think they act much more as a distributor.

—ROSALIE MULLER WRIGHT, *SAN FRANCISCO CHRONICLE*

They are the ones that keep the trains running on time.

Also, since they are in the closest contact with the cartoonist, they

*are the ones who say, "Your readers won't really understand this."
They have to be the readers for the cartoonists.*

—RON PATEL, *THE PHILADELPHIA INQUIRER*

*When the syndicates market-research something and come in with
something that's tailor-made for their demographics, I guarantee you
they'll never have a success doing that. They'll never have it.*

*It's got to come out of some individual's creativity, market be
damned. The market will respond to genius, but it is not going to respond to something contrived. It just isn't. You've got to have that
spark there.*

*You might get something that's mildly successful for a short period
of time that's been market-researched, but you're not going to have
something that endures and becomes part of people's lives.*

Peanuts *is absolutely part of our lives, and that never came from
market research. I'm not saying that the syndicates shouldn't do market research, but when you see something good you get a feeling about
it. If that feeling's not there, chances are it's not good.*

—JAY AMBROSE, *ROCKY MOUNTAIN NEWS*

HOW THE CARTOONIST VIEWS THE SYNDICATE

Well, they're essential.

—JERRY SCOTT, *BABY BLUES* AND *NANCY*

*In really basic terms, the cartoonist is production and the syndicate
is sales/distribution.*

*They are supposed to be partners. Unfortunately—this is the other
bad aspect of syndicates—these are the guys who wear the suits and
ties. They take the power positions, and like to treat cartoonists as
toys. Cartoonists—being the nerds that most of us generally are, especially when you're young and inexperienced—are very ready to accept
that role, that hierarchy role where the syndicate is the boss. They're the
ones telling you how things are supposed to go, and you say "okay" and
produce.*

*Once you're syndicated, once you've had that initial sales push,
they don't want to hear from you again. They just want you to keep
pumping out the cartoons.*

*Well, they're not your employer. You have a contract. You are sup-
posed to be equals. You are both supposed to be working equally hard
at the success of this strip.*

—WILEY MILLER, *NON SEQUITUR*

I don't know about other syndicates, but at my own, if the syndicate was a person he would be a counselor and a lawyer and a mailman and a researcher and an editor and an adviser and a salesman and a diplomat and a go-between and paymaster and—above all—a good friend, all rolled up into one person. One person would be all these. If you find a guy like that, marry him.

—JOHNNY HART, *B.C.* AND *THE WIZARD OF ID*

Being a cartoonist and working with a syndicate is very much like being in a band and working with a record label. You're constantly trying to get those guys to do stuff for you and promote you and make calls, but they have other things to do, so it's a constant battle.

I don't know one cartoonist who is absolutely pleased with their syndicate. We always think they can do more.

—PETER KOHLSAAT, *SINGLE SLICES* AND *THE NOOZ*

I think that syndicates are less likely to take a chance on something that's different. I think that they like to be safe, and they see themselves as a business. I disagree with them. I think that perhaps a little variety in the comics pages would do as well as this kind of sameness they seem to want, but I understand that's what they consider a business decision. And it is a business.

—NICOLE HOLLANDER, *SYLVIA*

I tried self-syndication, and I lived through it. Look at your average daily newspaper. Pick it up and look at how many self-syndicated strips you see. They almost don't exist.

—JERRY SCOTT, *BABY BLUES* AND *NANCY*

I thought it was an industry, an art form, where generally the people in it, whether they be syndicate people or feature editors, had this wonderful little textured knowledge about cartoon art.

I thought they would have a general awareness of where cartooning has been historically, how the art form is evolving, where it is now and where the next step may be.

I thought when you would send the strip in, there would be learned, knowledgeable folks looking at it and saying, "Well, this is kind of our next thing here."

I found that the industry was far less driven by intellectual concerns—and interest and knowledge about the form itself. "If you take in X number of features, one or more will stick, and that's going to be good for us."

There may be something happening in the industry at the time. Some big new feature gets taken on, so everybody else can see that it's doing okay, so they see something that looks like it and they take it on.

—JERRY VAN AMERONGEN, *BALLARD STREET*

I consider the syndicate the agent. That's the role they hold, and as far as I'm concerned, that's always been their role, from the beginning. They are the agent.

   —MELL LAZARUS, *MISS PEACH* AND *MOMMA*

Syndicates turned the comics into big business, and they make the comics visible and profitable. Syndicates free the cartoonist from business matters to concentrate on the creative aspects of the job.

On the downside, because syndicates offer the only real access to the nation's daily newspapers, they are in a superior bargaining position when it comes to negotiating contracts with new cartoonists, and they use their power to demand outrageous terms. Syndicates are sales agents: They're the middleman between the comic strip producer and the comic strip buyer. Syndicates do not create the product they sell, and they don't need or deserve long-term contracts and extensive rights to the strip in order to do their job. Their one-sided contracts turn cartoonists into adversaries, rather than partners. A few of the top cartoonists are beginning to turn the tables, and I think it's long overdue.

   —BILL WATTERSON, *CALVIN AND HOBBES*

There's a grate that goes on all the time, and of course I can't bring this up in front of other cartoonists because they say, "Easy for you to say." One thing I think you have to remember is that the syndicate is basically a sales force. They're selling a bunch of other things in the same briefcase, so you have to realize you're kind of responsible for most of the selling. It's the work you put out. If your feature is in only two hundred newspapers, it may not be the fault of the syndicate. They may be doing a brilliant job. Maybe you're only worth fifty papers. Creators always say, "My syndicate—they don't do this, they don't do that." I try not to waste any energy thinking about that. I've had a really good relationship with the Tribune for years and years.

And then you get into the licensing thing. There are a lot of guys in the business that are trying to get licensing deals with their comic strip. The way I look at it, Shoe has been in front of just as many people as Garfield has. There may be a reason why I don't have a jet plane with Shoe on the tail. It's not the syndicate's fault that you're not a multi-millionaire, just because you can draw a comic strip.

So I try to really put the load on myself. I think the best thing is to do the best work you can, and it'll get out there.

   —JEFF MACNELLY, *SHOE* AND *PLUGGERS*

A cartoonist wants to be treated well, treated fairly and treated honestly.

Syndicate people tend to think that all they have to do is promise you money and everything will be fine.

We don't hear the word money *as audibly as we hear the words* fair, just *and* honest. *And so they're beginning to realize now that we're not twits. A lot of us have trouble reading contracts and thinking in literal, financial and legal ways, but we are very perceptive. We're perceptive in that we know when we are being lied to, and we know when we're not being treated fairly.*

Our response is generally very gentle at first, and then becomes so personal and destructive that we find it awfully hard to work. And I think that is where a lot of the conflict arises.

They talk about partnership and equal partners, but they never see us as partners. They see us as producers. Often we feel that the handshakes and the warm chummy stuff is insincere, because for years we've learned that it is insincere in many ways.

Some syndicates are starting to realize this. Other syndicates don't. There are still people who cannot distinguish between loyalty and the dollar. Everything is based on the bottom line. They actually think loyalty is the dollar.

A lot of people have been doing a lot of fighting, and things are changing. Fortunately, at long last.

—Lynn Johnston, *For Better or For Worse*

The Newspaper

Newspapers and comic strips have a relationship that is documented at a hundred years old, and in that time, it has been an exciting if unnatural alliance.

Many successful volumes have documented that particular history lesson, but the aspect of comics that put them in the newspapers and keeps them there still exists.

Comics sell papers. While the content, appearance and presentation of comics has evolved, its purpose has not. Comics still sell papers. While this fact should not be catered to, it cannot be ignored.

There used to be newspaper comics editors who were responsible for the comics pages. Now, more often than not, the features editor is the contact person for the syndicate salesperson.

The primary market for comic strips is daily newspapers, although I think weekly newspapers, for a variety of reasons, are becoming more and more viable.

For strips that are particularly offbeat, there are some very credible alternative newspapers and weeklies out there that provide a pretty good market.

College newspapers run some cartoon material, usually not a lot. The problem there is that the editors change every year. When the new editors come on board, they usually like to bring their own sensibility or their own agenda into the newspaper. It is an academic learning process, and there's a lot of turnover at the college level. Unless you're somebody like Doonesbury, it's hard to keep strips in the college paper.

—STEVE CHRISTENSEN, LOS ANGELES TIMES SYNDICATE

I think that ultimately, in this day and age, you have to be very, very glad of that space, even if it's small. It's such a precious commodity now.

—LYNN JOHNSTON, FOR BETTER OR FOR WORSE

If cartoonists don't know much about the business, I think they would be unpleasantly surprised about the realities of the market-place, especially in today's world where the comic pages are not getting any larger, and in most cases they're getting dramatically smaller.

The number of newspapers are shrinking, and the number of good cartoonists is rising pretty dramatically. So you put all of those to-gether into a mix and it's hard to pick up hundreds of newspapers quickly.

—STEVE CHRISTENSEN, LOS ANGELES TIMES SYNDICATE

I guess the other thing the cartoonist doesn't understand is the de-gree to which syndication is incredibly difficult. There is not a lot of room in newspapers. They don't have a lot of room to just try things out. There are very few competitive markets anymore, so it has changed the business enormously. Bidding wars are very rare, to the point of not hap-pening anymore.

In order to be successful, a syndicate has to hit very well and have very good ties with editors. If they don't have that, they aren't going to be long-term successful. If the comic artist doesn't realize that that's part of it, he's not going to be successful either.

—JANE AMARI, THE KANSAS CITY STAR

The cartoonist's first challenge is finding a syndicate that is willing to invest in him. His biggest challenge is getting on—and staying on—

the comics pages. Competition is so tight and space is so limited the only way to get in is to replace another comic.

—ANITA TOBIAS, CREATORS SYNDICATE

The biggest objection by editors is about space. That's by far the biggest problem in selling something: "I don't have enough space to add a new comic." The second thing is: "I don't have the budget to buy a comic." Those are the biggest complaints.

I think the salesmen start at a disadvantage, because the assumption on the editor's part, in most cases, is: "I don't need to make changes." So the salesman starts with a hurdle to overcome. Space and money.

—JAY KENNEDY, KING FEATURES

It is a sad reflection on our national artistic pride that the comic strip has been wantonly suppressed and debased by the very people who exploit the medium out of necessity. Better than 99 percent of the newspapers in this country need the comics to sell their newspapers; a dynamic testimony to the popularity of the art form.

Many editors, seemingly resentful of this fact, have in recent years reduced the comics in size to the point of illegibility and have even resorted to distortion lenses to crowd more comics into smaller areas to appease the demands of their readers. Such disdainful practices point to a grim future for one of America's most popular art forms.

—JOHNNY HART, B.C. AND THE WIZARD OF ID

I would probably feel funny if the newspaper didn't have comics. Of course, the New York Times *doesn't, the* Wall Street Journal *doesn't, so there are some people out there who don't have comics and are successful, but I think it would be very difficult for most of us to be successful without them.*

—JAY AMBROSE, ROCKY MOUNTAIN NEWS

TERRITORIAL EXCLUSIVITY

Did you ever wonder why small papers surrounding big cities that have big papers don't carry very many of the really terrific comics?

It isn't because they don't have taste. It's because they've been locked out of the opportunity to buy certain strips and panels. This lockout is called "territorial exclusivity."

It works in our area to whatever degree we can negotiate it. Think of the TV networks. TV networks contract for a show, say "NYPD Blue." They don't want it to show up on the other networks. They have no competitive advantage. You're paying for the rights to bring something exclusively to your readers that can be found only in the Free Press.

—JOSEPH "CHIP" VISCI, DETROIT FREE PRESS

I remember being told that the Chicago Tribune *used to take most of the Midwest, and the* L.A. Times *took everything but San Francisco. There was a time when big papers really took a lot of territory. Now* New York Newsday *and* New York Daily News *and the* New York Post *practically share features. It's really broken down a lot.*

—RICHARD NEWCOMBE, CREATORS SYNDICATE

It's a dinosaur. It doesn't work. It's like buying a McDonald's franchise. You don't want another one springing up next door to you, so there are certain territorial requirements, like you can't have a number of McDonald's for X number of miles.

That was a very important thing to many of the newspapers in the early days. I think the Des Moines paper bought the entire state of Iowa. That was some years ago, not anymore.

This meant we would pay premium prices to keep certain comic strips out of what we said were competitive neighborhoods.

By the time I got here the territory had shrunk to a fifty-mile radius around San Francisco.

—ROSALIE MULLER WRIGHT, SAN FRANCISCO CHRONICLE

WHAT NEWSPAPERS PAY

A small paper can pay as little as three to five dollars a week for dailies, plus postage and handling.

A very few extremely large papers could be paying hundreds of dollars a week for dailies, especially after years of annual increases on certain individual premium features.

For the launch of a premium strip and territorial exclusivity, one extremely large paper pays $250.00 a week for dailies and $250.00 for Sundays, plus postage and handling. That's the exception, not the rule.

Mid-size city papers can pay twenty to sixty dollars a week for dailies, sometimes more and sometime less, plus postage and handling.

The average price paid by newspapers seems to be about twelve dollars a week for dailies, plus postage and handling. Of course, this average is probably more true in a calculation that exceeds one thousand papers than a calculation that is less than one hundred papers. Since papers with larger readerships pay significantly more than papers with smaller readerships, a strip with relatively few papers but a strong urban appeal could have a much higher average price than twelve dollars, but don't take that hope to the bank.

In towns with competing papers, the syndicate salespeople can strive for premium rates. Even then and otherwise, they are usually forced to negotiate for what the market will bear.

You buy a lot of relatively new stuff at a low rate, because you want to see if it is going to catch on. Of course, the syndicates always tack on a little percentage every year, so features you have for a long time have compounded over the years, like Peanuts. *If you bought it for three dollars, at the end of forty years you'd be paying a whole lot of money.*

So that's really why some things are outrageously priced, and others are bargains.

—ROSALIE MULLER WRIGHT, SAN FRANCISCO CHRONICLE

All the newspapers sign on thirty-day agreements. Thirty-day till forbid. If I ever found the person who invented the thirty-day till forbid, I'd love to give them a good talking to, or worse. But it's the industry standard, and it's widely accepted. Thirty TF, meaning that either party can cancel on thirty days' notice. Everybody uses it.

—ALAN SHEARER, WASHINGTON POST WRITERS GROUP

MARKET AWARENESS

God, stay away from bad taste.

—JAY AMBROSE, ROCKY MOUNTAIN NEWS

The newspaper features editor has a responsibility to his or her paper and readership. Since the interpretation of the scope of that responsibility is different with every editor on every paper, it makes it tricky (impossible) to anticipate their specific needs—and it would drive you nuts if you could.

This said, it's important to recognize the general scope of a newspaper editor's concerns. Since editors help to define the edges of the sandbox, they may not want to play with the cartoonist who steps outside that sandbox.

Does this mean the cartoonist shouldn't test limits and try to enlarge the size of the sandbox?

In his TV show, Red Skelton played a mean little kid in an ongoing comedy sketch. When the mean little kid considered doing something he knew was "wrong," he posed the problem, "If I dood it, I get a whipping. I dood it anyway."

You have to remember all the time who you are drawing for. Whether or not it is true, most readers have this conception of the comics pages being someplace where children go, and a lot of comics these days really aren't for kids. You have to have a certain amount of maturity and sophistication to understand them anyway.

Even while you draw for those people who have more sophistication, you have to avoid offending their sensibilities when it comes to something their children might read, and that's not easy.

—JANE AMARI, THE KANSAS CITY STAR

We decided from the beginning to show breast-feeding. Wanda and Daryl were a couple that chose breast-feeding when Zoe was born, and we just did it. It wasn't a big deal. Wanda was breast-feeding the baby, but of course she was always covered up. We did a couple jokes about it, but we didn't make a big deal out of it, so I guess the newspapers didn't either.

Daryl and Wanda have just started potty training Zoe, who's two years old, and I'll be very careful about that. First of all, I don't think bathroom jokes are funny, but the concept of little kids learning to use the bathroom is funny.

When you really think about it, you have to put yourself on a totally alien planet. You don't understand the language or really understand how to move your body, because the gravity is different. You don't know how to breathe. You don't understand what anything is for. It'd be pretty hysterical for you to get used to the way these beings go to the bathroom. Suddenly they're wanting you to train your muscles, or do this or that. They want you to sit on a what? What? Where?

I think that approach is funny, but I don't know that I can do it yet though, so that's a challenge creatively.

—Jerry Scott, *Baby Blues* and *Nancy*

Editors don't really like to see content in a strip or a panel that is going to be offensive to readers. It's the biggest thing you could have a problem with, and obviously every editor is different as to what they think that threshold of tolerence is.

—Steve Christensen, Los Angeles Times Syndicate

Once in a while—it hasn't happened very often with me because I don't really do the hatchet job–type cartoons—every once in a while an editor will say, "Gee, that goes over the edge a little. I don't think we're going to run it."

The question I get from people is, "Weren't you outraged?"

And I say, "Well, you know, it's their newspaper. I do the cartoons, and if it doesn't fit into their newspaper they don't have to run them." It's not a First Amendment issue, as far as I'm concerned.

—Jeff MacNelly, *Shoe* and *Pluggers*

We have been experimenting with a local cartoonist who hopes to get syndicated, and we're running him on one of the lifestyle pages. He is pretty funny, but two or three times he has overstepped the bounds. Stay away from anything that smells of bad taste. It doesn't do you any good. There is enough bad taste in this world without adding to it.

It is very hard to get away with bad taste in newspapers. They go into every kind of home. It's not like an X-rated movie where only people who want to see X-rated movies will go.

The newspaper is something that goes into homes, and the thing that makes them great is that they reach every segment of society. You've got to keep that in mind, and you've got to stay within the bounds of good taste.

—Jay Ambrose, Rocky Mountain News

I don't know if one is able to say that there is anything that really turns editors off, because that is projecting that they're not going to like something. They may have been waiting for this something they just don't know about for a long time.

That's up to the syndicate. The syndicate has to take a good hard look at it and say, "Hey, whatever this strip represents, it represents it for a purpose. This is the way that the character is best portrayed and projected." And I think that to go in saying this would turn an editor off, or that would turn an editor off, is shortchanging the editor.

Traditionally, for example, overwriting or busyness in a strip has always been a drawback. So the syndicate has got to create the good reason why this has more writing, why this art is what it is. There has to be a reason why it is an animal strip. You just don't throw it out to the wolves and say, "Sell it." There has to be a purpose and intent.

—John McMeel, Universal Press Syndicate

Decisions on How Newspapers Purchase

Since purchasing a new comic feature almost always entails dropping a feature from the comics page, the decision to replace one with another—and replace the angry readers with a greater number of happy readers—is very important.

Some editors at papers just shoot from the hip and buy what they feel. Those papers tend to have the best comic strips, because those editors tend to be the ones who know what they like and what they don't like in comics. They are confident enough to make that decision.

Over the last few years, a great many newspapers have decided to turn this over to committee, so there is no one person making the decision.

—Richard Newcombe, Creators Syndicate

Today, some editors say they want to show a strip around. It's a committee type of thing.

—JOHN MCMEEL, UNIVERSAL PRESS SYNDICATE

More increasingly it is by committee. They often function as the first filter. If the editor you're calling upon likes it, then it will be shown around.

As a group, they make a decision on whether to add it to the paper or not. That's the real mechanical answer to the question. The answer calls for the fact that they use their judgment on what they decide upon.

I think they are looking to see if the addition of the strip will bring in more readers than the dropping of whatever strip they dropped to make room for it.

—JAY KENNEDY, KING FEATURES

Most newspaper editors don't make a decision on the spot. They've got a committee, and they show it around, and it's a matter of taste. It's a matter of committee votes, usually.

I think we have a very, very large initial influence in making the presentation with a sparkling brochure, by visiting them, by demonstrating that we're behind the feature, by telling them why and by giving them some insight into who the cartoonist is.

Beyond that, they just go with their guts. The newspaper can get really scientific with surveys, but a survey ought to be one piece of evidence. The number of other newspapers ought to be another piece of evidence, as well as the recommendation of other editors and the recommendations of staff.

Ultimately, an editor has to decide, using his best instincts to say, "Yeah, I like this strip."

—ALAN SHEARER, WASHINGTON POST WRITERS GROUP

We operate here with a committee of three or four people who hopefully have a sense of humor and look at everything that comes in.

—RON PATEL, THE PHILADELPHIA INQUIRER

The feature editor's function is to be the guardian of the initial comics page and any changes in that comics page, so he is going to be very choosy and very careful about taking on another strip. That's a very important change for a newspaper, replacing one comic strip with another.

—JOSEPH D'ANGELO, KING FEATURES

Editors are ill-equipped to make judgments on comics. That's why so many of them are resorting to polls to make a decision. It's an admission they don't know what they're doing. The paper gives these editors so many different responsibilities—with comics one of them—that just makes it that much worse. They just don't want to think about the comics unless there is a problem.

—Wiley Miller, *Non Sequitur*

Decisions on Why Newspapers Purchase

The newspaper editor's got a good antenna.

—John McMeel, Universal Press Syndicate

Once again, we come to the question of art versus commerce. Do newspaper editors buy a comic feature because it may help them sell their paper, or do they buy a comic feature because they think it's a good comic feature?

The answer is "Yes."

Most newspaper editors want to buy syndicated material they think serves two purposes: to attract new readers into a section or into the newspaper by offering something that was not there before, and to provide some kind of service to the reader, whether that's an entertainment service or a consumer's service.

Some newspaper editors make their own unilateral decision as to whether those two things are occurring or not.

—Steve Christensen, Los Angeles Times Syndicate

I truly believe that the editors universally—I don't care if it's a big city or a small city—look at a strip, and if they laugh—because today everything is humor, there are no more continuities—if they relate to the text initially, they'll look at the graphics quick and say, "Oh, yeah. That's good art," and if they laugh, they've got to seriously consider it, because they are the toughest audience in the world to get to respond to something. They've already got sixteen, eighteen, twenty-four, fifty-two comic strips.

It really depends on the quality of the strip, regardless of the subject matter. You can't go in and convince an editor he's got to buy it for any particular reason, unless it was to be able to supply a certain part of their readership. But other than that, it's just got to be good.

—Joseph D'Angelo, King Features

About fifteen years ago, an editor called me up to his office at the Daily News *and said, "Okay, I've got one space, and I've got two possible panels to fill the space.*

"One is a strip called The Far Side, *and the other is this panel called* Love Is . . . "

He said, "Now, I love The Far Side, *but I don't think the people will understand it. I think it will go over their heads. I don't like* Love Is . . . ,

but I think that is the kind of thing people will put up on their refrigerator."

And I grabbed his collar, and I said, "Ed, you're a 'people.' You're a 'people.' If you like The Far Side, *run* The Far Side. *If you don't like it, run the other one. You're a 'people.'"*

—MIKE PETERS, *MOTHER GOOSE & GRIMM*

It depends on what else you've got running. Part of it depends on the competitive thing, but often you look at your page and you try to balance it out.

—JANE AMARI, *THE KANSAS CITY STAR*

There are a whole range of factors I try to keep in mind. Is this strip going to address a segment of readers that our current lineup doesn't do very well, or is it going to do it better than one of the existing strips? Is there some diversity? Does it show people of color? Strips are woefully white, and it would be good if there were more folks of color. Does it cover gender issues? Does it portray people in a nontraditional role?

—JOSEPH "CHIP" VISCI, *DETROIT FREE PRESS*

There are a few levels.

One is that they read the sample and see if they like it. Sometimes they just hate it, without any question.

Sometimes they think it's like another strip or fills a niche that they already have filled.

Sometimes they just don't think it's strong enough.

Sometimes they really trust the salesmen. They are ready to give the salesmen a shot, and those are the editors who may cancel a lot more.

If a newspaper has twenty strips, I prefer the editors who have a core of twelve or ten, and eight or ten that are moving around, with the ones that catch on fate. I think that's how a newspaper ought to be run.

—DAVID HENDIN, LITERARY AGENT

I think that the biggest mistake that they'll make is the analytical part. They try to analyze cartoons. They overthink it. They don't go with their gut, which is ironic, because that has always been the stereotype of a good editor. They go with their gut feeling. But with comics, they keep trying to pigeonhole all these things and try to figure out which readership such and such is going to go to.

What they end up doing is overthinking the process, instead of just looking at a comic and making a judgment whether that comic is successful at what it's attempting to do.

You don't compare Shakespeare with Jerry Lewis. They are two completely different things, but are they successful at what they are trying to do? That's what you make a judgment on.

You can't compare Gothic novels and children's books. Obviously, people who prefer Gothic novels aren't going to like children's books as much, so it's the job of the editor to make the judgment if either are well done or not.

If you have a strip that is obviously geared toward kids, you try to make an assessment of whether it's well done or contrived. The same with other types of strips. Along the lines of what I do, I already have a clone out. It came out a little after Non Sequitur *and it's such a blatant and obvious rip off, which is a high compliment, but an editor should be able to judge what is original and what is a copy.*

—WILEY MILLER, NON SEQUITUR

The best person I ever saw at this was my predecessor's editor at the Rocky Mountain News.

His technique was simply to buy everything, but then he had to make the decision whether to run it or not because there's not room for everything.

Of course, by doing that the syndicate salesmen always came to him first, because he'd hang onto everything until the syndicate salesman got his commission off of it. In a competitive market that makes a certain amount of sense, because over a certain amount of time he was able to build one of the best comic sections in the country.

He relied on his own instincts, and I think an awful lot of it just comes down to subjectivity. Do I like it, or don't I? Does it make me laugh, or doesn't it? Does it make me feel warm, or doesn't it? Does it make me feel good? Is there some real entertainment value here?

He would show it around, and get people to react. He would show it to just about everybody in the newsroom, and he liked to watch you while you were looking at it. He'd notice not just what you said, but also whether you laughed.

He would experiment a little bit and test drop things for a day or two to see how much objection there would be.

We have tried to analyze our comics. Okay, these are comics for women. These are comics for the elderly. These are comics for minorities. These are serial comics. These are funny comics. These are sophisticated comics. These are less sophisticated comics, and so forth.

But when all that is said and done, you still have to ask whether it is a good one or not. In the final analysis, you don't get a comic just because this fills your niche for children or whatever, unless you feel it is really a good comic. That's what finally counts, and there is always going to be some degree of subjectivity there.

Any good editor is going to let that be overridden by the facts. I may just absolutely love something, but if there is absolutely no evidence at all that it's getting any response or building readership or building loyalty, then you've got to let go of it, even if you do like it. and vice versa.
—JAY AMBROSE, ROCKY MOUNTAIN NEWS

Sometimes, we'll look at a strip that addresses a target audience we may not have any or many strips addressing.

Also, we'll look at something a little different.

But the number one question would be: Is it funny? Do I like it? Does it strike me when I first read it? Does it have possibilities?
—SUE SMITH, DALLAS MORNING NEWS

Generally, if a comic strip is successful in a major market, then the other markets usually follow along.
—LEE SALEM, UNIVERSAL PRESS SYNDICATE

Some papers will buy a strip, sit on it and never use it. It never sees the light of day in that particular market.

Then the paper cancels because it says, "Why are we paying for this and not using it?"

Then the competitors see that as damaged goods. I think that's really unfair. It's very disheartening to the cartoonists and the people at the syndicate. I don't think that's fair, and I don't think they should do that.
—ANONYMOUS

WHY NEWSPAPERS CANCEL COMIC FEATURES

Cancellations? What cancellations? [laugh]
—BILL AMEND, FOXTROT

This should be a bumber sticker: *Cancellations* happen.

As a result of underachieving cartoonists, unexpected left turns in content, losing out to someone else, edgy material, bad taste, no taste, angry readers, angry editors, apathetic readers, apathetic editors, quality drop-off, creaky bones and acts of God, comic features get canceled. Ultimately, there's nothing you can do about it, except keep your eyes open, hold on tight and hope you gain more papers than you lose.

I usually don't find out about the cancellations until about two months after they've happened, and I appreciate that. Every cartoonist differs, but knowing my personality, if the syndicate were to say, "The paper canceled you because you used the word 'butthead,'" then in the back of my head I'd be scared to use "butthead" again, and that's not necessarily good for the strip.

Now, if half my papers canceled because I used the word "butthead," that would be a different story. I would want to know.

—BILL AMEND, FoxTROT

That's another secret. When you see cancellations on your sheet, it really affects you personally.

They may not have anything to do with your cartoon or the sales of your cartoon. In the initial launch, that's just how it goes. A lot of people buy in, and after the initial six weeks pass, they just cancel. It's not unusual, but to me it looks like a cancellation, and it affects me very much.

It affected the way I was writing, so I don't concentrate on the numbers anymore. I do the work for the paper, and my wife concentrates on the numbers.

—STEPHEN BENTLEY, HERB & JAMAAL

We give a strip no less than six months to prove itself, maybe a year. We have pulled some quicker than that, but mostly because they veered violently from the course they were supposed to be following.

—RON PATEL, THE PHILADELPHIA INQUIRER

I think it is a painful process. Very often, if editors decide to drop something, they have a vague feeling that it is not as popular as other features, or maybe another feature has come along that has made a great claim on attention. That new strip will push out what seems the weakest on the page. Very often, they're proved to be wrong. I know there are columns and comics with an unsuspected readership, completely unknown, until you have dropped them from the paper.

—STUART DODDS, CHRONICLE FEATURES

If you read the comics page day in and day out, after a while you know what's making it and what's not, what's coming together, what isn't, what's moving forward, what seems fresh, what's hitting its mark, what's delivering on the basic idea and hasn't pooped out, and what has.

Most places I've been, I asked opinions of those I worked with and put their opinions alongside my own. In some cases, we took the strip out of the paper to see what happened. In other cases, it could be that its relevancy had run out.

Now, I have to say that I have bought strips without running them by somebody, but I have not canceled anything without saying, "This is what I'm going to do; what do you think?"

—SUE SMITH, DALLAS MORNING NEWS

Usually, they see something they think they like better, because it's rare I hear an editor say he thinks a strip is starting to fade. I rarely hear that. Usually they say, "I've got something else I like, so let's see what has been in a while and maybe is just not having much of a following."

A lot of times it comes to a test drop. "We'll take it out and see what happens." In fact, an interesting thing has happened lately. For several years, King Features has come out with a four-week Christmas feature from Disney. This year was the "Lion King," and I find a lot of newspapers using that as an excuse to test drop. The "Lion King" will go in place of something, and they'll see who complains during the four-week period. It's kind of fail-safe, because if they get a lot of complaints, they can say, "Well, we just took it out for a month." If they don't get a lot of complaints, then they have space for a new strip.

—ALAN SHEARER, WASHINGTON POST WRITERS GROUP

I think many times, somebody out in the newsroom says, "Hey, Jack! You still carrying that crap?" [laughs] That's only a theory.

I think sometimes, the editors' antennae start to wave that this feature or that feature may not be holding. If they don't like it, then they start asking questions of others. And all of a sudden, they may move it a little bit, see if there is any reaction. Then they do more than move it. They take it out of the newspaper for a day or two, to see if there is any reaction. Then all of a sudden, boom!—it's gone.

Sometimes the reaction is delayed and it goes back in. I have always felt the editor has to talk to his associates, and the associates will tell him, "Boy, you picked a good one," or "you picked a bad one." And the thing is earmarked that way.

Another way—just recently, in fact—a paper carried a little reader's note between two features: "Which do you like? Just call this number."

They ran it for a week. They got over ten thousand responses. They got seven thousand votes for one and three thousand votes for the other.

So, they have many ways to decide to cancel a feature. But many times it is internally generated. It's somebody saying, "You really think that thing is funny?" That starts the challenge. Hopefully, it will survive that type of adversity, but it's tough to say how exactly. Salespeople go in, and they'll mention track records, and they'll mention if they know a feature is not holding. They will plant the information. This is an age where there is no adding on anymore. If something is going to go in, then something else has to go out.

—JOHN MCMEEL, UNIVERSAL PRESS SYNDICATE

When something gets canceled, you can't really blame the syndicate. The syndicate can get something sold, but if they sell a feature to three hundred newspapers and then 250 cancel, it's not time to complain to the syndicate.

—DAVID HENDIN, LITERARY AGENT

It's very difficult and here's my theory on it: You can put almost anything on the comics page, and over time it will build up a constituency.

If you test drop it, you're going to have a certain number of objections. What you have to do is weigh that against the greater following another strip might have.

You never drop a strip without a strip you think is going to have a bigger audience over time and build a greater and more intense loyalty.

There are strips that have an intense loyalty but aren't appealing to a large audience. For Better or For Worse *appeals to certain women readers, more than anybody else, not to all women readers and probably only to some men readers. I happen to like it somewhat. To those people it appeals to, it's very important. It could be one of the really important reasons they get your newspaper.*

The sports sections are like that. People tend to think sports sections are read by everybody, and that's why you put so much emphasis on them. It's not true. Sports sections are read by less than 50 percent of your readers in almost any market in the land on a regular basis, even in a place like Denver, which is a sports-crazy city.

So why is it so important? It's the intensity. Those people decide whether or not to read your paper on the basis of your sports section alone. When you've got a competitor like we do, who is pretty good, and in a lot of ways you're pretty close on things, that comic strip could be the deciding factor for people.

Readers figure your national and international news is roughly the same. Your local news is roughly the same. Maybe one day one is a little better than the other. But over time, it equals out. The crossword puzzles are about the same, and so on and so forth.

But by God, we've got Peanuts, *and they don't. We've got* Doonesbury, *and they don't. But they have* The Far Side. *. . . (Well, they don't anymore, which delights me.) For that reason, comics are hugely important for readership. I get letters from people who say, "I would quit your paper except that I like* Peanuts." *They will flat-out say this to me and it is discouraging, because you put so much of your effort into headlines and developing good stories and into staff development and all these things.*

Only roughly half the readers hardly ever look at the comics, but for those who do it is very, very, very important.

—JAY AMBROSE, *ROCKY MOUNTAIN NEWS*

The Late Delivery

Producing, printing and delivering comic features is an extremely time-sensitive business. If a feature misses its delivery to the newspaper, the results can be more than disappointment.

Strips that are consistently delivered late are a pet peeve. You call a syndicate on it and they say, "Well, it's just that the cartoonist tries to be so up-to-the-minute on it." Well I appreciate that, but a deadline is a deadline.

—Sue Smith, *Dallas Morning News*

That kills us. You've got to have your stuff on time, and we've got to have the syndicate be very responsive to us when anything goes wrong.

We're a time-driven business, and we can't mess with that. That can be a killer for a strip. Anything, anything that you depend on that you're getting late can be a killer. People on newspapers are very busy, and we don't have a lot of time to mess around with that.

—Jay Ambrose, *Rocky Mountain News*

The Newspaper Readership

The 1993 Metropolitan Sunday Newspapers' commissioned survey reported that 86,323,000 people read the Sunday comics over a four-week period. That averages to over 21,150,000 people per week.

As reported in the study, 45 percent of the comics readers say that the comics contribute very much to the enjoyment of the Sunday newspaper. Three-quarters of all comics readers say that reading comics is a good way to start people reading the newspaper. Eighty-seven percent of the comics readers agree that comics help children learn to read.

You can find further details of the study in Appendix 5, but it clearly shows that comics have a wide and diverse national readership.

If editors are effectively communicating with their readers, the readers will let them know what they like and what they don't like, and

EVOLUTION of LITERACY

I think that can play a pretty big role in whether a strip stays in the newspaper or not.

—STEVE CHRISTENSEN, LOS ANGELES TIMES SYNDICATE

I think you have to be aware of your audience and their acceptance of you.

I see a lot of young people saying, "Aw, the heck with them. They don't like it, they don't have to read it." That's okay if you want to do an art form and you don't want to be successful. They even look down on being successful. I've heard this attitude expressed numerous times in cartoon publications, "Just because a strip sells well doesn't mean it's any good."

Growing up in the Depression, in poverty, I've always had dollar signs in my eyes. I want to reach the biggest possible audience, and I want to be a successful cartoonist. You have to listen to the public. You have to be aware of what they like and don't like.

—MORT WALKER, BEETLE BAILEY

Melissa's only hope is that Mike sees her letter today in Dear Abby.

When I was an editor in El Paso, there was a strip I just didn't think was funny at all. El Paso is just a 30,000-circulation paper, and we didn't ordinarily get much response on anything we did.

I dropped this strip and we got four hundred phone calls in a day. I don't know if in the history of that paper they ever got four hundred phone calls. Naturally, I stuck the strip back the next day. I didn't like it, but I tell you, everybody else did.

—JAY AMBROSE, ROCKY MOUNTAIN NEWS

Tastes change. Demographics change. Political viewpoints change. So if you are an editor, I think you have to be very aware of that, and your own demographics.

—JOSEPH D'ANGELO, KING FEATURES

I did a little panel. There were just two of us, me and the guy who does Dilbert, *Scott Adams, whose work I like very much.*

We were talking to an audience of newspaper editors, and they talked about readers who called in. There seemed to be rather an unnecessary degree of fear about telephone calls from readers objecting to things that were said in cartoons.

I told them about the one experience—a very positive experience—I had with a newspaper editor. He sent me the front page of the editorial section where he had printed my cartoon, very large over an angry letter about the content.

I called him up immediately and asked, "Were you trying to offend anyone who might not have seen the cartoon the first time?"

He said, "Yes. That's my job."

Oh, I really admired him for that.

—NICOLE HOLLANDER, SYLVIA

"IS THE *NEWS* SOMETHING THAT'S OKAY FOR KIDS LIKE US TO WATCH?"

There are two levels of complainer criticism. The first one is where the reader has just looked at something and said, "Oh, that's not working. That's not my taste. I'm not going to read that." And they just blame the cartoonist for not being funny that day or too stupid that day or whatever.

The next level of criticism and complaint is the one that brings out action. When the readers decide it's the newspaper's offense to have brought this to their doorstep that day, that's where it takes courageous newspaper people to keep things in the paper, in spite of the clamoring that it's bad.

—RON PATEL, THE PHILADELPHIA INQUIRER

RESPONSE TO THE READERSHIP

I don't want to see language that I know is going to give me a problem. However, I don't mind seeing themes that are difficult. I think there is a place for that.

What I hate are the words that are going to be problematical for my readership. I know I'm going to get questions from the editor like, "How come they put this word in the strip?" It's just going to give me a pain.

The word "sucks" is going to get me in trouble on the comics page. It depends on your market, but I guarantee you we won't say "sucks" again in this city's comics.

Comic strip artists who tend to be young, tend to be pretty hip and *live in a different world, they just don't realize what we have to deal with. It's the nature of youth to test limits, and the problem for people like me is I'm sitting in the middle between an artist who is screaming First Amendment, a syndicate who is a marketing arm but is also basically speaking for the artist and trying to kind of keep their talent happy so they don't pick up and leave and go somewhere else, and enraged readers.*

I can't win. It doesn't matter what I do. When there is something that I think has value, I don't mind defending it, but I really hate to waste the energy on "Reagan sucks."

—JANE AMARI, *THE KANSAS CITY STAR*

Another challenge, somewhat unique to my strip, is that I have a strip with teenagers, and I'm trying to make it a reasonably realistic portrayal of an American family.

The problem, of course, is that teenagers don't always behave in a way that is suitable reading for a family newspaper. There is a balancing act between being realistic in a way that young readers will identify with the strip and it will read as being true, and not wishing to offend the more sensitive.

There was a period when I couldn't say "butthead" in my strip without a number of newspapers screaming and yelling. There were some newspapers who would white it out. The Kansas City Star put "jerk" in, which didn't fill up the white space very well.

—BILL AMEND, *FOXTROT*

We have people who write us constant commentaries about the comic pages.

In one instance, we made a very subtle change in the Sunday comics page. We switched Prince Valiant *to the bottom of the last page, and we got a number of phone calls. There were maybe twenty comics in this reconfiguration, and we got maybe two hundred to three hundred phone calls. I guess we got maybe 150 letters from people who said, "We noticed that you put* Prince Valiant *on the last page. Does this mean you're thinking of dropping it? Don't you dare touch that strip. I have been reading it forever, and I am not going to buy up this paper unless it has* Prince Valiant *in it."*

That kind of thing happens all the time. A lot of these letters are signed, Horatio P. Algier, Vice President Providence Bank or so-and-so attorney at law. As a matter of fact, we get an awful lot of letters from attorneys. I think they must feel that they have been educated to argue, so they're going to argue with the comics page part of the paper.

—RON PATEL, *THE PHILADELPHIA INQUIRER*

The Comics Survey

Bob Greenberg is the guy who said, "Well, I'm gonna tell you how I'm gonna do surveys. Every once in a while, I'm going to pull a strip out, and I'm going to see what the squawk factor is. and if nobody squawks, I'm not putting it back in."

In the end, it is the most accurate way.

—David Hendin, literary agent

There are many different types of comics surveys or reader's polls, some scientific, most not.

Most readers' polls are popularity contests, and the strips with the highest rankings and most intense loyalty ratings win the contests.

Is that bad? It depends how the poll results are utilized.

Is it fair that some percentage of the readership has more free time to respond to polls than the other percentage of the readership? Is it fair that newer strips have not had an opportunity to develop a strong readership base?

This is like asking if it's fair that the squeaky wheel gets the grease. Of course it's not fair. What's fair got to do with it? This isn't a game, and there aren't any rules, except for the ones the newspaper editors choose to make up.

The reality is that the newspaper editors have many uses for the reader's poll.

The poll is a way to get readers involved. And I think the newspaper is looking for more and more ways to do that, with the comics page as well as other sections of the newspaper.

—Lee Salem, Universal Press Syndicate

We periodically survey, and we look to see what did well and what didn't do well.

We figure out what we can kill without sustaining the horrendous wrath of the readers, which is useful.

It also allows us to let the readers interact with the paper, and it's a way of showing them that we care what they think, that we're interested in their thoughts.

—Jane Amari, The Kansas City Star

I think editors are basically trying to tailor the comic page. They are having a popularity contest for the comics page. They're trying to get the most cartoons with the most popularity with the most readership. What they are trying to do is to get as many different people to like as many different strips as possible.

—Bruce Beattie, Beattie Blvd.

You've always got artists out there producing new stuff, and you know you'll die on your comics page, just like you will on any other page of your paper, if you never change.

You've got to have some way of measuring what is working for you and what isn't. The problem with comic polls is that they are not scientific, and even if they were, you have to know how to interpret that data.

There might be something that is not widely read, but it is very intensely read, and you'll lose every one of those readers if you quit carrying it. You have to be very, very careful with it. If you use those polls as one indication among many, including maybe your intuition, then I think they can be helpful.

—Jay Ambrose, *Rocky Mountain News*

Different papers determine which strips to drop in different ways, and I think that for me that is one of the most frustrating things of all.

Sometimes they just simply take a reader poll by asking people to write in what their favorite strip is. This really gives papers a skewed view on how the strips are doing, because people who work nine to five or have heavy job schedules may read comics, but they are not going to take the time out to write a letter.

Some papers do it by telephone, but even then, who's going to call? You get the people who are superpassionate about a strip, or you get the people who have a lot of free time. You see the older people responding more, and of course, you don't see kids responding at all, unless they have a very sympathetic parent.

The better papers conduct better surveys, where they ask enough questions enough ways that they cover some of the bases that I just talked about. But I don't know that they accomplish a great deal by asking readers, because readers aren't even aware of the strips that are available to them, other than the ones that are in their paper.

So what a newspaper accomplishes is, at best, to identify the ranking within the strips that they carry.

—Jay Kennedy, *King Features*

The editors are taught to recognize that there may be panels and strips and features that have their own readers that may not give them much of a showing in the survey, but they are still a part of the overall readership of the paper. I hear them talking about how the readership in a paper is full of lots of little readerships, and there's some truth in that.

—STUART DODDS, CHRONICLE FEATURES

The poll makes your readers believe you are caring about them. It's really less for us than for the readers. It's more to say, "We're willing to listen to you. Tell us what you think."

Since we already know we get this much mail every day, we know people want to be involved in things, so by encouraging them we hope to encourage people to help bring out a balance.

After that, it's just to see if something shows up as radically weak. If you do these things consistently, like every two years, you can see these things starting to fall.

—RON PATEL, *THE PHILADELPHIA INQUIRER*

Every two years, in April, we run an in-paper comics poll which is, as you can imagine, not scientific.

People have to clip it out. We say, "Mark your favorites from 1 to 10, 1 being your favorite, 10 being your least favorite." We show a little icon of the strip to remind people.

We get twenty thousand responses, which is a lot, because people have to cut it out, put a stamp on it, fill it out, and they usually attach reams of suggestions. "Well, now since you asked . . ." And this is very interesting and very helpful.

We tabulate them every two years. It's too time-consuming to do more often, but we see what's rising and what's falling over time. And the next time something wonderful comes in we say, "Well, the one on the bottom of the list is the most vulnerable."

One year I was skeptical of the mail-in ballot idea. The paper was doing some telephone surveys for other reasons, so I said, "Why don't we tack on a comics survey?" It turned out that we got the very same results as the mail-ins. So now I trust it a little more, because even though there are probably statistical peaks and valleys—glitches, across the board—it seems to be reliable.

And that's why I did it. I could be making decisions based on very faulty stuff, but the survey held true. At least that one time.

—ROSALIE MULLER WRIGHT, *SAN FRANCISCO CHRONICLE*

OBJECTIONS TO THE SURVEY

Marketing data have a long history of misuse. The cliché is that you can make the numbers say whatever you want them to say.

If the readers get to vote, who's doing the newspaper editor's job?

If a strip does well in a poll in one city, that unscientific result is used by a syndicate salesman at another paper with a different readership as the primary reason the editor should buy the strip.

These questions go beyond a question of fair play. They question whether the paper and the readership are being well served.

I think it's the coward's way out. I think a lot of the editors will justify that this is the readers' page, so that they get what they want in there.

Well, it's not a scientific survey. The people who are really busy and who still enjoy comics don't participate, and the people with a lot of time on their hands participate, so you get a real skewed response.

If any poll company operated like that, they would go out of business in about a day, but the editor can say, "Look, we had a poll, and this is the most popular thing."

—PETER KOHLSAAT, *SINGLE SLICES* AND *THE NOOZ*

Most of the polls I've seen are really flawed. One of the biggest flaws is the length of time the comic strip has been in the paper. There is almost no way to account for that. Say one strip has been in for twenty-five years, and another one has been in for six months, and yet they are treated as equals. It doesn't seem fair.

—RICHARD NEWCOMBE, CREATORS SYNDICATE

It's a very unscientific poll. Only the people who have the time or are really interested in comic strips (or their favorite comic) are inclined to answer a poll. And they may not like your cartoon, because it hasn't been in the paper as long as other strips.

—STEPHEN BENTLEY, *HERB & JAMAAL*

The thing that frustrates me about the use of readers' surveys is that once again you're in the situation of letting demographics run the page.

Several years ago, there was a phase where some of the syndicates tried to develop strips. They went out and got the demographics and said, "Okay, let's do a yuppie strip. The demographics poll we've taken indicates this and this and this, so we'll find a cartoonist and have him do it, and we'll all be millionaires."

Well, it doesn't work that way, and when you look at the comics page, it should reflect more than just readership surveys. It ought to reflect something of the editor there. A lot of the comics pages across the country have the same ten to twelve strips. Not that many readers travel from one place to another, but it is sort of a shame.

—BRUCE BEATTIE, *BEATTIE BLVD.*

I kind of like the old way of doing it where the comics editor ran what he thought was funny and took the gas for it. In general, I think we rely too much on polls, and you can see this in politics especially. If I'm a congressman, I run a poll in my district to figure out how I'm going to vote on an issue. That basically provides you cover. And you don't have to argue. You can say, "Well that's how everybody feels about it, so that's the way we're going to do it."

And the trouble with readership polls, and the aftermath, is that it's all subject to manipulation. What they are doing now is trial stuff. They cancel something and see if anybody notices or squawks. So if you're a cartoonist and you're smart, you call up everybody you know in that city and have them complain to the paper.

Polls strike me as a useful tool, but I don't think you should rely totally on them. If I were the comics editor who loved Pogo, I would say, "The hell with you readers. I like it. We're leaving it in."

I've always said the key person to impress is really the wife of the publisher. If she thinks it's a great strip, then it will stay in.

—JEFF MACNELLY, *SHOE* AND *PLUGGERS*

It's hard to say what you really accomplish.

While a lot of newspapers have a tremendous response, it's hard to know exactly who is responding. By that, I mean we all know if you run something in the newspaper for people to respond to, you get probably the most conservative arc of your audience. That would be the people who have the time and the inclination to respond, because a lot of people are so busy they wouldn't even give it a second thought, so I'm not sure what you're proving.

—SUE SMITH, *DALLAS MORNING NEWS*

This is the editor bypassing his or her duties as an editor. By doing these polls, they are having somebody else do their job for them.

This has gotten even worse in recent times. Some newspapers are conducting polls of new strips for readers to choose which new strip they want. Editors are going on the basis of just a handful of samples, and by readers who bother to take the time to write in or call about which one they like.

Fortunately, this works very well for Non Sequitur, *because it's very easily understood. Each cartoon stands on its own. There is no cast of characters to get involved with. There's no setting you need any prior knowledge of. So whenever they have these surveys,* Non Sequitur *always finishes number one, because the reader understands it right away.*

This is really unfair to the traditional comic strip, where you have to get involved with the characters. Trying to make a judgment on just a sample of a couple of strips is stupid. It's really unfair. Like I said, it works out great for me, but it's a bad practice.

—WILEY MILLER, NON SEQUITUR

The one risk you run with readers' surveys is they can be stacked like any kind of nonofficial voting process, and it eliminates those who do not have the time or inclination to write in.

—STEVE CHRISTENSEN, LOS ANGELES TIMES SYNDICATE

The polls I've never quite understood are the ones that tell you how many papers carry such and such a comic. I'm not sure what that tells you about your readership. All that tells you is about the judgment of other editors. You're not selling your paper to other editors.

—JAY AMBROSE, ROCKY MOUNTAIN NEWS

THE RESULTS OF THE SURVEY

So what's the fallout from the comics polls? What do they tell us? What disasters have they wrought in the lives of unsuspecting cartoonists? Will a comics poll and a dime still buy you only a cup of coffee?

Have the characters in the feature developed that rapport with the readers? If not, it should show up in the survey.

—TONI MENDEZ, LITERARY REPRESENTATIVE

I don't know if the editors learn anything, but I think it is a good promotion.

—HANK KETCHAM, DENNIS THE MENACE

Depending on how sophisticated the poll is, some people really do get tremendous results out of polls. The important results—and the poll has to be structured this way—are the ones that don't go just for the numbers. They're the ones that go for the intensity of readership. It's a very key ingredient, because the comic page has got to be made up of a number of different approaches and tastes to readers.

—JOHN MCMEEL, UNIVERSAL PRESS SYNDICATE

Every so often it reestablishes the fact that the comics page has a readership that is an undeniably strong one. It also serves to weed out those strips that are tired and need to be replaced. Because it's such a small surface on which to push your wares, you have to drop one in order to accept another. So I think the comics polls are invaluable.

I think we all look forward to them and we all want to know how we're doing. I have been very fortunate. Whenever my strip appears in the poll, I am usually within the top five or six, and that's nice. I want to know that, because if I slide down, I have to be honest enough with myself and say either it's time to kick yourself in the behind and work harder, or go play the accordian for a living.

—LYNN JOHNSTON, *FOR BETTER OR FOR WORSE*

Over the last fifteen years now, we take an occasional survey, and we take stuff off that falls to the bottom of the list. I have discovered that the readers pretty much mirror my own taste. So it gives you some room to work in, and we have been able to make some surprising moves as a result of reader intensity on a couple of strips. We've had a couple of war horses just drop out of sight.

—JOSEPH "CHIP" VISCI, *DETROIT FREE PRESS*

I think that polls probably confirm the feelings of the public about which strip they like the most.

I think editors always feel that they have to upgrade and add to their features. If they find features not very well read or very well liked, they will replace them with new ones.

You've got to make room for the new, although it scares the heck out of a veteran like me. I'm so happy I'm such a survivor. Beetle *is still in the top ten, number seven in the survey the Metropolitan Sunday Newspapers took.*

And after forty-four years, I feel very good about that, but still you see these new guys coming along, like Bill Watterson, who does Calvin and Hobbes, *trying to knock you off all the time. Each one of the syndicates brings out two or three new ones a year. Every one of those guys is a potential rival. It keeps you on your toes. I work twice as hard now as I did when I started.*

—MORT WALKER, *BEETLE BAILEY*

It is astonishing how much mail you get. For example, over the holidays we ran the King Features serialization of Lion King. *I ran it in the space that* Funky Winkerbean *was in because a lot of our polling and other syndicates said* Funky *was getting weaker.*

So we ran it—perfectly innocent, a thing for children over the holidays—and we got sixty to seventy letters in the first three days saying, "Why are you messing with my Funky?"

*Afterward, we got four or five letters saying, "Thank you for bring-
ing Funky back. It means so much to me to have him with me every
morning."*

—Ron Patel, *The Philadelphia Inquirer*

*I think they can determine what comics are being read from their
selection of comics.*

*Sometimes they don't have the sense to evaluate. Just because a
particular feature shows up at the bottom of a survey doesn't mean it
doesn't have an avid following. Like when* Pogo *was in the newspaper.
That used to show up pretty low on the readership polls, and yet there
were people—"Pogophiles"—who followed* Pogo, *and it was a well-
done feature. Walt Kelly was a genius. But if newspapers go strictly by
the number of readers, they could be losing a very important part of
their comics by dropping their low-rated strips.*

—Bil Keane, *The Family Circus*

*I guess it tells you what strips are pretty well read. But you can't to-
tally go on that. There will be strips that have a small readership, but
those readers are absolutely avid about that strip, and you don't want
to lose them.*

*I don't think you can cancel or eliminate comics totally based on
the surveys.*

—Sue Smith, *Dallas Morning News*

Well, it gives a lot of kids something to do.

*There are a lot of people who enjoy something a lot in newspapers,
read it regularly, and yet it would never occur to them to clip out and
vote for it. By the time it does occur to them, it's too late, so what they
have to do is call up or write to the paper.*

—Mell Lazarus, *Miss Peach* and *Momma*

Three Views of the Newspaper

Okay, back to the elephant.

What's the role of the newspaper in the process of newspaper
syndication?

Three Views of the Newspaper

How the Newspaper Views Itself

*The newspaper is the movie theater, the place where you pay your
money and get your* Garfield *fix.*

—Rosalie Muller Wright, *San Francisco Chronicle*

The role of the newspaper is to recognize who your readers are, and bring to the comics page those cartoonists you believe your readers will enjoy.

To be perfectly silly about it, let's say you're doing a farm paper for a farm community. I think somewhere in that comics page you ought to recognize you have farmers who are reading this newspaper, so there ought to be a strip that's funny to farmers.

Sometimes the best strips are funny to everybody, but sometimes you also want to look at one that is a little more in line with your reader. That's not possible with big papers, because you have too many types of readers. There you're just trying something that's funny for everybody. But in the smaller markets, I think there are some chances of taking on some features that might be specific for your area.

—RON PATEL, *THE PHILADELPHIA INQUIRER*

Stan Arnold was the person to discover Gary Larson. Gary Larson walked in off the street. He had come down from Seattle, and I guess

Stan thought, "Well, he's in town. I might as well talk to him," and on the spot signed him up. There has always been sort of a tradition here of looking for new talent, looking for the original idea.

For then, The Far Side was fairly risqué. It was very strange, and it was so different. But Stan was willing to take a chance on this young guy.

That's kind of a history here, that we do like to seek out new talent.

—ROSALIE MULLER WRIGHT, *SAN FRANCISCO CHRONICLE*

HOW THE SYNDICATE VIEWS THE NEWSPAPER

The newspapers are what it's all about. I suppose someday there will be other ways to get our material to readers, but the papers are the traditional vehicle, and I think they're going to be around for an awfully long time.

—ANITA TOBIAS, CREATORS SYNDICATE

They're the Holy Grail. We want to get as many of them on a list for every cartoonist as we can. That's the primary market, the initial market we target.

We don't sell to readers. Readers are often allies in the polls, but often not allies when we get canceled. We're there to help the newspapers keep the current readership, maybe even increase readership. So we try to work closely with newspapers in ascertaining their interests and needs, and be sure the cartoonist we bring out or the cartoonist we handle is doing the job the newspapers want them to do.

It's an uneasy relationship among the syndicate, the cartoonist and the newspaper. We all have overlapping interests, but we all have interests that are apart. Sometimes that's where we get into difficulties or discussions or arguments, but I think we're all moving along in the same direction, and we're all interested in one of the goals we share.

—LEE SALEM, UNIVERSAL PRESS SYNDICATE

The role of the newspaper—from the role of the editor—is to come up with the features he feels are the most entertaining features for his readership, depending on the kind of newspaper and where he is. Is he in a major urban city like New York, Chicago, Philadelphia and Detroit, or is he in a small town with a circulation of about fifteen thousand versus eight hundred thousand? He has to know his readership. He has to know the type of humor and the sort of things that appeal to the people of that small town or big city. How large and broad a group is he trying to reach? Obviously, New York, Chicago, Philadelphia and Detroit pose a different kind of problem than some small town in Illinois. So I think

*it's the function of the editor to try and anticipate, by reason of his de-
mographics of his readership, what kind of features would be appealing.*

—JOSEPH D'ANGELO, KING FEATURES

HOW THE CARTOONIST VIEWS THE NEWSPAPER

Well, they're essential.

—JERRY SCOTT, *BABY BLUES* AND *NANCY*

*I value my space in the newspaper more than I can say. I think
that's why I torture myself so much about what the strip says, because
I really think that space I'm given in the newspaper is so valuable. I
want to feel that I deserve it on as many days as I possibly can.*

—CATHY GUISEWITE, *CATHY*

*They are very apathetic, the editors. They get used to a bunch of
comics in their paper—that have been there a number of years—and
they're hesitant to throw them out. They're hesitant to make room for
new ones. They make it a hard club to join.*

—HANK KETCHAM, *DENNIS THE MENACE*

*I would like to see the newspapers get back to giving comics the re-
spect they deserve.*

*In every general survey ever taken, comics and sports are always the
highest-rated sections in any paper. If you ask the average editor what
they would love to get rid of, they all say the comics. It's just a big
headache for them. The reason they don't is because the readers love
the comics—they're too popular—and it drives the editors crazy that
they can't get rid of it.*

*To them it's a catch-22, but it really isn't. It's just that they don't
take comics seriously. It's not taught in journalism school. In their up-
bringing as journalists—especially when going through journalism
school—they all aspire to the highest—that's human nature—the highest being the* New York Times, *and the* New York Times *doesn't run
comics. They have had a policy for over a hundred years which means
comics are beneath contempt of real journalists. Real journalists don't
bother with comics.*

—WILEY MILLER, *NON SEQUITUR*

*The newspaper editors are frustratingly silent, unless they feel
that we have done something that they don't agree with. Then they will
open up.*

*I once worked in an animation studio, where the head of the studio
never talked to those of us in the studio, unless he wanted to criticize*

us. "This isn't right, and that isn't right." He would show us the films and complain about this and complain about that, and morale went right down the tubes.

And so I find myself not working for the editors. I'm working for the readers, because I know a lot of the editors don't read what I produce anyway. They just want to fill the space in the paper. They might be happy with the polls that come in, but I almost never ever hear from an editor. Ever.

Editors are very silent partners, and they rarely read our work. I feel it's sort of like the olive in the martini. If it's there, it's nice. If it isn't, well, it's the drink that's important.

There is not an editor out there that I have a bone to pick with. I just think that editors have a lot on their minds, and they have consistently felt that the comics page is not really something that they should worry about reading or care about the contents, unless readers oppose or applaud something.

—Lynn Johnston, *For Better or For Worse*

They're a reluctant partner, which is evidenced in their uncaring attitude.

Look at comic pages, thrown together pretty sloppily in a lot of cases, not all, of course. There are exceptions in every case, but it's sloppiness when they have wrong names over stuff. One day I looked in the newspaper, and it said *Hagar the Horrible* over my comic strip, and I wondered, "Do I draw so much like Chris Browne that the guy couldn't tell?" They do that a lot. And they cut off the tops and bottom of strips, to make them fit in the already overloaded pages. Then they reduce them. I don't know why they do that. They pay so much money for these things, and then they reduce them down as far as they can. I know that's so they can get more of them in.

Once, they cut up one of my Sunday strips and wrapped it all the way around an advertisement, like a frame. One of the panels was a long panel, so they just cut it in half and stacked the back half under the first half. That's really cute.

So you know how much they really think about the importance of what we're doing. I think they are a bit miffed that comics play an important role in selling their newspapers. They consider them a kind of low-class thing. "An intellectual wouldn't stoop to reading comics." That's an old stigma, a myth that they perpetuate by reducing the comics in size and making them insignificant.

When somebody takes exception to something I do, newspaper editors rarely take our side. They take the reader's side.

You know that old bit, which applies to all life, follow the money. They begrudgingly pay to put my strip in, and they take the readers' side *because the reader pays them to look at it. That's where they get their money, then grudgingly their money goes right out of their hands and comes to me.*

—JOHNNY HART, *B.C.* AND *THE WIZARD OF ID*

I think cartoonists should be more open-minded than an awful lot of guys I have met over the years—which is funny, because you think of cartoonists as being the most open-minded people in the world. But I think there's a reason why editors are the editor of the paper. They know a hell of a lot about newspapering. We might just, by holding our breath, not scream and maybe listen once in a while. We might learn something.

—JEFF MACNELLY, *SHOE* AND *PLUGGERS*

Part 2—The Product

The Cartoonists are at bat, and Coach Syndicate sends in his signals. The Newspaper Editors are in position. The infield and outfield are covered. The Readers are in the stands, screaming for a hit.

New Idea is at the plate. She's a rookie. She looks back at Inspired Cartoonist, standing in the dugout. He's been in the business for years and keeps coming up with new strips. He gives her the thumbs-up. She takes the encouragement, then turns to face the pitcher and starts daydreaming.

The pitcher, Shrinking Market, has been around for a while, but he continues to throw new pitches, wild screwballs called Market Needs that skirt the strike zone, often miss and get called for strikes anyway by the blind umpire.

The pitcher sets. There's the windup, and the pitch.

New Idea hasn't been paying attention to the pitcher, Shrinking Market, or the pitch, but suddenly she's got a really fun idea, and she swings.

She's not swinging for a home run. All she wants is a hit, to run the bases and do what she likes to do best.

Let's discuss what she swings.

The bat. That's what New Idea is hoping to use to get a hit. New Idea has learned how to stand at the plate and learned how to hold and swing the bat.

Unlike baseball, there are no rules about what material this bat needs to made from. It could be made of Styrofoam, and if she manages to hit the ball her bat will explode. Her bat could also be made from fine

hardwood, and when she hits the ball with her smooth professional stroke, that ball could go sailing out of the park.

COMIC FEATURES

I think cartoons have the potential to be art, although obviously they very rarely rise to that level. Cartoons are a combination of words and pictures, the most powerful tools of communication we have. Cartoons are an unbelievably versatile medium, and they offer tremendous possibilities for personal expression. That said, it has to be acknowledged that the newspaper business puts severe constraints on what comics can be. Comics are produced on an inflexible daily deadline, given very little space for writing or drawing, and are often poorly printed. To attract a diverse national audience, comics must generally avoid controversial subjects and opinions. Comics were invented to sell newspapers, and the commercial, mass-market needs of newspapers are not sympathetic to the needs of art. The business encourages comics to be a formulaic, crudely crafted, juvenile entertainment. Even so, a great strip comes along every generation or so that offers a glimpse of what comics can do, and that's where my hopes for the art form lie.

BILL WATTERSON, *CALVIN AND HOBBES*

CONCEPT

With the potential to utilize panels, characters, word balloons, captions and an unlimited special effects budget, the comic feature is a unique vehicle for humor and self-expression.

The lead horse that guides and helps to pull your comic strip vehicle along is the concept. Be careful how you select and treat your lead horse, because if it comes up lame, your vehicle will almost certainly slip off the narrow mountain road and crash onto the craggy rocks below.

We were trying to come up with a really great strip, making the same mistakes everybody else makes, and all the time Rick was this new father.

Tired, beat, and he used to feed me these stories on how he could survive on three hours' worth of sleep a night, and about this kid that's just sort of oozing all sorts of different liquids from every different orifice.

Not being a father, I was just sort of horrified, and fascinated at the same time. Why would anybody do this to themselves?

Watch all the people—without exception—who are introduced to somebody who has a new baby—and that's the subject they stick to.

Rick and I looked at each other, and we said, "Okay, here's the baby . . ."

We did not say, "Hey, twenty-two million people have babies every year in this country."

We just thought it was a nifty idea, and thought people might relate to it, and that's what newspapers are looking for, so we got lucky because of the timing. This whole second baby boom was just starting, and we had no idea about that.

JERRY SCOTT, *BABY BLUES* AND *NANCY*

Comic strips are one of the most extremely personal forms of creativity there is, but editors and syndicate people just don't comprehend that, and I don't know why.

CHARLES SCHULZ, *PEANUTS*

Drawing a comic strip is one of the last pure creative forms that is around. If you get into the movies or television, you've got to work by a committee. When you're writing a book, you're writing for an editor's approval, and it is only when you are completely successful that you get back your independence.

MORT WALKER, *BEETLE BAILEY*

In the traditional comic strip, you are locked into a certain space and time because of the setting and characters.

You have certain characters, and obviously, they have characteristics. They can only do certain things.

In your settings, you are locked into certain settings. You are not going to have Hagar going to the Moon. It doesn't work, and this was the genius of Calvin and Hobbes. *You have a traditional setting, and, through the imagination of a six-year-old boy, you can go anywhere. That's what opened it up.*

So when I set out to create a comic strip, I wanted to have as broad a base as possible, so there wouldn't be any of the limits to my imagination or creativity, and that's what Non Sequitur *did for me. I can do anything with it. I can go anywhere, have any characters. Nothing is irrelevant in the strip.*

WILEY MILLER, *NON SEQUITUR*

If you can have a feature that appeals to every age, then you have it made.

BIL KEANE, THE FAMILY CIRCUS

There's that strange synthesis among the character and humor and art that there are no rules for. As you know, there aren't any five rules we can give people, or else we'd all be retired by now. It just doesn't work that way, and you look for an element of imagination and something that's different from anything else out there. It could be something as simple as friendship between a boy and a stuffed tiger. Or it could be a whole generation facing political and social issues. These can be broad canvases. They can be very small canvases. The key is the artist being able to take that vision and make it funny to a whole lot of people.

LEE SALEM, UNIVERSAL PRESS SYNDICATE

One of the things that has bugged me a long time about strips—and it hasn't been solved yet—is that the comic artists seem to be totally nonadept at dealing with cultural diversity.

You either have a strip by a black artist, starring all-black people with a token white person, or you have a strip by a white artist with all-white people with a token black person.

Very rarely do you have a strip that kind of mirrors society. Now, I know this would be a tough nut to crack, because you would have to portray a whole lot of cultural points of view, but I wish the strips were not all white and all black. Apparently it is harder than one would think.

JANE AMARI, THE KANSAS CITY STAR

I think a strip has to be true to the artist. There have been a lot of strips that come and go that rely on the fad of the time or the demographics. I don't see how you could draw a strip like that unless you are totally engaged with the concept. Just to do a strip that you think would be salable, even if you got it in a bunch of newspapers, if it really wasn't you and your life, you're really going to run out of ideas pretty quick.

It has to be something that's pretty flexible, and I think visually exciting, even though the strips are getting smaller and smaller. The artwork is what really appeals to me. People—even unsophisticated, untrained eyes—will be attracted to fun artwork, so I think that will always be a key to it.

JEFF MACNELLY, SHOE AND PLUGGERS

People tell me all the time, "I created a comic strip."
I say, "Great, let's have a look."

They say, "Well, I'm just waiting. I have to find an artist."

I say, "Well, what did you create?"

Well, they created a story that they think can be illustrated, and that's not a comic strip.

The comic strip is writing and drawing in one, two, three or four little boxes every day. It's not a lot of words. It is a very challenging form of entertainment and communication.

DAVID HENDIN, LITERARY AGENT

There has to be more than just three panels and a gag. There has to be truth.

JANE AMARI, *THE KANSAS CITY STAR*

If a strip's not just outright funny, it has to have a germ of truth about it, something that makes you realize the human condition.

ROSALIE MULLER WRIGHT, *SAN FRANCISCO CHRONICLE*

I think what makes a good strip or panel is the degree to which that strip enables you to put your personality and your vision, your view of the world, down on paper.

The best cartoonists—the most successful ones—are doing stuff that is very autobiographical, stuff that can take the form of somebody's personality and come out in the form of Peanuts. Each strip has its own little language that unlocks the key to the creator, so I think if I had one rule as to what I think makes a good strip—beyond whether it's funny or not, or consistent or not—is the degree to which it gets to the heart of who that creator really is.

Ultimately, if your work is not funny, or if it is not consistent, or whatever, if the work stinks and that's the best you can do to express your personality, well then, the marketplace is going to weed you out.

BRUCE BEATTIE, *BEATTIE BLVD.*

Simplicity. This is it for me: Simplicity. That's a word I hung up over my drawing board years ago. It just said, "simplicity." That's in art and composition and humor. [laughs] And I carried it to the full extreme, didn't I? I took it back to the beginning of time. I thought, "What excites me?" Well, actually it's the simplicity of man's mind that excites me. That's what's so funny. We don't do anything that's intelligent. [laughs] We just go around pretending things we do are intelligent, because we fit them into intellectual categories.

JOHNNY HART, *B.C.* AND *THE WIZARD OF ID*

A truly unique outlook on the world and humor. A very distinctive voice.

JAY KENNEDY, KING FEATURES

Maybe I'm off-base here, but think about what makes a great story, and I don't mean a neat story. In the annals of literature, in all the things that are wonderful, what emotions and motivations are often there? Love, sex, money, religion and death. Well, sex is definitely off-limits in the comics, or pretty much so. And religion and death. So in a lot of ways, by that very simple formula, cartoonists are constrained. They get love and money.

JOSEPH "CHIP" VISCI, *DETROIT FREE PRESS*

Personally, I like character development. I like the interplay of the characters, and how personalities affect one another. There seems to be a popular trend with some cartoonists to do more of the noncharacter, avant-garde, gag-a-day kind of stuff, but I'm the kind of guy that likes to have one character talking to another character.

A good strip definitely reflects their own self and their take on the world. Where Herb's and Jamaal's lives may not reflect what I do or how I perceive the world, it is definitely my interpretation through their eyes.

STEPHEN BENTLEY, *HERB & JAMAAL*

I think it's nice when the strip has some sort of insight into human behavior, not just flat caricatures and two-dimensional stereotypes. I tend to enjoy the strips where the characters seem real, behave in real-istic ways and offer me an insight—maybe reveal things about myself, about my friends, human nature—that I might not necessarily have thought of until I read the strip.

BILL AMEND, *FOXTROT*

I think there's got to be some depth of humor. I don't think just gags are enough.

Character development. There has to be something in them for people to identify with, something people feel is real.

Think of almost any of the great characters. To mention one we don't have, Dagwood—the competition has him—he is everyman, and he has the problems of every man. And there is no mistaking who Calvin is. We all know that little boy. Smart, smart, smart, but you know he's got the devil in him. The character development in a strip is just as important as in a play or a novel. You've got to really have that. The character has to be real and has to have lasting power.

You don't want to do what everybody else has always done. You gotta have your own slant on things. There has to be some individual-ity to it. There has to be a uniqueness to any strip that is going to be really wonderful.

JAY AMBROSE, *ROCKY MOUNTAIN NEWS*

With people who are trying to get started in this business, I see the

same thing all the time. They send me samples of strips they're work-
ing on, and for the most part, the strips are really pretty much rehashes
or variations of strips that have already been done or are currently
being done.

Unfortunately, this is a two-prong problem. One: cartoonists are
trying to come up with something that will get syndicated. Yet this is
mainly the fault of the syndicates, who look at comics strictly in a mar-
keting viewpoint rather than as an art.

What I try to explain, to both young cartoonists and syndicates, is
that basically syndicates are door-to-door salesmen. They have their
products, and they're going to all the newspapers around the country to
sell. Now, when you're a door-to-door salesman, and you have a prod-
uct you're pushing, you go and knock on that door—no matter what the
product is. If the person on the other side of that door has five or ten of
virtually the same product, what incentive is there for them to buy your
product?

What you have to do is come up with something completely differ-
ent than what's already out there. Why would editors just want to buy
another variation of another family strip?

This is how I went about creating Non Sequitur. *When I sat down*
to start creating comic strips, I went through the same motions. What
kind of characters do I want? What kind of setting? Yada-yada-yada,
and everything came out very formulaic.

I got to wondering what was it about all the strips that really made
it big, the ones that became icons like Peanuts, Doonesbury, The Far
Side, Calvin and Hobbes? *You go on down the line,* Bloom County. *You*
go back some. Pogo *and* Li'l Abner. *What did all these strips have in*
common? They're all completely different from each other. What did
they have in common?

Suddenly it dawned on me that they came out with something com-
pletely different than what was being done at their time. That was their
viewpoint. They weren't trying to do another variation of something. This
was their perspective, through the eyes and mouths of their characters.

So I went back, and I just started doing some material that I liked.
The kind of thing that I wanted to see. Get my voice. And that's what
works, getting your voice out there.

WILEY MILLER, *NON SEQUITUR*

There needs to be a thought-through idea, something that brings
home to the reader some irony of life and sometimes tries to educate
and to identify with people. Something that touches on the human fac-
tor, whether it's people or animals doing these things, it still touches you
as a human being.

SUE SMITH, *DALLAS MORNING NEWS*

Behind the jokes, I try to talk about life in a serious way. I don't look at cartooning as just an entertainment. It's a rare privilege to be able to talk to hundreds of millions of people on a given day, and I don't want to squander that privilege with mindless chatter. There is an opportunity here to talk about real issues of life with sensitivity, warmth and humor. This is where the greater significance of the comic strip lies. Many cartoonists consider their strips a commercial product and are therefore able to justify turning the strip into factory work, hiring a team of writers and illustrators to crank out whatever the public will consume. That kind of cartooning holds no appeal to me. The strips that interest me are always the personal, idiosyncratic strips that reflect a unique and honest sensibility.

BILL WATTERSON, CALVIN AND HOBBES

CREATIVE FREEDOM AND THE FORM

There are two types of boundaries: Those that exist in the form, and those you create in the cartoon universe of your own design.

It is important to understand the boundaries that exist, to keep abreast of how the boundaries change and, in order to effectively test them, to know where the walls are thick and strong or thin and penetrable.

Boundaries may be viewed as restrictions on creative freedom or the outermost extremities of a sandbox. While I prefer the latter, take your choice. Either way, you'll have lots of company.

I can't have someone run over by a steamroller and bounce back. I have given myself that limitation.

LYNN JOHNSTON, FOR BETTER OR FOR WORSE

Total creative freedom only exists for the guy who streaks through a football stadium, and he ends up getting arrested. Total creative freedom is not really something you want.

Is it creative freedom if somebody looks at your strip and says, "Listen, this is great, but I think you can improve that gag if you cut out these three words at the end"?

You know, the words aren't, "[bleep] you, Charlie." It's just tightening it up. So it gets down to the issue of what's the difference between editing and censorship?

DAVID HENDIN, LITERARY AGENT

There are two major limitations. One is space, and the second would be language.

I think the changes have been so slow, one has to go back in ten-year leaps to see how it has changed, rather than in one-year leaps. But I think the comic pages have opened up a bit in terms of the language they allow, and I think that trend will develop. The impact of television is so tremendous on the field of humor that it's had an impact on the comic pages as to what newspaper editors will allow and what newspaper readers will accept.

The more challenging problem is one of space, and that's the frustration that some cartoonists deal with constantly. Others have just learned to accept it as part of the art form

LEE SALEM, UNIVERSAL PRESS SYNDICATE

I think we get lazy because of the size. We're drawing for such a small size, you say, "Why in the hell should I beat my brains against the drawing board trying to get my character flying in an airplane or something?"

JEFF MACNELLY, *SHOE* AND *PLUGGERS*

There are a lot of strips where the writing seems to take over. I wouldn't say whether that's a good thing or bad thing, but I observe that. It seems possible these days, especially in a highly verbal, highly literate kind of strip, to get away with drawing being very average.

STUART DODDS, CHRONICLE FEATURES

It's easy to draw something thirty-nine picas wide that may reproduce badly, so I think cartoonists need to keep in mind that the medium it's going to be printed on has to be compatible with the art. There are very few strips that can get away with breaking those rules.

JANE AMARI, *THE KANSAS CITY STAR*

My only limitation is the amount of space that I can have for the words. I am a writer first and foremost, and that's a problem in my strip, because my strip tends to have a lot of words in it. I know my strip is hard to read. And I wish there was a way to—I don't know what—either for me to write shorter or get bigger boxes.

As far as content matter, I am not inclined to do anything more radical, or racy, or controversial than what I already do, so I don't feel any limits that way.

CATHY GUISEWITE, *CATHY*

I find it easier to create for a limited space than if someone said, "You have all the space and all the time in the world. Do something with it." It's so much easier when someone says, "This is all the space you have. This is all the character can do. Go for it." Somehow that limited space generates ideas.

Mike Peters was saying that he was talking to Chuck Jones, and Chuck Jones said, "It's like putting water in a bag and then squeezing the bag, and the water comes out so fast because you've limited every-thing." It's like ideas are generated faster by the limitations that are put on you.

It makes your mind work much more efficiently, so I'm used to the limitations now, and I love to grumble about it, simply because that's the thing to do. Absolutely nobody on earth should be or will be totally happy with their job, and that's what draws us together—bitching.

LYNN JOHNSTON, *FOR BETTER OR FOR WORSE*

I would certainly expect to have a certain amount of free-dom. On the other hand, if I was on the syndicate side and I saw material I didn't think was in good taste or good quality, I would want to be able to say, "No, give me a replacement on that one. I don't think that's what we want to give to our customers."

I've been very lucky and have always considered the newspaper space my own private space, and I'll do what I care to do in it. A few times they've rapped my knuckles, but not too many times.

HANK KETCHAM, *DENNIS THE MENACE*

I know King Features has the attitude that they like low-mainte-nance strips, because editors will quake and coil or recoil under the pressure of one letter. You get one angry person writing to you, and the editor will write you a letter and say, "Stop this. Don't do this anymore."

You have to maintain a certain amount of thick hide about that, be-cause everybody is angry about something, and I find that if you try to mollify them sometimes it just gets worse.

MORT WALKER, *BEETLE BAILEY*

I'm interested in adventurous content, in going beyond the con-ventions of just a happy family kind of humor, but readers are a mighty

---

militant lot. They don't see the humor in some of these things. They really do enforce a standard on the comic page. It's the result of the readers writing and calling, annoying you with hate mail. You really are a servant of your readers in this area.

RON PATEL, *THE PHILADELPHIA INQUIRER*

We don't put any restrictions other than liability, obscenity and taste.
The last one is the interesting one. For example, there have been a number of comic strips that have appeared in Bloom County *and* Outland *that have drawn reader response, pro and con. Sometimes it's a fine line, but we don't in any way try to restrain our people from using controversial subjects. And sometimes we argue, but I always count on that argument, because once we pass on a cartoon then we defend it. Once I know the cartoonist's reasoning for the topic or for doing it the way they did, then I understand it, too, and in case it comes up, it gives me something to stand on.*

ALAN SHEARER, WASHINGTON POST WRITERS GROUP

I would say cartoonists have a lot of leeway, not to be mean-spirited, but to poke about in the spirit of fun. I think cartoonists can get away with an awful lot, especially if they show a little sensitivity and finesse.
However, I guess there are some cartoonists out there who just don't get the difference between humor and the boundaries of mass media–style good taste. I would ask these cartoonists what media they want to show in. There are some very fine alternative and college publications.

SUE SMITH, *DALLAS MORNING NEWS*

I'm totally allowed to express myself. Okay, editorially there are think-limitations you learn to live with. And what's worse, I think each of us puts ourselves into a particular box. And if you stray out of it, if you try to get out of it, it doesn't work. You have a certain readership, and they expect a certain performance from you, so you're sort of restricted.

MELL LAZARUS, *MISS PEACH AND MOMMA*

It's troubling when I try to put together a comics page that will reflect our community. When I go looking for things that a little boy who is black will find fun to read, I don't want it just to be a black kids strip where there aren't any white people.
That's the annoying thing. Why can't a strip have different kinds of people in it without it being a multicultural strip? If there was any one thing that the artist and the syndicates could solve, it would be this thing.

JANE AMARI, *THE KANSAS CITY STAR*

The Uphill Battles

The cliché says you're always better off facing your problems than running from them. I like to think I'm better off facing the train that's roaring toward me, because it gives me the opportunity of knowing when to jump out of the way.

The question is, have you looked down and suddenly discovered you're standing on the railroad tracks, or did you purposely step on them?

There are things that set off many newspaper editors' warning bells; aspects of strips or panels that may make them review a new feature with a negative bias and make it more difficult for you to climb your particular mountain.

You may have a reason you want to play Sisyphus and roll a boulder up a mountain, but it's important to recognize this is what you are doing. You should have no misdirected anger if the boulder repeatedly becomes too heavy to push any farther and rolls back to the bottom.

Clones

Whether it be in concept, writing or art, should you create a comic feature that's similar to something out there, you may meet resistance based on this observation alone.

For a brief moment, when Gary Larson retired and newspapers scrambled to find a comparable replacement, there was a commercial advantage to being a *Far Side* clone.

If you have a strip that is similar to something else, your strip needs to be that much more original in other areas to compensate for the perceived comparison.

The early *Bloom County* is a good example of a strip that suffered by comparison to another strip *(Doonesbury)*, but it overcame that comparison with a powerful new voice, fresh characters and quickly evolved drawing style. Its place in comics history assured, *Bloom County* is the exception, not the rule.

Generally, editors want fresh material, not imitations. And they understand pretty well the trend of humor, and what may have worked in an initial launch ten to twelve years ago certainly will not work today.

LEE SALEM, UNIVERSAL PRESS SYNDICATE

A strip or panel really needs to be unique. It needs to come from the imagination of the creator himself. It should not be based on somebody else's work.

A lot of what we see are people who are fans of another cartoonist. They try to re-create that other cartoonist's work. That's never effective.

ANITA TOBIAS, CREATORS SYNDICATE

The one thing I really dislike is a clone. A Gary Larson rip-off.

I want something fresh, and I want a voice. I want something where people reading it say, "Gee." If it's not a laugh, they're going to say, "Yeah, life is like that," or "I can relate to that situation." If it's not a joke, then there should be a little epiphany, and that happens very rarely in the cartoons that are out now.

ROSALIE MULLER WRIGHT, SAN FRANCISCO CHRONICLE

They don't like things that are derivative. You're going to have a lot of trouble with a strip or a panel that looks like it's trying to cash in on the concept or the art style or the gag-writing style of a Bill Watterson or a Lynn Johnston.

When sitting across the desk from a syndicate salesperson, I think editors tend to make snap judgments as to whether something seems to be unique or appears to be a deliberate knockoff.

STEVE CHRISTENSEN, LOS ANGELES TIMES SYNDICATE

THE UPHILL BATTLES

THE MARKET-RESEARCH STRIP

What's the difference between a strip that's contrived to fill a niche in the marketplace, and a strip that's inspired and happens to fill that same niche?

The answer probably involves those words "contrived" and "inspired."

In the middle of the '80s, some of the syndicates would present strips that were based on market research. They would say, "Well, there's a strip for this age group, and there's a strip for that age group, and here's an age group we're missing, or here's a working mother with two kids."

When they'd come with that sales pitch, I would just blanch. This is the cart leading the horse. Because they are setting out to fill a niche, there's no creativity. To me, a market-research–driven comic is a failure.

ROSALIE MULLER WRIGHT, SAN FRANCISCO CHRONICLE

EDITORS in the AFTERLIFE

CONTROVERSIAL CONTENT

If your strip is founded on creating controversy or addressing sensitive issues, it would be very appropriate for you to make that evident in your samples.

Otherwise, addressing controversial subjects so early in your feature lets editors know how much fun you're going to be to work with. This isn't a bad thing, but you should know the potential ramifications of what you're doing before you do it.

If it is important for you to deal with sensitive issues, the characters and the world of your feature should be designed to accommodate the full range of your topics. The more the editors are prepared for the editorial content of your feature, the less they'll be surprised when they see it. Along this line of thinking, it is extremely important that your feature not veer too sharply away at once from what it was sold to be. This makes editors feel like they've been sold a bill of goods.

In the initial stage of a comic strip, I think it is probably very unwise to do anything controversial.

ANITA TOBIAS, CREATORS SYNDICATE

USE OF LANGUAGE

Even though we're adults, we can still have our mouths washed out with soap.

The objections we would most come up against are the use of words like "hell" or "damn," which sometimes creep into a comic, and we have to be careful about them. That would be the biggest concern among editors.

LEE SALEM, UNIVERSAL PRESS SYNDICATE

WORD COUNT AND LETTERING LEGIBILITY

Both of these concerns stem from the same premise. A comic strip should be fun to read, not hard to read.

The quality of your lettering will raise the level of your strip up a notch or knock it down a notch. That's a fact.

Still, even if your lettering is good, don't think you can count how many words *Doonesbury*, *Cathy* and *Calvin and Hobbes* have in their panels and use the same number of words yourself. Trudeau, Guisewite and Watterson can use a lot of words because their strips are fun to read. If you want to use the same number of words, your use of words needs to be just as good as their use of words.

The main thing that will put off an editor is if it's hard to read. The legibility of the lettering, and the size of the lettering.

Also wordiness. A lot of words will put off an editor right away.

ALAN SHEARER, WASHINGTON POST WRITERS GROUP

My first thought is about those strips that are so text heavy as to drive the drawing out of the space.

At the same time, some of the better cartoons—the social commentary things I've seen in alternative publications—are really neat because of all the language in them.

Still, knowing how small these comics are going to run, you have to look at them immediately and think, "Why are the cartoonists doing this?"

RON PATEL, *THE PHILADELPHIA INQUIRER*

THE UPHILL BATTLES

"UGLY" DRAWING

The cliché: Beauty is in the eye of the beholder.

The reality: It may take the rest of the world time to catch up with you, or you may need to learn to draw.

I think sometimes editors are are put off by a bizarre drawing style, because they know every newspaper has a ton of conservative readers, and they know that an avant-garde–looking comic strip is going to produce a reaction from those conservative readers.

On the other hand, we look for avant-garde strips, because we think they are different, and they are fresh, and they attract younger readers.

ALAN SHEARER, WASHINGTON POST WRITERS GROUP

I don't like bad art or derivative ideas.

ROSALIE MULLER WRIGHT, *SAN FRANCISCO CHRONICLE*

THE UPHILL BATTLES

ANIMAL STRIPS

Yes, yes, yes, I know animals are fun to draw.

Yes, yes, yes, I know it isn't fair that some editors don't think readers relate to anthropomorphic animals.

Yes, yes, yes, I know your cat is different than Garfield and Heathcliff because she's got a different personality.

Yes, yes, yes, I know no one's done a giraffe strip.

Yes, yes, yes, I know.

An animal strip scares newspaper editors because they're afraid some segment of the population will latch onto it so tightly it'll never let them let it go, even if the quality turns to fertilizer.

In essense, editors fight this formula for success by being very choosy about the animal strips they purchase. An animal strip needs to be more than cute. It needs to be a contender for the crown.

There's the old saw about, "Don't bring me any animal strips." Heard that? "Put an animal strip in, you can't get it out." I think that's just an old saw.

ALAN SHEARER, WASHINGTON POST WRITERS GROUP

There is this risk with running an animal strip that we talked quite about when we started this comic Mutts. *You have this great big risk you can never kill it.*

RON PATEL, THE PHILADELPHIA INQUIRER

Once an editor buys an animal strip—like a cat or a dog strip—God, it's hell to get rid of. The readers come out of the woodwork.

SUE SMITH, DALLAS MORNING NEWS

THE DAILY AND SUNDAY FORMAT

At a creative level, there are some fascinating differences between the daily black-and-white strip or panel and the Sunday full-color, multifunctional grid.

First, since the multipanel Sunday strip is larger, there is more room to develop an idea. There are more panels to utilize for variations in timing, which is a luxury compared to the limitations of today's daily. As a side note, Mell Lazarus once did a sixteen-panel daily strip in *Momma,* and his use of space and timing was brilliant, but this isn't a corner you can paint yourself into very often.

The downside to the traditional Sunday format grids is they are designed to have removable panels and be stacked into different configurations. This means you have to create panels that won't be missed when they're removed. Also, the Sunday may be stacked in a configuration that doesn't read as smoothly as when you created it.

Some cartoonists have dealt with this by creating Sunday pages that exist only with a single fixed rectangle of space. *Calvin and Hobbes* is a half-page size only, and Wiley's *Non Sequitur* is a one-fourth-page size only.

The second difference between dailies and Sundays is the use of color.

On the face of it, the flat, limited color palette simply adds a new dimension and makes the comics easier to read. In reality, the addition of color adds an entirely new facet for storytelling. Simply put, the choice of color can add to a desired mood or complement it. This is not the place to address in depth this particular aesthetic, but it is an extremely important tool and should be studied.

Traditionally, cartoonists use a color chart with a limited palette to indicate on a black-and-white photocopy of the Sunday which color they want in which location. The syndicate sends your color indication guide to another company that creates the color separations for the newspapers.

Several cartoonists have experimented with the process of producing the separations for the printed color strip. Take a look at Bil Keane's *The Family Circus* and Wiley's *Non Sequitur.* There are some production tradeoffs you can discuss with your syndicate when the time comes, but their use of color is quite effective.

The formats and size restrictions of today's strips limit what a strip can do. I don't think it's any coincidence that the "Golden Age" of comics was fifty years ago, when a Sunday strip could have an entire newspaper page to itself. Newspapers have been shrinking the comics for decades, and now we're at the point where comics can no longer entertain with beautiful artwork and extended dialogue.

Because of the space limits, I use the dailies for continuing stories or one-shot gags, and I try to vary the pace and tone to the extent possible. The Sunday strip offers a chance to take advantage of the power of pictures, so I try to set off fireworks when I can. The comics are a visual medium, and drawings can do a lot more of the work than most people think. Obviously, the better a cartoonist can draw, the more effectively he can design the space, and the more flexibility he'll have to keep his strip interesting.

BILL WATTERSON, *CALVIN AND HOBBES*

I like to think the Sunday page should have more action in it than is necessary in the daily strip. The daily strips don't necessarily have to have any action. They can just be people talking to each other, but you better not have that happen on a Sunday page too often.

So, I think lots of funny action is important in a Sunday page. I love drawing scenes when there's wild action or whatever I can think of. I wish I had the ability—and I wish we all had the room—to produce some of the great action things that cartoonists used to be able to do in their Sunday pages. But boy, they're even shrinking those down on us now, more and more. That's disgraceful, isn't it?

CHARLES SCHULZ, *PEANUTS*

The advantage of a daily, obviously, is that you get six shots to the reader. You get six chances during the week for the reader to see it and bond with the strip. The flip side is that people spend much more time with their Sunday paper, and circulation figures show that daily is declining, while Sunday is increasing.

RICHARD NEWCOMBE, CREATORS SYNDICATE

Well, first of all, a Sunday takes a different kind of gag. I try to use more repartee and more of a time lapse. Sometimes, I try to make a ministory out of it. I think they are harder to do. Plus, you have to write a couple of panels that disappear in a lot of the papers. That part's a pain in the ass, but otherwise, it's a nice change of pace.

Initially, when I'm writing gags, I don't think about whether they'll be dailies or Sundays. If it works mechanically as a daily, some things you just can't stretch out. If it needs more development, then I'll reserve it for Sunday.

MELL LAZARUS, *MISS PEACH* AND *MOMMA*

You're still telling a story, but you have creative elbow room in the Sunday page to tell a little bit longer story. And there's use of color, change of attitudes, use of time changes. It gives you a great deal more opportunities.

HANK KETCHAM, *DENNIS THE MENACE*

With the Sunday strip, I have much more freedom to explore new ways of illustrating the joke. I have more space. I have more panels. I can toy around a little bit more visually. I also have more room to set up a joke.

I think my characters are naturally blabbermouths, and I am always paring down their dialogue to keep things readable on the daily strip. I think with the Sunday I'm allowed to be a little more verbose.

BILL AMEND, *FoxTrot*

HEIGHT-TO-WIDTH RATIOS FOR DAILIES

There is currently no standard aspect ratio for the size of the rectangle that dailies are drawn. There are boundaries—heights you should probably not exceed—but that's different.

Strips and panels are distributed by syndicates at fixed widths, but the heights are all over the place.

Why is there no standard? How did it get this way? I have an opinion, and others have opinions, and some opinions are probably better than others.

The advantage here for you is that you can pick the height you wish to draw.

I wish somebody had told me this when I started out.

We just picked out a comics page, Xeroxed it bigger and said, "Well, geez, these are all different sizes. Let's take a strip that we like and make ours the same size. Automatic success. On Baby Blues, *I think we picked* Calvin and Hobbes, *but made it not quite as tall, because he was really tall.* Peanuts *is really squatty, so we went kind of in-between. It was one of those things where, if there was some unwritten rule, we didn't want to look stupid.*

JERRY SCOTT, *Baby Blues* AND *Nancy*

After I got the contract to do the strip, I said, "How big should the boxes be?"

I think they sent me back a copy of somebody else's boxes and said, "Make them this big." In eighteen years it's never occurred to me to even ask if I could change it. Thank you for mentioning it.

CATHY GUISEWITE, *Cathy*

You're welcome.

I'm certain newspaper editors across the country will be very excited to discover *Cathy* will soon be twenty feet taller.

I think I took the newspaper, cut out a Garfield, *and then I did the old trick of drawing the lines from one corner to the other, and then I made it a larger size.*

SCOTT ADAMS, *Dilbert*

I measured somebody else's strip. I got out my ruler and said, "How big are these supposed to be?" Then I think the syndicate told me what an actual size was suppose to be. They gave me a size, and I cut a little template out of cardboard.

JEFF MACNELLY, *SHOE* AND *PLUGGERS*

The amusing little anecdote is that when I was first syndicated by Universal Press, I asked Lee Salem what size I should be drawing my originals, now that these are really going to run.

He said, "Oh, I don't know. Grab a Calvin *and* Hobbes *in your newspaper and just double the size." I was expecting Universal to have these very rigid size requirements, but that's basically what I did.*

The size I use now actually is the same as Calvin *and* Hobbes. *I went with it because it works out conveniently that the size of bristol I work on is half an eleven-by-fourteen-inch sheet. I buy it in eleven-by-fourteen pads, then cut them in half, which is easier than pulling out the big twenty-three-by-twenty-nine-inch sheets and chopping them up with a big paper cutter. That's what I used to do, and I used to go nuts.*

My strips are three and three-quarter inches high and twelve inches wide. I used to draw them a little bit bigger than that. When I went down, I noticed I was still drawing the characters the same size, and I was cutting off their legs. They're standing a little closer together now.

I think you had a question, "What sacrifices have you made for the format?"

I was going to say, "Well, my characters sacrificed their lower legs."

BILL AMEND, *FOXTROT*

There may be many reasons why you chose the size to draw in. The important thing is that it works for the printed page as well as for you.

Beetle fits on my copy machine. That's how things are determined these days. I used to draw a lot larger, until I got my copy machine. The strips wouldn't fit, so I had to change. I think it's about thirteen inches long and five inches high.

MORT WALKER, *BEETLE BAILEY*

THE "HARD EDGE" AND THE "SOFT SEAT"

As the world changes, art and artists note and often reflect upon the changes. New artists have their first opportunities to comment on what's around them. Established artists see the world as well as the change. New artists will become established artists, and newer artists enter the picture and complete the cycle.

Extending this to comics, as the world continues to change, new cartoonists and established cartoonists reflect upon the changes, but

they come at them from two completely different perspectives. The same is true for the established reader and the new reader, and that's the way it should be. That's the marvel of a medium that reaches out to such a diverse audience.

THE HARD EDGE

It is difficult to think of the medium of newspaper comics as having a hard edge, and perhaps it doesn't. But it does have boundaries that have been pushed out and redefined the use of the medium. These boundaries continue to be pushed, and the use of the medium continues to change.

Whether it's an evolution or devolution is open to interpretation.

I think the envelope has always been moving along, and newer strips are always going to be at the forefront of that push. At least the good newer strips. The envelope moves along because of a variety of forces, not the least is competition with other media. You've got "Beevis & Butthead" and "The Simpsons" on TV. You've got comic books. I mean, there are a lot of things competing for the humor reader out there, and if newspapers want to remain competitive in that arena, there is going to have to be a little bit more freedom as far as what can be done in the comics page.

BILL AMEND, *FOXTROT*

A lot of these geniuses push limits. And that's what it's all about. Pushing limits.

DAVID HENDIN, LITERARY AGENT

I would say, if anything, the main trend as far as envelope pushing was for strips to become more topical, more political, led by Garry Trudeau and Berke Breathed.

At some point, a lot of this stuff will start getting done on computer, and the question is whether or not you'll see it in a newspaper, but we're not really a medium that tends to push the envelope.

BRUCE BEATTIE, *BEATTIE BLVD.*

I don't think there are many newer strips pushing the envelope, and unfortunately very few of us get to see the ones that are. I think the ones that are in the alternative press, they're the ones breaking all the new ground.

PETER KOHLSAAT, *SINGLE SLICES* AND *THE NOOZ*

I don't think the issue is pushing the envelope. I think it's just finding a new voice. It's reaching people in a way that no one else is currently reaching them.

JAY KENNEDY, KING FEATURES

I think the success of The Far Side *and other panels like it has really prompted a dramatic increase in the number and percentage of submissions you get from people who are trying to duplicate that same kind of off-the-wall, bizarre kind of concept, which was very difficult for guys like Larson to sell in the first place.*

And I think you see more strips that try to be contemporary, that try to talk about life in the nineties, families in the nineties, and work in the nineties, rather than taking a concept that is more timeless.

STEVE CHRISTENSEN, LOS ANGELES TIMES SYNDICATE

I think you can get away with a lot of things "now" that you couldn't "then," in terms of material content and subject matter. And I think it's good.

The whole beauty of the comic page, these hundred years, is that it has always sort of reflected American mores, and better than any other medium, because it is ongoing. I once said, if you flipped through them fast you'd see the history of our culture. And so it's fun. It has to be that way.

MELL LAZARUS, *MISS PEACH* AND *MOMMA*

I'm not aware of things being pushed the way they could be. I think once an artist earns a following in the newspaper and the right to do certain things, then the newspaper is generally supportive, but I think overall cartoonists are apprehensive.

LEE SALEM, UNIVERSAL PRESS SYNDICATE

I think people today are more willing to tackle some social commentary and social issues—serious subjects put in the context of their characters.

ANITA TOBIAS, CREATORS SYNDICATE

There seems to be a trend for minimal art now, and the editors treat it as the vanguard.

I see a lot of strips coming along that look like just a tossed-off sketch. In the long run, I don't think they are going to be successful because I think the readers are going to like well-constructed figures.

MORT WALKER, *BEETLE BAILEY*

This is a touchy situation for me. This is where I become very opinionated. I don't fault the syndicate for what they're trying to do—they're trying to please the audience—but I find that new cartoonists just getting into the business aren't taking the business seriously or the idea of art and comic strips seriously.

They want to throw some kind of weird cosmic idea out there and consider that humor, or they comment on something that is going to be very sensitive to some people and not humorous to others. That isn't humor. The manipulation of words, the manipulation of characters, how people perceive ideas and how those ideas can be twisted is something that is funny.

To me, the word "cartoonist" implies that they are going to do something visually funny, and I think there has to be better art, much better art than we're seeing. I don't know whether that's talent, or whether we're giving up the idea that what they draw can be perceived as funny. But the idea of art—fine line, pretty pictures, pretty funny pictures—is now no longer being conveyed the way it used to, and I think we need to come back to it.

I think that might be something that's drawing a lot of people away from the comics.

STEPHEN BENTLEY, *HERB & JAMAAL*

THE SOFT SEAT

What is the reason for an audience's perception that a mature comic feature has ceased to grow?

In some cases, this may be true.

In other cases, it may be that the audience has come to know the cartoonist's sensibilities and the feature so intimately that the pleasure of being with that feature has less to do with the twist, the punch line or the surprise, and more to do with visiting an old friend.

I think it's easy to fall into a comfortable pattern. You think that if it has worked these last several years, then it is going to continue to work.

I think a strip has to change.

MELL LAZARUS, *MISS PEACH* AND *MOMMA*

For a lot of people, I think there is comfort in that they like a strip, they enjoy it and it is exactly what they expect.

ANITA TOBIAS, CREATORS SYNDICATE

When people wake up in the morning, they're groggy, they get a cup of coffee, they don't want to be shaken up. They don't want anything new. They want to read their nice little cartoon strip, and it's like waking up with a roommate. There's something to that.

PETER KOHLSAAT, SINGLE SLICES AND THE NOOZ

A new suit feels new, but when you've worn it a while, it feels more comfortable. There is always a tendency, when you've seen characters for a long, long, long, long time, for them to get a little old.

It's a real challenge to a cartoonist to try to keep being fresh. Because you're not drawing for new readers every day. You're drawing for the readers who follow you every day. They get to learn your sensibility.

ALAN SHEARER, WASHINGTON POST WRITERS GROUP

Once a cartoonist has mastered his characters and knows what needs to be done with them, then a pattern of character behavior in certain situations becomes predictable. And I don't think that's necessarily a bad thing.

The downside is that that can become complacent. Then the readers no longer come to the strip, unless they want to be reminded of things, and then the readership starts to taper off.

LEE SALEM, UNIVERSAL PRESS SYNDICATE

When it is all said and done, each strip has its own little view of the world and universe, and the challenge of being a cartoonist is to keep presenting that—your own unique view of the universe—and do it in different ways. But it still is your own unique view of the universe.

In my case, after eighteen years of doing it, I know there are people who look at my strip now and say, "Geez, Cathy, she's moaning about being fat again" or whatever. That is my view of the universe, and I think that the people who like my strip like it because they are struggling to lose five pounds.

The familiarity of the subject matter, and the frustration of "here we are again" is part of it.

On the other hand, I think that one of the great, great functions of comic strip characters is to be a real unit of familiar friends and faces for people. I think that's why comic strips have endured. They are one area of the newspaper where you can turn to it and there are always the same faces, and you always know—kind of—where everybody stands on what. If you are curious on that day, you will read further and see what their particular comment is that day. But wherever you go in this and many other countries, or whatever is going on in your own life, or whatever hideous thing is going on in the newspaper, the comics are something you can open up to and say, "Oh, well, now there's my friend Charlie Brown." I think there is something very comfortable about that, and for me, this has always been an argument for expanding the comic section. You can hang on to some of the old, comfortable, familiar, albeit sometimes redundant, faces, and still make way for some new voices.

CATHY GUISEWITE, *CATHY*

Part 3—The Process

C harting the process of newspaper syndication would be like charting the course of a golf ball from the first tee to the eighteenth hole. You can pick certain places where a ball is supposed to be and certain places where the ball is not supposed to be, but the journey each ball takes is going to be unique to that particular ball and the person who drives it.

So let's discuss where your ball is supposed to be, and we'll point out some of the sand traps and other obstacles that can get in your way.

NEW FEATURE DEVELOPMENT

Let's start by assuming you already have something resembling a golf ball (a mass market comic strip or panel). If you're trying to tee off a tennis ball (adventure strip), football (comic book) or basketball (alternative market feature), your journey to the eighteenth hole may be much more circuitous than we have the space to explore. I'm not even going to begin to propose how you should putt a basketball down a hole fit for a golf ball.

So we're at the beginning of the first hole, and you tee up the best golf ball you can possibly make.

THE SUBMISSION

The strip has to sell itself, so a set of photocopies, a cover letter and a stamp are all the aspiring cartoonist needs. The strip is either good or it isn't, and no amount of fancy packaging and salesmanship will

change that. For serious consideration, a proposed strip must be better than the strips already in the newspaper, because those are the strips it will have to replace. If the submission isn't up to that standard, the cartoonist is kidding himself about the odds.

First of all, I think a new strip must be original. The world doesn't need second-rate imitations of what's already successful.

After that, I think characterization is the most important part of any strip: Do the characters have real personality? Are they rounded individuals with unique voices, or are they cardboard stereotypes? Do they reveal themselves through their actions, or do they tediously explain themselves?

Next, I think syndicates look for consistency. One funny strip will not carry you through five mediocre strips. The strip must demonstrate an ability to surprise day after day, week after week.

After that, a strip must demonstrate flexibility and room to grow, so that it doesn't exhaust its material in a year or two.

On a slightly more esoteric level, I think a strip must create its own world and be true to itself. The writing must fit the characters, and the tone of the strip must communicate itself naturally and unself-consciously.

And finally, a strip has to be fun. Assume that readers have better things to do than pore over a self-indulgent comic strip. A comic strip must entice, and that means polishing one's craft until the strip is an attractive product. A poorly drawn, ugly strip will have trouble bringing readers into its world, even if the writing is good. Strips with heavy-handed or preachy writing do not fly. The trick is to produce a strip so incredibly engaging that people will make an effort to seek out its company.

Any cartoonist who expects to pull all this off on the first try probably has some disappointment ahead of him. Persistence is important, but so is a willingness to learn from mistakes and start over from scratch.

BILL WATTERSON, CALVIN AND HOBBES

THE EDITOR'S NEEDS

There are two ways to get a syndicate editor's attention.

First, jump up and down, wave your arms, drop your pants and do anything else you can think of to offend him. This won't get you anywhere—except possibly out the door—but it will get his attention.

Second, you can show him a commercially viable comic feature that is unlike any comic feature he's seen before. Not only will this get an editor's attention, but it will also sustain his attention, and this should be your goal.

Like book manuscripts, film scripts, and TV scripts, your presentation needs to be as plain vanilla as possible. This allows the syndicate editor the opportunity to look through submission after submission and concentrate on the material without being distracted.

If you want to waste your time and money on an expensive presentation, you are welcome to do so, but it will not help you syndicate your strip. In fact, if your presentation is more elaborate and well executed than your feature—and I've seen this more times than I can count—you may want to consider a career in promotion or advertising, since that's the area in which you seem to be more inspired.

The cartoonists need to make the syndicate editor's job as easy as possible. A pack of strips, roughly the size they are going to be run in the newspaper. Cover letter. The cover should explain the artist's vision.

The large oversize packages tend to collect dust in my office. I understand the desire to want to capture someone's attention, but with the way we operate, it's the writing and art that count.

If you only want to put one strip on a page, that's fine. You have to stay to standard size paper, but at some point—and it might be before we even write somebody back—we may reduce those strips in-house to the size they can be run. So if it's there up front, it is going to make the syndicate's load that much easier.

LEE SALEM, UNIVERSAL PRESS SYNDICATE

It is important to have the right amount of material, just enough to demonstrate what the feature is. I'd say the most important thing is to have a clear presentation of the work without gimmicks and without an overly long introduction.

STUART DODDS, CHRONICLE FEATURES

Please make it easy for me to read. I really don't want huge pieces of paper or teeny, tiny pieces of paper or anything that is folded, spindled or mutilated. This would seem like a really basic thing, but it's not.

What I want is a cover letter to let me know who you are. You can give me a concept sheet on the strip. Sometimes that can be helpful, but it is not necessary.

I need at least two Sunday comic strips and four weeks of dailies in a clean form that I can read. Personally, I like two strips, laid out horizonally on an eight-and-a-half by eleven sheet of paper. Do not send originals. and remember the only thing that really matters is the quality of the work.

ANITA TOBIAS, CREATORS SYNDICATE

PROFESSIONAL QUALITY

Since there is such a wide, seemingly acceptable range of quality in the drawing and writing of a professional comic feature, this makes it very hard to quantify that range. So instead of discussing the space inside the definition of professional quality, I'm going to talk about some common problems in submissions that are outside this space.

Draw your comic feature so that it will cleanly reproduce at the size and proportion of a comic feature. I've seen comic strips drawn in pencil, stacked two on two on an eight-and-a-half by eleven–inch sheet of paper and colored with crayon.

Your writing needs to stay on the course of communicating the story or the point you're attempting to make. If you step off this particular road you will most certainly be standing in quicksand. Since this is your story or gag, and since it's a road of your own design, you wouldn't think it would be so hard to stay the course, but it is.

Your drawing needs to be executed from a single vision. For example, unless you've got a reason, don't put a two-dimensional face on a three-dimensional body in a two-dimensional room with three-dimensional furniture. If your characters and world are two-dimensional, they should stay two-dimensional.

If you've created two-dimensional characters but need to execute them in a three-dimensional manner to show action, then you need to seriously reconsider your character design.

The visual filter a cartoon world is viewed through is what gives the cartoon world life. If the filter is flawed, the world is flawed and lifeless.

Your lettering should be uncluttered, easy to read and consistent in its interpretation of the alphabet. Lettering, letter spacing and word spacing should be practiced over and over and over.

Your balloon placement should be clean and unobtrusive. If you need to have two separate balloon pointers crossing one another, you should have a better reason than "that was the easiest way to do it."

Since this is not intended to be a how-to book, I can offer only one last piece of advice on the subject of professional-quality work. Photocopy your work down to the size of a comic strip, put it on the comics page, see how you measure up and be as hard on yourself as you are to any comic feature you dislike. You have to be honest with yourself, because if you're not, you're the only one who gets hurt.

About 1 percent of strip-related submissions are professional quality, and it's a little frightening that the other people that are drawing can't recognize professional quality. Obviously, some of them are closer than others, but the vast majority—well over 90 percent—are just not close.

People have to be realistic about their skills and talents. That doesn't mean that they can't improve. Another thing, they should not be going to the syndicates or the agents every step of the way saying, "Am I good enough yet?"

They ought to be able to tell when they're ready. If somebody comes to me and says, "I'm ready," I say to them, "Well, geez, I'm ready to look." And then, when I look, they're nowhere near ready. Then the next time they tell me they're ready, it's like the boy who cried wolf.

DAVID HENDIN, LITERARY AGENT

I have had several people send me things at different times. I don't want to come right out and say sarcastically, "You know, I'm not running a correspondence school here," but I am appalled at their lack of ability to judge their own work.

I have one man who has sent me things several times. He doesn't get any better, and he keeps saying, "I'm not going to give up. I'm going to keep after these syndicates."

And I want to tell him, "What's wrong with you? You can't see what's wrong with your work? It's so obvious what's wrong with it. The person in the mailroom is rejecting your work just by looking at it. Can't you look at your work and see what's wrong with it?" It amazes me.

Aren't you also amazed at the lack of historical knowledge that some of the young people have? I am astounded at those who have never heard of Percy Crosby and Skippy. And never seen Roy Crane's work.

CHARLES SCHULZ, *PEANUTS*

Well over 90 percent of the strips submitted are just clearly amateurish and aren't going to get more than a moment's consideration.

The strips or panels speak for themselves. The submission package needs to be a professional presentation, but too many cartoonists spend much too much time with elaborate pages and pages of describing the characters, pages and pages of explaining the concept, putting them into extremely fancy folders and having them professionally printed. Most syndicate people who review submissions scan that material, then go to the heart of the strip and start to read it. and the strips will pretty well sink or swim on their own.

STEVE CHRISTENSEN, LOS ANGELES TIMES SYNDICATE

THE PACKAGE

In order to properly present all your hard work and to show you are serious about being a professional cartoonist, the operative word about presenting your work is KISS. Keep It Simple, Stupid.

Yesterday, we got a submission in a plastic trash can. I don't know exactly what the gimmick was, but that was sort of annoying. You wonder whether to return it. One does get some very odd-shaped submissions. They're difficult to handle, and it really is a distraction from the work itself.

STUART DODDS, CHRONICLE FEATURES

Mailing tubes bug me. Anything that's not of a pretty standard size is very irritating.

Steve Christensen, Los Angeles Times Syndicate

We've gotten everything you can imagine. Somebody just recently sent us cookies—home-baked cookies. The gimmicky things aren't going to get you syndicated. They are just large, and cumbersome, and strange-looking. I was sent a toilet seat once, and when you lifted the lid, you saw the character on the inside. It's been years—I don't remember what the comic was, but that was the initial submission. That type of thing really doesn't work.

Anita Tobias, Creators Syndicate

We see a lot of odd-sized things. Oversize things.

We get too many original submissions.

We get things without a return address on them. Maybe the return address is on the envelope, and we don't keep the envelope, and we don't notice it's not there, and we don't know how to send it back.

We sometimes get handwritten letters, a scrawl on lined paper, like from a school notebook.

I would like to see the submissions all rather uniform in size. Eight-and-a-half by eleven is sort of easy to manage, because at this stage, we're looking at concept and character and humor and artwork. and it shows on a Xerox.

Alan Shearer, Washington Post Writers Group

The Cover Letter and Character Sheets

How much should you say in a cover letter? Not much.

Be courteous and explain briefly that you are submitting a comic feature for consideration. It would not hurt to touch on the the concept of your feature, but you should not embellish this. The feature needs to speak for itself, and you're not doing yourself any favors by announcing you've created the next *Calvin and Hobbes* or *Peanuts*. You can offer information about any cartoon-related experience you've had in the past. It's good, but it's not necessary. The editor is more interested in the feature you are currently submitting.

It can help to present your cast of characters on separate sheets of papers, but the effort in introducing your characters and your world will be wasted if you do not keep your character descriptions to one to two sentences. If you don't immediately grab the editor's attention, he will ignore your introduction and jump right to the strips. This is a case of less is more.

I don't like submissions where the cartoonist is telling you why their strip should be syndicated and why readers will like it. That strikes me as a very defensive posture for the cartoonist to take.

STEVE CHRISTENSEN, LOS ANGELES TIMES SYNDICATE

SEND PHOTOCOPIES, NOT ORIGINALS

Professional cartoonists mail photocopies of their submissions, never original art.

I won't go into the potentially tragic results of sending original art in your submission, but if your original art is damaged, lost or destroyed in the mail, it's not the syndicate's fault.

It does not matter how the art was lost. It matters what form the art was sent in. If a secretary accidentally dropped your submission into a shredder—no, I've never seen this happen—if you had sent photocopies, it would not have been any form of a tragedy. Clumsy, yes; tragedy, no.

Since photocopies are what you are supposed to send, if your original art is damaged, lost or destroyed in the mail, no matter what the syndicate's part has been in this process, you have only yourself to blame.

Don't take chances with your art. Be professional.

One thing that can cause some aggravation, it is important not to send things that can't be easily handled or returned. For instance, large originals. Original drawings. Send copies. The strips should be reduced to newspaper size.

STUART DODDS, CHRONICLE FEATURES

THE STRIP SAMPLES

Some cartoonists who've been syndicated sent in the first samples they created and others culled their best work from a much larger selection. The reconciliation of these two extremes lies in the fact that each was confident in their final selection of material. In developing this ability, you need to be your toughest or most honest critic in evaluating your work.

When I get an idea for a new comic strip, I want to make sure that I will sustain the idea stream. I usually do a hundred to two hundred ideas, to make sure that I will be able to write it over a long period of time.

I always sketch my ideas out, so that I can show them to other people, pass them around the house, pass them around to my staff, have them vote on them and see which ones are the best.

Then I usually draw up a couple of weeks' worth with a regular pen like a regular submission, then I include some initial sketches in the package—the better ones—so the syndicate gets a longer view of it.

I don't try to draw out the characters and tell everybody what the characters are like, or what I intend to do, because the strips should tell that by themselves.

MORT WALKER, *BEETLE BAILEY*

I don't think you should even send anything to a syndicate until you've done at least about two months' worth, and then don't be afraid to throw half of it away.

I can't remember what my submission was like. I just remember it was really primitive. Drawing's like your signature. It just changes. The first time you write your name in script it's kind of primitive, but after a while you get faster, and I think you express yourself more naturally. It happened to me, but it took me four or five years before the characters really started rolling off my hand, and now it's impossible to draw them any other way.

JEFF MACNELLY, *SHOE* AND *PLUGGERS*

I basically wanted six or seven weeks' worth of stuff. That's what I've always thought was the rule of thumb. It's not too many that you don't work for ten years and get it in payback, and it's not too few that they can't take a look at it and know that you can come up with and sustain a strip. As far as editing it down and working on it, your best forty-two cartoons will give the syndicate a chance to read between the lines and discover what may or may not be a diamond in the rough. Ultimately, that is what they are trained to do.

BRUCE BEATTIE, *BEATTIE BLVD.*

For the physical presentation of the samples, it's important they be comfortable to read.

While some syndicates request samples reduced to the size comics print in the paper, you can send your samples in significantly larger for easier reading. One or two strips on eight-and-a-half by eleven-inch sheets of papers make for a very easy read, especially for someone who's just looked at ten, twenty or thirty submissions.

If a syndicate considers your feature it will ultimately need it reduced down to the printing size. There are two ways to look at this. Give the syndicate what it wants in the first place because it will ease the process, or present your feature in a slightly larger, more attractive and easier-to-read form.

My view is that if a syndicate is really interested in your strip, it will not mind reducing it down. If it minds reducing it down, it isn't really interested in your strip.

This said, beyond the material itself, you have very few opportunities to sell yourself or your potential in a strip sample, so avail yourself of the one opportunity you have. It would not hurt to show your strip at seven, seven-and-a-half or eight inches wide.

So many submissions are drawn in the wrong size and proportion, they cannot be reduced properly.

ALAN SHEARER, WASHINGTON POST WRITERS GROUP

I made kind of a little booklet. It began with a letter, and then I commented on life at that time and the state of womanhood, and then you would turn the page and there would be a drawing summing up or contradicting what I had just said. and then there would be a little bit more about what was going on, and then you would turn the page and there would be another drawing.

The drawings that I sent were all different shapes and sizes. The only two characters that were really viable in the strip today were Cathy and her mother. There were some miscellaneous men and girl-friends.

CATHY GUISEWITE, *CATHY*

We sent out maybe six weeks' worth of dailies, put them into one of those binders you put reports in, added a cover letter that just said this strip is about parenting.

We purposefully didn't do the twenty-five-words-or-less character sketches, because we don't believe in that. We wanted people to read the comic strip, to meet these people.

It's limiting to say, "Daryl is a thirty-eight-year-old executive who works at a company and makes some sort of wing flaps for airplanes. He makes ninety-two per week and drives some kind of car. He was always a precocious kid and that kind of stuff." Phhhfh! The hell with that.

They're two people. They're probably in their mid-thirties, and I liked that approach a lot. It worked for us. It may not work for anybody else.

We thought we could just write ourselves into a corner if we gave these people some preconceived personality. Since we didn't really know who they were, we didn't want to model them after anybody in particular right off the bat.

It's better for us to get to know them with the readers. The premise of the strip was so strong, so organic, it's just one of those things everybody goes through, we didn't think it was all that damn important.

We wanted the strip to be as identifiable to the readers as possible. Daryl could have the same job as my neighbor. He could have the same job as the guy who lays bricks. Who really cares what he does for a living?

JERRY SCOTT, *BABY BLUES* AND *NANCY*

I believe there were thirty-six dailies that I had reduced by 50 percent, and put three on a page, and stapled together with a nice cover letter.

I sent that off to six or seven syndicates. In that first batch I did not necessarily know what FoxTrot *was. It was more a free flow of ideas. I think what was in that package was a good broad range of humor. There were five characters and an iguana, but it wasn't as carefully thought out as some might imagine it would be.*

BILL AMEND, *FOXTROT*

SEND FINISHED STRIPS

A cartoonist's perspective: Why can't the syndicate just look at the first week's worth of finished strips and know that the other five weeks' worth of rough pencils will be finished just as well?

A syndicate editor's perspective: How do I know the cartoonist can sustain the quality?

Another syndicate editor's perspective: If the cartoonist isn't interested in finishing the sample, how interested is he going to be in working on the strip day after day after day?

Another cartoonist's perspective: I want to make certain this sample represents the best work I can do.

While it would be nice if a syndicate could read your mind to know just how consistently wonderful your feature is going to be, it can't.

While it would be nice if a syndicate could study one or two weeks' worth of finished strips and trust that you will continue that quality in subsequent weeks, it can't.

The reality is a syndicate only knows what you show it, so you had better show it the best work you can do. If you don't have time to finish your work, then a syndicate may not take the time to look at it.

I find it pretty irritating when people include only a few finished strips with a lot of pencil roughs. I feel if you're not really willing to put the time into the submission to finish the pencil roughs, how serious are you?

STEVE CHRISTENSEN, LOS ANGELES TIMES SYNDICATE

If you want to be syndicated, it doesn't necessarily do you a service to send in roughs.

ANITA TOBIAS, CREATORS SYNDICATE

Goals to Strive for in Your Sample

When the curtain goes up on stage, it's time to go into your act, and you need to sustain your performance until the curtain goes down.

In a comic feature sample, from the first daily to the last, everything counts. In that time, you are expected to deliver a portrayal of your characters, their world and how they behave in it. Like the lowering of the curtain at the close of a wonderful play, your comic feature sample should leave the reader aching for more.

Make sure you create a character so that everybody knows almost immediately who that character is and what his role is going to be. You can't say Beetle is going to be lazy and then not show it. He's got to perform the way he's going to be in a way that captures the editors and readers so they say, "Wow, that's a funny idea. That's a funny character, like Calvin."

MORT WALKER, *BEETLE BAILEY*

I think the important thing was getting across the relationship between the characters. I concentrated just on Shoe and the Professor, how they related and just what they were about. And I think that's key. I think you should do that, just kind of keep it simple at first, just kind of work on the relationship between two or three main characters. And then you can bring in the other characters later on.

JEFF MACNELLY, *SHOE* AND *PLUGGERS*

So many of these people who want to get into a comic strip feature are always trying to second-guess what the readers want. They're always saying, "Oh, God, I hope they like this."

MIKE PETERS, *MOTHER GOOSE & GRIMM*

I was trying to be funny. I'm sure at the time I was trying to convey intelligence on my part, but I did not know really what I was doing. I mean, I had read a book, How to Be a Cartoonist, *but that is one of the beauties of this whole business. You don't necessarily have to know*

what you're doing if you're talented. Joe Blow can send in his submis-
sions, and six months later his strip is in the newspaper.

BILL AMEND, FoxTrot

*My commercial considerations were to tap into a market that had
not been tapped into, and there still aren't many strips that use ethnic
characters as featured characters.*

*That was primarily the focus, to tap into that market, hopefully to
create characters that people of color could identify with and appreciate, and bring them to the comics page.*

*When I was growing up, there certainly weren't any black charac-
ters I could identify with, unless they were stereotypical in nature. I
wanted to make sure I created characters who had a positive role, presented with a more positive image.*

STEPHEN BENTLEY, Herb & Jamaal

*What you're trying to show with your sample is the creative essence
of the strip and that you are a professional and can handle the workload.*

BRUCE BEATTIE, Beattie Blvd.

*I wanted to look a little bit different than the usual cartoon. Instead
of the regular square panel, I put it in a circle so it would stand out, and
I originally called it "Family Circle."*

BIL KEANE, The Family Circus

*You have to do what you find funny, what you enjoy doing, and
hopefully an audience will find you. You can't find an audience. You
can't please an audience.*

WILEY MILLER, Non Sequitur

*What we really wanted was for the syndicate editor or somebody to
say: "This might work. Newspapers might buy this," and most important, "Gee, this is funny."*

*I thought it was funny, because it was Rick in every strip, as far as
I was concerned—and he was probably just going through some kind of
self-analysis by drawing it.*

JERRY SCOTT, Baby Blues AND Nancy

*Syndicates should be looking for creative material, something new
and original. What the they have been doing for several years is choosing
comics based on what they think newspaper editors want. What they
don't realize is that editors don't know what they want. All editors know
is that they want something different from what they already have. But the
syndicates can't quite seem to get that through their heads, so they see
something has become successful and they immediately jump on the
bandwagon, rather than trying to find something different.*

That's what happened with Non Sequitur. I sent it out to all the different syndicates, and they all said the same thing. "Oh, we love the art. We love the humor, but we would like to see a central character."

I said, "You idiots! That destroys the entire foundation of the format."

WILEY MILLER, *NON SEQUITUR*

WHAT THE SYNDICATE IS LOOKING FOR

Editors don't say, "Oh, I really want you to do a strip about kids/pirates/giraffes/elves/bugs." If they do, they are really just trying to prompt you to think for yourself.

There are aspects of strips that catch an editor's eye, but each editor is different, so if you try to appease each one, it will be like trying to chase a rainbow. It's important for you to understand why certain things catch an editor's eye, but these are their professional considerations, not their wish lists.

The prime directives are: Is this a cartoon product that we can sell to enough newspapers to make it worth all of the effort and expense that a syndicate goes through in marketing it and producing it, and make it worthwhile for the creator in terms of the very hard work that they have to go through in producing it every week? And does the strip have merchadising potential?

STEVE CHRISTENSEN, LOS ANGELES TIMES SYNDICATE

There is no rule. Some people just fall into it. It's just luck. They're in the right place at the right time with the right thing. Greg Howard—never cartooned before, never was an artist—had an idea. Boom! He hits it.

PETER KOHLSAAT, *SINGLE SLICES* AND *THE NOOZ*

We get excited when a creator really has a focus, really has an identity, really has a good approach in mind with strong characters and strong writing.

JOHN MCMEEL, UNIVERSAL PRESS SYNDICATE

The concept, the quality of the artwork, the briskness and vibrancy of the writing are all things you can intuitively spot quite quickly.

STEVE CHRISTENSEN, LOS ANGELES TIMES SYNDICATE

The first thing we look for is originality. We don't want to see carbon copies of existing comics. We want something that's fresh and new. The writing must be first-rate and the art must be good.

ANITA TOBIAS, CREATORS SYNDICATE

I always look for three things. Good writing. The artwork is really something that catches my eye. And something else, some kind of truth in the comic strip, some new way of looking at the world that, through humor, makes me understand it a little better.

Berkley [Breathed] wrote in the introduction to one of his books: "The most important dynamic in a comic strip is not shock and satire but character and truth. The truth of Charlie Brown's anxiety, for example, is a mirror of our own. The truth of Calvin's manipulations of his world. The truth of Opus's vanity and naïveté."

I think that's pretty good. I think truth gives a strip broad appeal.

ALAN SHEARER, WASHINGTON POST WRITERS GROUP

I can tell you what has to happen in order for us to take on a strip. Everyone who sees it must be absolutely ecstatic about it. That means that it truly has to impress six or seven very different people with different tastes and backgrounds, so it has to have that compelling quality. Now what that is, to analyze it, is very difficult.

STUART DODDS, CHRONICLE FEATURES

THE DEVELOPMENT PROCESS

Once you've sent your submission, there are four basic potential responses from a syndicate.

The first response is a form letter that says your feature does not meet its needs at this time.

The second response is a personalized response that says it'll pass on this submission but the editor would like to see your next feature.

The third response is a phone call or letter, asking to see more material, and there may or may not be some indication about the direction the syndicate would like to see you go in.

The fourth response is a development deal or contract offer.

THE SYNDICATE EVALUATION

Every syndicate works differently and to its own strengths. Some make new-feature evaluation a group process so that everyone is involved. Others keep the departmental functions separate.

Regardless of how the syndicates operate, the new comic feature goes through a filtering process that separates the wheat from the chaff.

There is a process we go through when we evaluate comic submissions. A number of people who are on staff are involved in that process, and each individual in that circle looks at all of the submissions.

If anyone feels passionate about one of them and says, "I know this is it, it's going to work," our philosophy is: Back that individual, even if we don't agree. It has happened before, where only one person really saw the potential, but that person felt strongly enough that the others said, "Okay, if you really believe in it, I'll take the chance."

Nobody is the absolute barometer of success and quality in cartooning, or anything else for that matter. If one individual feels passionately enough about it, then we'll support that individual. That person is the one who's most critical in developing and marketing that comic, talking to the creator and handling the whole account.

ANITA TOBIAS, CREATORS SYNDICATE

We try to involve as many people as we can in searching out new ideas and new products. We try to collaborate as closely as we can on development of new products so that we can bring a lot of different perspectives into the process: salespeople; editorial people; outside newspaper editors used as consultants; new-product development people.

We try to bring a lot of people into the mix.

STEVE CHRISTENSEN, LOS ANGELES TIMES SYNDICATE

I was taught that sales has its noble calling, editorial has its noble calling, and the two don't necessarily meet.

LEE SALEM, UNIVERSAL PRESS SYNDICATE

First and foremost, we don't syndicate anything that everyone in the organization isn't behind. They've got to be behind it. The worst thing is to have something show up and say, "Now go sell it." So everyone is involved, from the first time we see something, through development, until the time it's ready to go.

We're also involved in planning the sales strategy. Who are we going to call? What are we going to say? How are we going to position it? When are we going to do it? What's the timing of the mass mailings? And so on.

ALAN SHEARER, WASHINGTON POST WRITERS GROUP

WORKING WITH THE CARTOONIST

If your feature happens to be the wheat, the syndicate may want to keep it as it is, or they may want you to turn it into bread, bagels or Wheaties.

One of the first syndicates that considered Baby Blues *wanted us to make some changes. Put two kids in the strip right away, give details of Daryl's and Wanda's personalities, background and all that sort of thing.*

With Creators, there was no development period at all, outside of calling us in August and releasing it in January.

JERRY SCOTT, *BABY BLUES* AND *NANCY*

Once the strip comes to our attention and we like it, we work with the writer to try to hone the writing and the art. We make sure there is a common understanding as to the direction we want to go, then we will have the artist send in roughs on a continuing basis, which we will comment on.

Normally, with this process, we might ultimately produce 50 percent to 60 percent of those roughs for the public, and then, in the space of a year or two or three, it might be up to 100 percent. It takes a while, but it depends on each individual artist on how quickly that comes about. But we do want to be sure that person's best foot is always forward.

LEE SALEM, UNIVERSAL PRESS SYNDICATE

The syndicate committed to a development contract. It was supposed to run six months. After one month they said, "Oh, heck, let's just launch the thing." I'm not sure what I did that was so spectacular that first month, but I was happy.

BILL AMEND, *FOXTROT*

I think that different cartoon editors help people develop strips in entirely different ways.

STEVE CHRISTENSEN, LOS ANGELES TIMES SYNDICATE

I'm afraid that oftentimes—and I've had this experience myself— that if you take other people's opinions, they seem to water down your zeal, and you end up with the old story about a camel is a horse designed by a committee. You begin to put other people's ideas and other people's thinking into it, and you do end up with a bastardized version of your idea.

MORT WALKER, *BEETLE BAILEY*

It doesn't happen very often, but if an aspiring cartoonist got positive feedback from several syndicates at one time, which is reasonably rare, they would benefit from asking the syndicate questions of their own, like: How much development do you think this will require? Or can you give me some ideas as to where you think it needs to be developed? This way you can see whether it is going to be a good collaborative match.

STEVE CHRISTENSEN, LOS ANGELES TIMES SYNDICATE

THE CONTRACT

I was overwhelmed. I really was. I was terrified. I was absolutely sick. In fact, the day I signed the contract to do the ship everybody wanted to go out and celebrate, and I went back to the hotel and was sick. I said, "I'm sorry, I can't go to lunch with you." I was absolutely nauseous sick, because I didn't know if I could be what they wanted me to be.

LYNN JOHNSTON, *FOR BETTER OR FOR WORSE*

I suppose my biggest fear about my contract was that I couldn't figure out how I would ever color the Sundays, because I would look at the Sunday's color, and I would think to myself, My God, you need to be a major artist to handle the color and paint with their watercolors or whatever they used. I didn't know how they did it.

I was scared to death, and my editor finally said, "You don't do that." I swear to God that was almost a big enough fear to make me want to quit.

SCOTT ADAMS, *DILBERT*

The syndicate contract is one of the most difficult pieces of the syndicate puzzle for the uninitiated to immediately comprehend.

The skills and perceptions required for a cartoonist to achieve newspaper syndication have very little to do with the skills and perceptions required to appreciate the finer points of syndicate contract negotiation.

A further difficulty is that since the industry of newspaper syndication is relatively small, there are few lawyers outside the syndicates who are familiar with all the aspects of the business.

Since each syndicate has different needs—now more than ever before—it is extremely important for the cartoonist to have counsel with either a lawyer or a representative who understands the finer points of explaining and negotiating a newspaper syndication contract.

When I first started—and I'm sure that Mort Walker and most of the others will tell you the same thing—we had no choice. We were given a contract. We just signed it and were delighted. We were told this is a standard syndicate contract and that's it, so I just signed it.

CHARLES SCHULZ, *PEANUTS*

Actually, it's the fear of fear of commitment that I fear.

When a very successful cartoonist's term was up, he started shopping his strip around. There were a number of people who were very interested in picking it up, but his syndicate said, "No, we want to keep you."

So he put together a contract that said, "Here's how we're going to split the revenue. For the list I have right now, I get to keep 80 percent of the revenue and you get 20 percent, but for every new sale you make, you get 75 percent of the sale and I get 25 percent of the sale."

Before this contact, they told him his strip had saturated the market. "We can't sell your cartoon anymore. We have approached everybody, and you have plateaued out."

Well, he signs his contract with the syndicate, and immediately picks up 450 papers.

This is what happens when the syndicate realizes it has to sell. He also put into the contract that once they re-sign him, they can't introduce any new comics for six months and can't do any new promotions on anybody else, so he pretty much had the salesmen's ears. I don't know how the other cartoonists felt about this—they probably didn't know about it—but he put the syndicate on the spot and picked up a ton of papers.

Now wouldn't it be nice if we all had that kind of clout?

ANONYMOUS

CONTRACT CONSIDERATIONS
BY ROBERT S. REED, FORMER PRESIDENT, CHAIRMAN AND CEO, TRIBUNE MEDIA SERVICES

It would be hard for me to discuss syndication contracts with total objectivity. After all, I was on the syndicate side for over thirty years, twenty of them as president of a major syndication company.

I do have some suggestions and ideas, however, that might benefit creative talent just entering the world of syndication for the first time. (The old pros know all the contract clauses and usually have savvy lawyers or business agents handling negotiations, so they are not going to learn much here.)

This may seem strange, but my first piece of advice has nothing to do with contracts. I strongly urge all talent to first find out how comfortable you are with the syndicate you are talking to. Do you like the people? Could you get along with them for ten years, the normal length of a syndication contract? Do you have access to the top man?

You will have a working relationship with the syndicate you select for a long period of time. That's why you need to establish early on your comfort level on a personal basis.

This doesn't mean you should neglect protections provided by a good, fair contract. You start the process by developing a good mutual relationship with the executives at the syndicate.

There is no "ideal" contract in newspaper syndication. I once tried to develop with our lawyers a "fill-in-the-blanks" form for writers and one for cartoonists. Neither worked. Every deal is different. Each writer or artist has his or her thoughts about what should be in a contract. Each syndicate has specific ideas about what it wants in a contract.

If you are sitting down with a syndicate for the very first time, here are some suggestions to which you need to find the answers:

As an artist, are you going to draw six daily comic strips as well as one Sunday page each week?

Whatever you promise the syndicate as a writer or artist, you'll have to deliver fifty-two weeks of each year. There are no vacations, as a general rule, although a few of the very successful creators have managed in later years to get some vacation relief. As a beginner, however, you cannot afford to let someone fill that space you have staked out on the comic pages or the op-ed pages of newspapers.

What rights am I going to grant to the syndicate?

Syndicates will try to get as many rights from you as possible when they present the initial contract.

You may want to restrict the syndicate to just selling your work throughout the world. It depends upon the deal offered you by the syndicate.

Will you let the syndicate sell your work in electronic media?

Today that question is much more important. You are no longer dealing with just television and films. The interactive age is here, and even cartoons are showing up in cyberspace.

You will have to decide these questions pretty early in the negotiating game. Many syndicates have very good book publishing contracts or outlets and you would probably benefit by letting them exploit the book rights for you, in return for a share of the revenues.

Likewise, many syndicates have excellent subsidiary rights operations, and if your partnership with the syndicate is working properly, you would be well served to let the syndicate handle all the marketing of your property.

The rights you grant the syndicate will be determined in large part by two factors: one, how good the syndicate is at selling the various rights you want to grant; and two, the financial arrangement offered by the syndicate.

I've always felt that if a syndicate had a strong vested interest in all elements of your property, it would work much harder for you.

Naturally, if you want a syndicate to represent you in all areas of exploitation, it will ask for a share of the revenues. Perfectly legitimate. We'll get back to the question of revenue sharing later.

WHAT AM I GOING TO TITLE MY FEATURE?

A mundane question, perhaps, but important from a marketing standpoint and a legal standpoint. The title should make it easier for a salesman for the syndicate to explain what the feature is about to prospective buyers. The title you select may belong to someone else. A legal check of registered titles is probably something you'll want the syndicate to undertake as soon as possible.

DO I HAVE TO WARRANT THAT MY MATERIAL IS ORIGINAL?

Yes, and the syndicate will probably ask you to indemnify it in case somebody claims you've stolen his work.

If you do indemnify the syndicate, that might mean you'll be paying for the lawyers. This is where a good lawyer at your side will definitely be an advantage in your negotiations with the syndicate.

WHEN WILL I HAVE TO DELIVER MY WORK TO THE SYNDICATE, AND WILL I HAVE TO PAY THE DELIVERY CHARGES?

The syndicates must meet deadlines set by newspaper customers. Most distributors of feature material want artwork in house at least eight weeks in advance of publication.

This is where I have a personal piece of advice for talent, especially cartoonists. With the exception of Garry Trudeau, the brilliant creator of *Doonesbury*, there is no good reason a cartoonist should be late in submitting material to the syndicate. If you turn out to be a chronic violator of deadlines, you'll just be giving your customers another reason to cancel your feature. It is just plain stupid to lose a customer because you can't stay eight weeks ahead of publication date. Lateness is a flaw that can be fatal to the long-term success of a cartoonist. Nobody's work is so good that it can't be replaced by something else that gets there on time!

Oh incidentally, it is your responsibility to pay for the cost of delivering your material to the syndicate. Be sure, however, to specify that delivery will be made to the syndicate's corporate office, not to some outpost in Canada.

AM I FREE TO SIGN WITH THE SYNDICATE?

Be sure you don't have any outstanding obligations that would get you into a legal bind if you signed to do a feature for a new distributor. If you do, be open with the syndicate, and maybe you can work out a suitable arrangement to the satisfaction of all parties involved.

I made an arrangement with a *New Yorker* cartoonist that worked well for over fifteen years. He was under contract to the magazine and was obligated to give it first choice of the cartoons he produced each week. Once it had made a selection, and this was done every Wednesday in New York, he would bring the remaining cartoons to our editors and we would pick six for our syndicated panel feature. After lunching with fellow cartoonists he would make his rounds of other outlets, trying to sell what he had left from his week's work at home. He was a true professional and followed the same schedule week in, week out, for over twenty-five years. (I envied him also because he came into New York only once a week. The rest of the week he worked out of his studio at home. What a great lifestyle!)

HOW MUCH SHOULD I GET PAID?

If you are just starting out, the best you can expect to negotiate with the syndicate is a fifty/fifty split of revenue.

The key here is defining what that fifty/fifty split really means. Are you going to get 50 percent of gross revenues? Or is your share going to be determined on a net basis after deduction of expenses?

Is your 50 percent coming from sales in the United States only or are you going to get 50 percent of worldwide sales? (Remember the foreign agent issue.)

You'll find it difficult to get a gross deal. Syndicates have production expenses and these, rightfully, should be shared by both parties and deducted off the top before the split each month. But you can insist upon defining those deductions and perhaps putting a limit on the amount of deductions that the syndicate can assess against your feature before paying you.

Usually, net receipts are defined in a syndicate contract as the gross sales of the feature less all or some of the following items:

1. Promotional costs. The costs of promoting your feature are normally shared between the syndicate and the talent. A good syndicate

will prepare a first-class brochure on your feature and make a major mailing to key clients. The costs of these items will be the ones you share with the syndicate. You shouldn't pay for any of the syndicate's sales efforts.

2. Commissions or sales charges by any agency appointed by the syndicate to sell the feature. This could be a foreign agent. It could be an agent representing the company in the sale of movie or television rights. It could be a licensing agent for merchandising sales. All such agents will affect your income; you'll get less. Therefore, you need to know precisely who's going to be selling your feature and who's going to represent you in every area of exploitation.

3. Bad debts. If a customer fails to pay, the syndicate can't give you your 50 percent of the sale.

4. Rebates or allowances. This item is questioned often by talent. But it really is a fair deduction. Sometimes a sale is booked to start one week, but the newspaper delays publication by one or two weeks for reasons beyond the control of the syndicate. The paper will ask for a credit if it got billed for the two weeks of nonuse. That is why a syndicate that pays on billings instead of collections will always be making adjustments on the monthly statements you receive. It's just the reality of the business.

5. "Other costs, expenses or liabilities." Syndicates try to insert this "catch-all" phrase which would allow them to deduct practically anything they wanted to deduct before paying you your share of revenues. If your lawyer pushes hard enough, the syndicate will probably give in on this clause.

WHEN WILL I GET PAID?

Usually the syndicates bill clients on a monthly basis and pay on collections within twenty days of the close of each accounting period. This applies to domestic business only. Foreign sales are harder to track because syndicates do not break down overseas sales by customer each month. They just report a lump sum share of foreign sales each month. I would press the syndicate to provide all customer information.

CAN I INSPECT THE SYNDICATE'S BOOKS?

Sure you can. But I would have a qualified person represent you if you have any question about the numbers. I must say that all syndicates are very honest in reporting actual revenues on individual feature sales.

SHOULD I GET A GUARANTEED WEEKLY PAYMENT?

Syndicates fight hard to avoid guarantees. If you are just starting out in syndication, your chances of obtaining a guarantee are slim. A well-known writer or cartoonist, however, is in a much better position on this issue.

On occasion, a syndicate may bend and negotiate an escalating guarantee with a new talent, but at the same time insist upon escape clauses in case revenues generated by future sales are not sufficient to cover the original guarantees made before the feature was placed into the marketplace. This is not really a guarantee, just a minimum payment as long as the syndicate wants to make it. You also might be able to strike a deal with the syndicate that gives you the first $200 or $300 per week in revenue, lets the syndicate take the next $200 or $300, and provides for splitting everything over $400 or $600 per week.

How many years should i commit to in a contract?

Some talent want very short contracts; three years or less. This demand doesn't sit well with syndicates because they pour a lot of development money and sales efforts into the first years of marketing a new property. It could take more than three years for a feature to really establish itself with readers and with editors.

I think writers and cartoonists must understand that syndicates want to reap the rewards of their hard work in building a property. It does take two to tango in syndication. The talent's work must be good; the syndicate's promotional and sales efforts must produce results.

I always negotiated hard for at least a five-year contract with an automatic five-year renewal clause if my syndicate met preestablished performance goals. My reasoning was this: If I go out and sell hard and build up sales to $4,000 per week by the end of the first term of the contract, then I want to enjoy the fruits of my efforts. And if the feature really catches on in the marketplace, growth could be spectacular in that second five-year period of the contract.

Both the creator and the syndicate should feel "comfortable" with the contract length once negotiations have concluded. The worst result of a contract negotiation would be an unhappy talent and an apathetic marketer. Each party needs to be enthusiastic about prospects for success. That's why you need to have a good working relationship with your syndicate from day one. And if both sides act properly, that relationship should endure for many years.

A good contract and a good relationship will make it easier for both parties to consider renewing the contract after the first ten years have come and gone. Usually syndicates will insist upon a first right of refusal clause to renew with its longtime creator. This doesn't mean the talent has to accept another fifty/fifty deal. It just means that the two of you need to sit down first and hammer out a new agreement that works for both sides. I see nothing wrong with the talent asking for a bigger share of the revenue pie on old business already on the books for five or more years. I do think talent must continue to give syndicates an incentive to continue making sales, and the best way to do this is to agree that the syndicate can still have 50 percent of all new sales or rate increase on old business.

Here are a couple of other suggestions about length of a contract:

• Make sure you have an "out" if sales aren't going well. Give the syndicate a year to reach a level of billing that puts enough bread on your table to compensate you adequately for your work. After a year, you should have a right to terminate the contract if billings are below the agreed-upon amount.

• Avoid short-term contracts that automatically renew only at the option of the syndicate. You want the same rights the syndicate has, regarding termination of any agreement.

SHOULD I OWN MY FEATURE?

Yes. Today the pendulum has swung in favor of the talent owning his or her work. I don't think that bothers the syndicates too much now. In the old days syndicates demanded ownership of everything, including the ownership of the feature even after the contract expired or the talent died.

During the contract period it is easier and less expensive to let the syndicate take the copyrights and trademarks. However, if the contract expires and you do not renew, be sure you get the syndicate to assign all rights in and to the property back to you personally or to your business entity.

SHOULD I MARKET THE SUBSIDIARY RIGHTS IN MY OWN PROPERTY?

No. You are not a salesman, and I don't think you want to hire people on your staff to do this work. But that may depend upon the deal you have negotiated with the syndicate.

If a syndicate can show you that it does have the expertise to market your property for books, stage, motion pictures, television, radio, etc., then let your "partner" handle this part of the business.

You should insist upon controlling how your property is used. If as a cartoonist you do not want your characters used on cereal boxes, you should have the right to say no. You should also insist upon creative control. You need to approve designs on all uses of your characters, whether it is for an animated television show or a stuffed doll.

On the other hand, the syndicate is the deal maker. Let the syndicate negotiate the contract and terms. It is its job.

CAN I DO OTHER FEATURES AND SELL THEM TO NEWSPAPERS THROUGH ANOTHER SYNDICATE?

Not often. Most syndicates require a first option on your new ideas for syndication. Should they say no, then you would be free to take the concept to someone else.

What's the best piece of advice you can give me about getting syndicated?

Get a good lawyer. I always told young writers and cartoonists to get a lawyer experienced in property rights to at least review the contract. You need to know exactly what you are getting yourself into and what your obligations and rights will be under the terms of the deal proposed by the syndicate you have selected.

This also protects the syndicate. I never wanted one of my authors to tell me he didn't understand the terms of the contract he signed.

Now, after reading all this advice, it is time to get syndicated. Good luck.

Contract Needs of Syndicate and Cartoonist

If you take some M&Ms out of someone's candy tray, he may be very upset because his tray is now half-empty. You might not see his problem, because you left the tray half-full. That's what it's like to negotiate, and initially you will get only more or less half the tray of candy.

During the negotiation, the important thing to know is whether you're interested in most of the red M&Ms, yellow M&Ms, orange M&Ms, green M&Ms or brown M&Ms. If you know this, you have a better chance of getting what you want—provided you're willing to give up some of the other colors.

Contract Needs of Syndicate and Cartoonist
The Syndicate's Needs

Their concern was to get me to sign the contract with no changes.
CATHY GUISEWITE, *CATHY*

If you know what's important to the syndicate, and if you know what's important to you, then you know how close or far apart you will be in your contract negotiations.

Protecting the Investment

It costs syndicates a lot to launch a new comic feature—costs in money, manpower and overhead.

Like any business, they expect a certain return for their dollar. If they don't believe they can protect their investment and get their projected return, they have no reason to be doing business with you.

I think the syndicate wanted to protect their investment. I don't mean this as a negative thing, but I think a syndicate—being a business—they're looking for everything they can get. I think cartoonists need to know this going into the contract. Most syndicates just don't charitably give things away. Some things need to be negotiated, and contracts are not set in stone.

BILL AMEND, FOXTROT

TERM

Should the occasion arise that a creator takes his feature to another syndicate, the new syndicate automatically receives the space and revenue from the feature's newspapers, and the original syndicate automatically loses that feature's space and revenue.

One of the strongest ways a syndicate can protect its investment in a comic feature is to have the longest possible term for the contract.

If a syndicate makes an enormous investment in launching a strip, they are entitled to some protection for having worked with the creator, having brought him along, having launched the strip, and more important, having made a success of it. So for this effort, it really has to be viewed as a partnership. They couldn't do anything without us and we could do even less without them. So it is in the true sense a partnership, and it should be viewed as a partnership.

So if the cartoonists own the copyright, they should at least be willing to give to the syndicate a reasonably long-term distribution deal, which means we syndicate it, with fair options to renew beyond the initial period.

There are all kinds of contracts out there right now. There are five-year contracts, with an option to renew for ten to fifteen, depending on performances. There are contracts out there for ten, with options to renew.

The important thing is the concept of partnership. God, the worst thing you can do to a syndicate is have them invest all that money, go out and kill themselves getting you in three hundred newspapers, and then leave, because somebody hiding in the bushes says, "You got a fifty/fifty deal. Give me your list, and I'll give you seventy/thirty."

To me that's piracy. For the syndicate that says, "I'll give you seventy/thirty," it's one sale, a sale to the creator. But we made three hundred sales, and every one to a tough newspaper editor. And that's effort, that's money, that's time. That's blood, sweat and tears. And then, when my contract with a cartoonist is up, someone says, "I'll give you a seventy/thirty deal," and 30 percent of a three hundred newspaper billing just drops in his lap. We spent five years developing the list, but some creators may make the change.

JOSEPH D'ANGELO, KING FEATURES

It has to be evident from the work that you submit that you are wor-

thy of the amount of money and effort that goes into producing a new comic strip—if comic strips is what you're talking about—because it costs thousands of dollars for a syndicate to actually syndicate and package you. And it takes a long time before they recoup their expenses. And so for the first five years in, at least, they are entitled to tremendous legal ownership and control of what you're doing.

After five years, if you've proven yourself, and you're doing an extremely good job, and it's your talent and your perseverance that's making this thing go, then other conditions could be arranged.

LYNN JOHNSTON, *FOR BETTER OR FOR WORSE*

We think long term, and that, in some cases, is more difficult for creators.

Our philosophy has always been that it's one newspaper at a time. It takes a while. It takes patience. In two years down the pike, or three years down the pike, I don't want our people or the company to be saying, "God, we're working our tail off here, and they're turning around and renegotiating a contract." Because then you start getting frustrated. You're doing a good job, you're building, then all of a sudden you're faced with a contract renewal.

Whereas, if both creator and syndicate are working together, they're going to give each other ample opportunity, reasonable opportunity to build this list. We have the confidence it can be accomplished, or we would not have gone into the relationship in the first place.

JOHN MCMEEL, UNIVERSAL PRESS SYNDICATE

So the syndicate's natural question is: "Why should we knock ourselves out selling you if we think you might leave us in five or ten years?"

The answer is that if they're doing a good job for the cartoonist and he or she likes the current management—and I mean the current management, because we sign with a corporate entity, and the people we sign with today are not necessarily going to be there in ten years—there is no reason for the cartoonist not to renew. I did. For thirty-five years I had options every five years but stayed with the same entity through all of its mergers, sales and amalgamations, because I liked the people. And that's very important to me.

MELL LAZARUS, *MISS PEACH* AND *MOMMA*

There are several things that are important: Obviously that the revenue split be equitable to both parties; that the revenue split and the anticipated market penetration are going to provide enough revenue to cover the expenses that the syndicate incurs in an ongoing way; and that it's going to produce an acceptable level of profit to the syndicate and an acceptable level of revenue to the contributor, and that's important.

I think term is important. If a syndicate really believes in a property, it needs to have enough term in the contract to build it over a period of time, to see whether it's really going to work or not.

STEVE CHRISTENSEN, LOS ANGELES TIMES SYNDICATE

Creators changed a lot of bad things in the syndication contract, by giving ownership right off the bat, and by making short-term contracts available.

We are never going to try to own the strips, but I would say we have longer terms today than we did five years ago for new cartoonists.

But I don't think it really matters how long the contracts are, as long as they're not fifty years or so. The real key is: At the end of the contract, whose asset is the client list? Is it the syndicate's, or is it the cartoonist's? That's the key question. It's taken me a lot of years to get this over. If the cartoonist has a fifteen-year contract, and at the end of fifteen years the cartoonist owns that list of subscribers free and clear (or if not free and clear, they may have to pay slight royalties to the founding syndicate), then that to me is a fair contract. If, at the end of fifteen years, the syndicate owns that list and can terminate the cartoonist and hire someone else to do the work and fill the space, then that's unfair.

RICHARD NEWCOMBE, CREATORS SYNDICATE

EDITORIAL CONTROL

Many syndicates feel they need to be the final word on whether or not an individual daily or Sunday is acceptable.

This feeling extends from two considerations. Most syndicates want to make certain "inappropriate" editorial content will not jeopardize sales. Also, since the syndicates are the distributors of the material, they feel it needs to be material they can support and defend.

Editorially, it's important to us to be able to reject an unsuitable piece of work. Having that in the contract saves a lot of arguments. If something's off the subject or out of character, we ought to be able to say no.

The other aspect of that is that we cannot insert things without the cartoonist's approval. And that seems to be a good, balanced relationship.

Financially, we think we should able to benefit from our work for years to come. I don't mean to be specific, but I don't think a one- or two-year contract is sufficient time for a syndicate to benefit, not if it's done good work.

STUART DODDS, CHRONICLE FEATURES

THE SPLIT

Traditionally, the newspaper syndicate offers a fifty/fifty split of the gross revenue. The gross generally describes those moneys left after the syndicate's expenses, but not the cartoonist's expenses.

The syndicate needs a fair share. We don't ever ask for over 50 percent. Fifty percent is a fair share.

It has been the practice of the Writer's Group to pay all production costs. Some of the other syndicates don't share that with the cartoonists. We just think it is simpler that way.

We also hold copyright and trademark for the length of the contract, because we defend it in court. We register it. That's important to us, although I think that's evolving. Control over the copyright may be more important in the long run than holding the copyright for the term.

What the syndicate really wants is assurance in the contract that if we really put our prestige on the line for this, and really bust our tails, that we're going to build a relationship with the cartoonist that will last as long as the strip lasts.

We don't sign super–long-term contracts. We don't believe in it.

ALAN SHEARER, WASHINGTON POST WRITERS GROUP

CONTRACT NEEDS OF SYNDICATE AND CARTOONIST

THE CARTOONIST'S NEEDS

When it comes to the contract, cartoonists have even more diverse needs than syndicates.

It is extremely important you be able to identify what you are comfortable with and what you are not comfortable with, because you will have to live with your decision for many years to come.

THE "REASONABLE" REQUESTS

I think you ought to start right off with reasonable requests. Own your own artwork. Get a decent guaranteed salary, so you don't have to work at the post office on the side. Ownership is very important, and the right to sell licenses.

MORT WALKER, *BEETLE BAILEY*

TERM

Term is a very different issue for cartoonists than it is for syndicates.

To many cartoonists, term is the length of time they are bound to their contracts, even if they don't like them. It's a commitment they cannot rescind for five, ten, or twenty years of their life.

My contract was ten years, automatically renewable for another ten years. That meant twenty years. And that seemed like an awfully long time.

LYNN JOHNSTON, *FOR BETTER OR FOR WORSE*

A cartoonist's primary concern should be the length of time, because if it were a five-year contract instead of a twenty-year contract, effectively a lot can happen in five years. You can feel a lot differently about things.

I think that . . . I'm pausing, because as the words come out of my mouth, I'm hearing the syndicate's rebuttal. I've heard many times about the investment the syndicate needs to make in the comic strip, and I respect that. I also feel, in the case of my syndicate—for me and other cartoonists I know—they really make the investment and stand behind it. And I also tend to think that's why their cartoonists tend to keep signing on, too, even after their bizillion-year contracts.

From a cartoonist's needs standpoint, a shorter contract is something anyone should try to fight for.

Also the secondary rights to the strip. Licensing, merchandising, TV, books. Any other form that the comic strip can appear in, besides the strip. I think that those rights should remain with the creator from the get-go. I thought that from the get-go, but it wasn't exactly an area where I felt I had a big vote.

CATHY GUISEWITE, *CATHY*

The creator is saying, "Geez, I can't go anywhere."

I think there is a balance. When I say, "We think long term," it is going to be a reasonably long term, where the syndicate can work with the creator, develop and sell the strip.

JOHN MCMEEL, UNIVERSAL PRESS SYNDICATE

I would want to get as short a contract as possible. A lot of syndicates will say, "God, we need ten years to develop this thing." I would say ideally you get it shorter than that, just so you can do something else with it at the end of the contract period if you felt you needed to.

Also you should retain ownership. The rights should be owned by you, but I think that's pretty much the standard now.

JEFF MACNELLY, *SHOE* AND *PLUGGERS*

I simply wanted something fair. It had nothing to do with money. It has to do with the terms. So I think that new cartoonists coming into the business are going to see tremendous change in their contracts' time lengths now. There's not going to be the ten-plus-ten years.

LYNN JOHNSTON, *FOR BETTER OR FOR WORSE*

OWNERSHIP

Ownership is less an issue with most (but not all) of the major syndicates than it was in the recent past.

The primary concern for any cartoonist who has been doing it a while or has a strip syndicated is, "Who owns my characters' copyright?"

ALAN SHEARER, WASHINGTON POST WRITERS GROUP

Ownership is no longer an issue. Ownership exists in some cases, but for the most part, contracts that are coming out today, ownership really rests with the cartoonists, and they own the copyright.

JOSEPH D'ANGELO, KING FEATURES

Ownership was probably the only thing we insisted upon, and of course that was easy because Creators is really founded on that premise. So that was offered right away.

JERRY SCOTT, *BABY BLUES* AND *NANCY*

I had two concerns. First, I wanted ownership, because, while you assign your ownership to the syndicate during the life of the contract, there is some subtle unwritten law that when you own your strip you get more respect. I've seen it happen. I've felt it ever since I got ownership. I had a different status with the syndicate.

The second thing I want to do is have some control over my licensing. I never have before. I can sell licenses now and I can say what products I like, what I don't like, and control the use of artwork. Before, to sell a product, the syndicate art department used to put the artwork together. I'd get the product, and I was never happy with it, so I think it is working out better.

MORT WALKER, *BEETLE BAILEY*

We have never sold a feature that the cartoonist did not own. Ever.

TONI MENDEZ, LITERARY REPRESENTATIVE

It used to be some of the old contracts gave the syndicates all rights forever. The right to use the trademark name, copyright, everything. But now that's broken down. I think we all realize that the contracts these days are more fair.

In areas where it counts, cartoonists should give the syndicates all rights that relate to its job in syndicate-newspaper relations and whatever on the licenses.

Usually after the term of the contract, the copyright is returned to the author. That's pretty standard.

STUART DODDS, CHRONICLE FEATURES

I was the first cartoonist to get ownership from King Features. Once they had ownership of a feature, they had not given ownership to anybody. A creator should own a comic strip and its characters because it it morally right. It's his baby.

Ownership is the bottom line. However, to be fair, I don't think a new artist can expect to have the clout others have in negotiating with a syndicate. I think ownership, split of revenue and control of the fea-

ture is important. You don't want the syndicate to have complete control where they can reject the work you're doing. That can nullify a contract. But if you own the feature, the syndicate is not going to allow the contract to expire when they're making money from it.

BIL KEANE, THE FAMILY CIRCUS

EDITORIAL CONTROL

Many cartoonists want editorial responsibility for what appears in their features.

With this editorial control comes the sole responsibilty for shepherding their visions, as well as the personal responsibility for papers dropping their features due to inappropriate or consistently inadequate material.

They want to make sure we make no changes without their approval, which we don't do anyway.

LEE SALEM, UNIVERSAL PRESS SYNDICATE

Their primary concern—overwhelmingly number one—is editorial control. Also, they want to make sure we don't enter into licensing agreements that they don't want or can't use or don't want to be embarrassed by.

RICHARD NEWCOMBE, CREATORS SYNDICATE

EXPENSES

You should make clear what syndicate expenses are to be deducted from your feature's gross income.

I think cartoonists are concerned about their share of the revenue and how production expenses are going to be handled.

STEVE CHRISTENSEN, LOS ANGELES TIMES SYNDICATE

GUARANTEED MINIMUMS

Freelancing is a lifestyle choice with some terrific upsides and terrifying downsides. One of the downsides is that you have absolutely no guarantees of how much you will make for a living, and whether or not it will even be a living.

The guaranteed minimum, depending on how it's set up, can be utilized in two ways. It could give you a minimum amount of money to live on, even if your share of the revenue drops below a certain point. It could also give you or the syndicate an opportunity to sever your contractual agreement if your income drops below that same point.

When you sign a contract with a syndicate, most contracts are going to have a guaranteed minimum in there. That really doesn't amount to anything, because if your income falls below the minimum and you demand your minimum—there's also a clause in there that says within

---

thirty days either can terminate the contract—then they'll just say, "Okay, we can't afford him," and they'll cancel you. So it really doesn't matter.

PETER KOHLSAAT, SINGLE SLICES AND THE NOOZ

Where I've run into trouble are with those cartoonists who view the syndicate as an employer. They want salary guaranteed, they want health benefits, and that's not what it's all about.

RICHARD NEWCOMBE, CREATORS SYNDICATE

PROMOTION AND MARKETING

The launch and continued promotion of your feature will have a large impact on its ultimate success. Since effective newspaper sales have quite a bit to do with book publishing and/or licensing ventures, and they in turn translate into additional newspaper sales, it's important to do everything in your power to have your feature promoted.

One way to help ensure an effective promotional campaign is to get a contractual guarantee for the amount of time and dollars your syndicate is willing to spend on the feature's initial launch, as well as a minimum amount of dollars your syndicate is willing to spend on an annual basis, as well as the amount of space your syndicate will guarantee in its annual syndicate directory ad.

You may not get everything (or anything) you ask for, but it will be important for you to know how far the syndicate is willing to extend itself on your behalf. If you know this, and you are unhappy with the depth of the syndicate's commitment to you, then that tells you the extent to which you will have to be your own promoter.

I think they are concerned about the promotional efforts the syndicate is willing to commit to, as well as the syndicate's marketing plan to sell the strip.

STEVE CHRISTENSEN, LOS ANGELES TIMES SYNDICATE

ORIGINAL ART

Syndicates have been returning original art to cartoonists for years. What I fail to understand is why a syndicate would have a policy of returning artwork to cartoonists and not have that in its initial contract offer.

Just to dot the i's and cross the t's, make certain your contract stipulates a timely return of artwork and guarantees an amount of money for any artwork in its possession that is lost or stolen.

There have been so many contracts where I have had to put in that original art will be returned to the cartoonist. We have always just done it routinely, but I guess there are some places that haven't.

LEE SALEM, UNIVERSAL PRESS SYNDICATE

King Features has never taken the position that we own the original art. I've got about sixty to seventy cartoonists who send me material. If it's the original, we package it after two to three months and return it to the creator. If it's a Xerox, we obviously just put them in the file.

In the past, other syndicates have taken the position that the original art was theirs.

JOSEPH D'ANGELO, KING FEATURES

<u>CONTRACT NEEDS OF SYNDICATE AND CARTOONIST</u>

MAKING THE EVALUATION

In order to make an effective evaluation of how far you're willing to compromise in your contract negotiations, you must know how important those red M&Ms are to you. Will it kill you if the syndicate takes them? Does only getting the yellow M&Ms in exchange sour you on the whole process?

When you create a comic feature, you own everything. At the moment of creation the feature is entirely yours.

When you sign a contract with a newspaper syndicate, you are signing over rights to them, and there is nothing that says you have to give them anything. However, until you sign over rights to them, there is nothing that says the syndicate has to do anything for you. This is why you're negotiating. You're trading M&Ms.

If there are M&Ms you are not willing to trade, then don't trade them.

If you do not trade them, be prepared for the syndicate to take its M&Ms and go home.

Unless you are already an extremely successful cartoonist, it is highly unlikely you will get more than half the M&Ms in the candy tray. If you cannot become reconciled to this fact, then you are probably trying to sell your work in the wrong medium.

If you are reconciled to the realities of the business, but you still want to keep your red M&Ms, then keep them. If your work appeals to one syndicate, then it may appeal to another, and the next place may be willing to let you keep your red M&Ms.

A caution: If you take your work elsewhere, looking to keep your red M&Ms, there are no guarantees that another syndicate will even be interested in your work.

The dilemma: If you are not willing to stand firm to keep your M&Ms, then you must be prepared to lose your M&Ms.

The most important concern should be what you want, both psychologically and practically.

I think you have to make a lot of choices. If you're getting a really tremendous guarantee, but the syndicate wants to own the strip, and if money is primarily important to you, you can go that way.

Barring that, I think the most important thing is to own your feature, and own it with a short contract that expires unconditionally. Especially for young cartoonists, because it is going to set the pattern for the rest of their lives. Clearly, if you sign the so-called standard syndicate contract, you'll be drawing under that contract for thirty years for the same 50 percent.

Fifty percent. Think about it. It's the only agency system in the world where they get 50 percent. Agents are supposed to get 15 percent. And if they have expenses they must absorb by themselves, then maybe 25 percent is reasonable.

But I don't think the cartoonist should lock himself into any situation. The creator should own the characters, outright, and sign the shortest possible contract that terminates unconditionally, without performance clauses or automatic renewals. It should simply end, giving the cartoonist a chance to renegotiate the deal on an equal footing, without their brain-children being held hostage.

At which happy time the cartoonist might rightfully ask for 65 or 70 percent of the billing—at least of the current billing, which comes from newspapers he's been able to hold on to and for which the sales commissions have long since been paid and have already been amortized by the syndicate. After all, the costs of distributing a strip are really very small.

MELL LAZARUS, *MISS PEACH* AND *MOMMA*

Basically, the overall thing that I was looking for was an agreement with a syndicate that I thought treated both sides fairly.

I wanted a contract with a fairly short duration. The money that we signed for I thought was reasonable. When you are in negotiation with a syndicate, you are selling a chunk of your life. You have to basically sit down and go through all the permutations and figure out where this agreement is going to take you, and whether or not you are willing to sell a chunk of your life for X amount of dollars, given the fact that you are going to be working on this thing for a long time. X number of hours per week.

You sit down and you make a very cold calculation. I'm fairly good at that, as far as stepping back and separating the creative side of myself from the business side. I thought we had a very good contract right from day one. Actually, I have always been happy with the way they have treated me, and that's a function of knowing what your needs really are. For me, the important aspect was the duration. We covered everything. There were no surprises later on, where I found out I had signed away rights I hadn't known about. There was none of that because I had an attorney to help right from the start.

The only real deal-breaker in my initial contract was ownership. We negotiated all the different parameters, and I tried to get ownership.

I went into negotiations, realizing I was bringing in a gag panel, and that's very, very different than doing a strip where you have continuing characters.

Let's say ten years down the line, I walk away from the strip or panel. What I am walking away from is very different than someone who is signing away a character that they have created.

For me, the ownership that was a deal-breaker for them was something I felt okay about. I realized if I ever left the strip and they retained ownership, they really wouldn't have anything, because what they are buying is what's coming out of me, as opposed to a character that may have a whole life and merchandising life.

BRUCE BEATTIE, *BEATTIE BLVD.*

Do You Need a Lawyer?

Yes.

We always recommend to anyone dealing with us, "Get a lawyer." They need to get one, as soon as they find out from us that we want to go to contract stage. They need a lawyer at that point, and they shouldn't agree to any terms until they get one.

ALAN SHEARER, WASHINGTON POST WRITERS GROUP

I think there is an absolute lack of good legal advice available in the country today for cartoonists' syndicate contract negotiations. I don't think the average lawyer knows much about syndication, or the personal possessiveness that is involved when a cartoonist creates something that is his property. Attorneys don't have a feel for what a cartoonist can't get and should get. They need to know a lot about the newspaper syndication business and about licensing, or have the ability to learn on the job. They need to be strong on negotiations, but not unreasonable, because a syndicate must be left with an incentive.

BIL KEANE, *THE FAMILY CIRCUS*

A lawyer is a much better guy to have on your side than an agent, if you can trust him, and if he knows the business. You want to be able to deal with contracts in a knowledgeable way. They need to know both sides of the business. Not any lawyer can do this. It's frustrating that some young person will go to a lawyer who is really good at drawing up wills or helping you sell your house, but doesn't know anything about this type of contract.

And not too many lawyers are honest enough to say, "This is not my field of expertise. Go to someone else."

Most of them will say, "Oh, yeah, yeah sure. I know all about this stuff."

And so you have to find someone good, and that's a real problem. One of the things that the National Cartoonists Society has been trying to do is have some kind of contact with legal people who will give us advice, help us out, and help new young people coming in. Not to fight the syndicates but to interpret those contracts, so a young artist knows their options and where the changes can be made.

LYNN JOHNSTON, *FOR BETTER OR FOR WORSE*

I absolutely would recommend to any cartoonist that has been offered a contract that a lawyer be obtained. I would rather have my tough discussions up front with a lawyer or a well-informed cartoonist than have someone sign a four-page document and two weeks later say, "Oh, my God! Is that what I signed?"

LEE SALEM, UNIVERSAL PRESS SYNDICATE

I think it's good for every cartoonist that negotiates with a syndicate to have a representative. It could be an agent, or it could be an attorney.

The fact is there are few if any attorneys who specialize or understand syndication. And there are few agents.

DAVID HENDIN, LITERARY AGENT

As a general rule, I would recommend to a cartoonist—assuming that they have already made the sale—that they should definitely have an attorney look at their contract before they sign it. Because you are getting together for a long time.

RICHARD NEWCOMBE, CREATORS SYNDICATE

Do You Need a Lawyer?

WHAT YOUR LAWYER NEEDS TO KNOW

If a lawyer doesn't know you should have ownership, he is in cahoots with the syndicate.

JOHNNY HART, *B.C. AND THE WIZARD OF ID*

It is vital that your representative have a working knowledge of the business of newspaper syndication.

A contract attorney who is familiar with book publishing or the entertainment industry, but unfamiliar with newspaper syndication, may introduce aspects of the negotiation that are based on his experience but are not germane to syndication. Since this could be intrusive to the negotiation and the retaining of rights that are far more important, it is important to have an informed adviser.

They ought to seek out a lawyer who already has knowledge of newspaper syndication, as well as the other aspects, such as merchandising, that would be covered in a contract.

STEVE CHRISTENSEN, LOS ANGELES TIMES SYNDICATE

Obviously, the best person you could have is an attorney who used to work for a syndicate. That would be ideal. Other than that, you'd need someone who is familiar with contracts, but they should have some idea of how features work in newspapers, how the fees are determined, what can happen to a cartoonist, what kind of trouble can he get in, things like that. That would be a good starting point.

PETER KOHLSAAT, SINGLE SLICES AND THE NOOZ

A lawyer doesn't have to know a whole lot about syndication, per se. He or she needs to know about basic business rights. Any good contract attorney—especially one from the entertainment business—will know about performance agreements and understand that a contract must provide for its own termination. A contract that keeps renewing itself is probably unconstitutional, in the first place. Basically, the cartoonist should know what he or she wants and the lawyer should make sure the document reflects that.

I've talked to a lot of cartoonists and am surprised at how little many of them know about the contracts they so cheerfully signed. They may not realize that in many cases the people who asked them to sign those things would never commit their own personal services under those terms.

MELL LAZARUS, MISS PEACH AND MOMMA

I think a lawyer needs to know that there is a huge, out-of-pocket start-up cost on the part of the syndicate. It could be as much as one quarter of a million dollars. If a syndicate is spending time on this strip, and forgoing the opportunity of working with another strip, that's very significant.

RICHARD NEWCOMBE, CREATORS SYNDICATE

When I have gotten various lawyers over the years, I have pleaded with them to get any information they could about deals other car-

toonists got, because I wanted a frame of reference. I wanted to know what other people got and that was—partially—to know what was reasonable for me, to know what other people had accepted. I thought that that was really valuable.

CATHY GUISEWITE, CATHY

A lawyer ought to know a bit about rights to a property, intellectual rights and copyrights, and what that means. A lawyer ought to have some experience with syndication contracts.

ALAN SHEARER, WASHINGTON POST WRITERS GROUP

A lawyer needs to understand the basic structure of individual rights, and I think if you're the creator of an idea then you ought to own the rights to that character.

A syndicate should have to reach certain levels for a period of the contract. As I said before, they get lazy about it, and once they get into a hundred papers that's it. They have covered their nut. They've covered their minimum guarantee, so they don't have to push anymore.

I think they ought to work as hard as we do.

MORT WALKER, BEETLE BAILEY

I have an entertainment lawyer. Basically I think the thing that the lawyers have to know is that the contract under negotiation has a potential for a tremendous financial impact and tremendous impact over the life of the creator involved.

When you're sitting there, with a property on the block that is in most cases the essence of who you are—and each cartoonist only gets one chance in life—I think the lawyer has to be cognizant of the fact that syndication is rather a dog-eat-dog world. This is something that needs to be protected and cared for, and the lawyer will have to approach it in such a way that the cartoonist isn't taken advantage of, because in most cases this is the cartoonist's entire life.

You have to have a "let the buyer beware" all around. The artist and the lawyer and the syndicate. This is a business deal, and one assumes that we all come to the table with a certain amount of knowledge. If people get taken advantage of, it is out of a position of ignorance, and that's dangerous.

What's fit for one cartoonist at one syndicate is not necessarily good for another. Ultimately, the agreement has to reflect the cartoonist's needs. If the lawyer comes into the situation and says, "Oh, you're not getting ownership, therefore the contract is bad," he isn't paying close enough attention to his client to be servicing it correctly. That's the lawyer and his ego getting in the way.

When a lawyer comes into a situation like this—let's say he is totally unfamiliar with it—he should say, "Okay, first of all, do you want to sign this agreement? Okay, let's talk about some broad financial parameters. I don't know anything about this. What are some of the other things coming up here. Ownership? How do you feel about that?"

You both go through the learning process, and God, I hope the lawyer is smart enough to say, "Do you know any other cartoonists, anybody that we could call?" That seems like the intelligent and diligent thing to do.

Something that is very important, and this is hard for a creative person to really swallow, is that their life is on the chopping block, and you can't come to the table without the ability to be able to get up and walk away. If you are coming without that ability, you are going to get screwed. That's something that I think is very tough for cartoonists to swallow, because the property is who they are, this thing that the syndicate is buying.

BRUCE BEATTIE, BEATTIE BLVD.

THE NEGOTIATING PROCESS

I believe in an honorable negotiation. You win, you give up, but you win the important things.

TONI MENDEZ, LITERARY REPRESENTATIVE

Psychologically, the cartoonist is at a disadvantage, and the people at the syndicates know it. They are already in business without you. You are just now trying to enter the business, and you need a syndicate to distribute your feature.

Your one advantage is that the syndicate may be in business, but it cannot be in business with your feature unless you let it.

Ultimately, the question becomes: How important does a syndicate think your feature is to the future of their business?

When you know who needs whom, you know who's going to get more of what each wants in the negotiation.

Frankly, the thing that made negotiating hard was my fear that I would raise one teeny weeny little objection, and Universal Press would say, "Well, you've blown it, pal," which is very naive. I've learned that now, but coming in, you spend two, three, four years sending in submissions, praying every night that somebody will offer you a contract, and when that contract comes, you're under a enormous amount of pressure to just sign on the dotted line.

This is something every would-be cartoonist needs to keep in mind: Every contract is negotiable. If they are offering you a contract, it means that they like your strip. They're not doing it out of charity. They'll be

---

willing to talk. That doesn't mean they are going to concede to your every request, but don't be afraid to raise your objections.

BILL AMEND, *FOXTROT*

I think cartoonists don't have much problem explaining their concerns, but that depends on their rapport with the person representing the syndicate. I think they are pretty good at saying, "I'm a little worried about this," or "How is this going to work?"

STEVE CHRISTENSEN, LOS ANGELES TIMES SYNDICATE

The contract was the most terrifying thing I ever saw in my life. I was concerned about how much of my life I was committing. That was really everything, because if the contract had been only for a year, I would have gladly done anything for a year, knowing that I could change it. But it was such a long amount of time. And when I signed the contract I know I felt like most new cartoonists feel, which is "I have no negotiating power whatsoever, because I'm completely unknown and inexperienced."

So I felt that I had no negotiating power. While I was not one of those people who had dreamed their whole life of being a cartoonist, I loved the idea of having a chance to do this. I really wanted to give it a try, and I loved that these people were willing to give me a chance. So I wanted to sign up, but of course it was terrifying to do it, because the contract was so long and so inclusive.

CATHY GUISEWITE, *CATHY*

I think negotiating's difficult for them, and that's why I encourage each artist to talk to an attorney. The attorney can negotiate on the major points we have. I'm no lawyer, and I certainly wouldn't sign a twenty-year mortgage without having a lawyer go through it. I wouldn't have them sign a twenty-year syndicate contract without having a lawyer go through it.

LEE SALEM, UNIVERSAL PRESS SYNDICATE

I don't think young cartoonists are in any position to negotiate at all. You have to take what is offered at the moment, and it's a fairly standard offer on the part of the syndicate. I think if the young fella has an acceptable idea, he ought to ask the syndicate to give him an advance so he can have some living funds while he's developing this thing, and it probably should be irrevocable. Most syndicates have a boilerplate sort of an arrangement, and I think they're all pretty sensitive to the needs of the creator.

HANK KETCHAM, *DENNIS THE MENACE*

If you're an unknown cartoonist with an untested strip, you are in a poor position to negotiate. Unless you are willing to sell the work your-

self, you will play on the syndicate's terms or not at all. It's very unlikely that more than one syndicate will be interested in your work, so shopping around for better terms is a nonissue in most cases. Consult a lawyer, but I don't know of any cartoonist who got a fair and balanced contract at the outset.

BILL WATTERSON, CALVIN AND HOBBES

I think that a new, young, eager person feels that if they don't agree to absolutely everything that's in the contract now, that they will look greedy and ugly and unappreciative—and all kinds of things—and therefore lose the opportunity. But that's not true.

If you have the wonderful situation in which a contract is presented to you, you're a very rare bird indeed, considering all the different projects that are sent in and submitted every week. You do have choices, and you do have room to move. That's the one thing that I found out a little too late, like a lot of other people. Yes, you can make changes. Yes, you can make your wishes known, and you can work it out much more equitably and fairly.

LYNN JOHNSTON, FOR BETTER OR FOR WORSE

I tend to think that cream rises across the board, so that for the most part those people I express interest in are very well-informed, educated, bright. I mean they are just smart people, and I think that smart people in general just say, "This is what I am concerned about. This is what I am not concerned about."

I don't find that to be much of a problem. They let you know what they want, because I've talked with them before we get to the point where we've offered them a contract. We have gone back and forth enough, so that I have a sense of who they are and they have a sense of who I am.

Hopefully, they are comfortable with my vision of their strip. If they're not, then they should certainly tell me—which they often do— or they shouldn't be working with me. I mean they shouldn't. This is a commitment they should be comfortable with.

JAY KENNEDY, KING FEATURES

I think a lot of cartoonists have a really difficult time negotiating.

Maybe it is not in their nature. I think that creative people tend to be most comfortable doing creative things, and they are often not comfortable dealing with the business aspects of what they do. Because of that, they find it hard to address certain issues.

Sometimes we encounter people who have wanted to be syndicated for a very long time, and they are so happy to get a contract that they don't want to jeopardize anything. They're afraid they'll blow it, and they don't want to lose their chance.

ANITA TOBIAS, CREATORS SYNDICATE

The thing is, when you are young and you are unknown, and you are submitting your strip and hoping somebody will take it, you have absolutely no leverage at all. The syndicates know that and the syndicates use that.

You generally end up signing a contract that the syndicate always benefits from. And that's just the way of the world. That's the way it has always been. Artists have always been taken advantage of by businesspeople. That's the way it always will be, until you get to a point where you have some clout. That's all you can do. You hope for the best.

The syndicates have gotten much better at it, over the last several years, and much fairer than they were. Before, it was a virtual ownership of everything. There are lots of horror stories, but syndicates have really cleaned up their act.

WILEY MILLER, *NON SEQUITUR*

The negotiation was very easy. I was working with a collaborator at the time, and he was already syndicated. He crossed out items on the contract and wrote in other items. Then we submitted the contract back to the syndicate, with our concerns quite literally on the page. And as long as our items were reasonable, the syndicate really had no problem with them.

I was surprised, because I didn't think this was something that you could actually do. I thought a contract was a contract hard and true, and whatever they offered you was set in stone. I found out that they were willing to negotiate, if they think they are reaping something, too.

STEPHEN BENTLEY, *HERB & JAMAAL*

I also feel that in a business conversation, if words are said and it is not by the creative person but by a third person, any negative feelings that arise during a negotiation are not taken personally. It stays in a business category, which is very important for the creative person. Very important.

TONI MENDEZ, LITERARY REPRESENTATIVE

SELLING THE NEW FEATURE

The promotion and the launch of the new feature are two of the most important determining factors of its initial success.

Quality aside, a feature can take years to recover from a poor promotion and launch, and it may still never get off the ground. However, a good promotion and launch can help propel a feature out of the pull of gravity and into outer space, where it can then keep going on its own momentum.

The Strip Samples

Traditionally the syndicate includes the first four to six weeks of dailies and Sundays in the promotion of a new feature.

When newspaper editors finish reading the strip samples, they should have a clear understanding of the strip, its world, its characters, its attitude, and they should want to see more.

I think the initial promotion package is very important. That's when a strip is introduced into the marketplace. You want your absolute best material, not one miss in the samples. If newspaper editors say "no" to your comic—as we all know most of them will—then the memory of not liking your comic is what they will keep stored in their minds. When the syndicate salesman comes back, his job is to overcome that memory and that is extremely difficult to do.

ANITA TOBIAS, CREATORS SYNDICATE

I go through the entire selection of what we call the inserts of the samples.

We will have been working on a development period, which can be usually in about nine months, and there will be three to four times as many strips done than I need. So I will go through my selection of what I think is appropriate, send it to the cartoonist, ask him to tell me which ones he thinks are weak choices, and then to give me a list of which ones he loves.

And then, together, we go through my reasons for choosing the ones that he thought were particularly weak. If he really thinks it's awful, I throw it out, because there are usually more to choose.

Why have anything in there we're both not happy with? And then we go through the list of the ones they like, and they may have caught something I didn't see.

JAY KENNEDY, KING FEATURES

How Promotions Are Produced

Each newspaper syndicate has its own internal process for producing promotions. Some are very departmentalized and others are very informal and free-form.

A comic feature promotion is a promise by the syndicate to the newspaper that it will distribute a certain feature with a certain perspective and a certain guaranteed quality. Anything short of these promises will be considered a disappointment or even a failure.

Regardless of the operating method of your syndicate, it is vital that the promotion sell your feature in the best and most truthful light.

It is up to you to determine how important it is for you to be either a leader or contributor to this process.

As a whole, syndicates have their own certain approaches in terms of sales promotions, and that procedure is one which I think most cartoonists not only adapt to, but accept as the way to do business. But we are certainly open to any other ideas.

LEE SALEM, UNIVERSAL PRESS SYNDICATE

I was very involved in my promotion. In my opinion, this is something a cartoonist should do.

Cartoonists today give away too much power to the syndicates. We let them run everything because we see them as the authority figure, daddy or whatever.

My wife put it best to me, she said, "Look, the syndicate is not going to care as much about your work as you do."

It is up to you—the cartoonist—to really look after your own ass, to look after that feature and make sure everything is done right. Because they don't care. They will make all the motions, but their livelihood does not depend on the success or failure of your feature. You are just one of a number of features that they run, so you have to get involved personally and oversee absolutely every aspect of it.

Go ahead and be a pain in the ass. Like it says, syndicates don't want to hear from cartoonists once the thing is launched. They just want you to send in the work and leave them alone. They don't want to be bothered, but you've got to bother them, 'cause this is your livelihood. And if you don't stay on top of it, you have only yourself to blame.

WILEY MILLER, *NON SEQUITUR*

Basically I had done the work. The promotion department put together a sales kit. To me, basically at this point, I felt that was their job. That's what they are making their money for.

BRUCE BEATTIE, *BEATTIE BLVD.*

The syndicate had commerical control. They are experts on that. That's a perfect example of where no two people would ever agree. There are lots of things I'd have done differently, but on an intellectual level I know that doesn't mean I could do it better.

SCOTT ADAMS, *DILBERT*

In producing the promotional material I like to be involved in every aspect of the creation, because this is my baby, and I know the syndicate has a real tendency to deal in cliché slogans.

MORT WALKER, *BEETLE BAILEY*

We'll support the cartoonist's promotional concepts. We usually show them the various kinds of promotional material we have used for other similar products, and we'll ask whether any of these things work for them. We'll ask if there's something different they'd like us to try, and we'll offer different ideas we have for this particular strip.

We try to make it a real cooperative effort.

STEVE CHRISTENSEN, LOS ANGELES TIMES SYNDICATE

I wasn't involved in my promotion as much as I would have liked, and I think part of that is because I was not knowledgeable in that regard.

I have been involved in this business for five years, and I still have yet to have a sales brochure. Part of that is because, when I first started in the business, we were trying to tap into a voice, a kind of product that was coming out at the same time we were just putting the finishing touches on my strip. We thought we might as well jump into that and take as many papers as we could at the time. It worked. I think I got about a hundred or so papers.

It was a good launch. Things tapered off a little bit, and then started to come back again.

STEPHEN BENTLEY, *HERB & JAMAAL*

There are times when we work together. There are times when the cartoonist will come up with a great idea for promotion, and we'll go with it. There are times when the syndicate art department will come up with a great idea, and the cartoonist will just go with it.

What I try to avoid are surprises. I've learned the hard way. I remember once paying $6,000 on a promotional package for Art Buchwald, and I was so proud of it. I was about twenty-nine years old. I sent it to Art, thinking he'd thank me, and he said, "Oh, my God! You used that one photo I hate." We don't do those surprises anymore.

RICHARD NEWCOMBE, CREATORS SYNDICATE

HOW STRIPS ARE SOLD

The syndicate salespeople at the larger syndicates try to sell a new feature to the larger-market newspapers in person.

After the syndicate has secured as many of the larger-market newspapers as possible, they use these sales as leverage to help influence the medium-size and smaller markets to purchase the feature.

For economic reasons, most syndicates rely on the phone and promotion mailings to reach many of the midsize and smaller markets. It's in this area that the syndicates with the larger number of traveling sales personnel have the decided advantage over other syndicates.

With a new strip, we try to visit every major market in person—especially the competitive markets—show them the new stuff and ex-

plain why we're doing it. What's behind it. Who we think the characters are. These days, you never get a decision on the spot. And then, once we've done that, and we've allowed the really major players to get a good look at it, it goes out as a mass mailer. And then we follow it up with sales calls, in person and on the telephone. Calling over the phone has really increased, because of the costs of travel.

ALAN SHEARER, WASHINGTON POST WRITERS GROUP

If the syndicate spends time promoting, you're going to pick up papers, and how many you're going to pick up is going to determine how successful your strip is. But once again, I think it boils down to how hard your salespeople are working for you.

PETER KOHLSAAT, SINGLE SLICES AND THE NOOZ

WHAT NEWSPAPERS LOOK FOR IN A PROMOTION

While it's an awful lot like the tail wagging the dog to produce a comic feature based solely on market needs, it's still important to be aware of what the people who purchase features are looking for in a comic feature promotion.

I like to see lots and lots of samples. Strips. I want to get as good a feeling for it as I can. I think I've been misled a few times by not seeing enough of something.

JAY AMBROSE, ROCKY MOUNTAIN NEWS

I don't really read sales packages. I read the strips. I don't really care about the hype.

I am more interested in what the cartoon is trying to do. Does it succeed? Is it a copy, or is it sophisticated? How does it fit into the mix? In other words, if I've got too many kids' strips, then I'm not going to be interested in another kids' strip.

Obviously, the salesperson is going to try to convince me that if I don't buy it I am really going to be up the creek.

ROSALIE MULLER WRIGHT, SAN FRANCISCO CHRONICLE

I like to get some sense of who the people are in the strip, what the characters are like. I like to get some sense that the artist actually

knows who they are. I like to get some sense that there is going to be enough tension and enough different situations that the strip can be sustained for a while.

JANE AMARI, THE KANSAS CITY STAR

I look at the six weeks of samples and also for the pedigree of the cartoonist. I want to know how reliable he is. Can I really count on him?

After that, I want to see the Sundays, even if I'm not buying it, because it helps me understand the cartoonist's abilities as an artist.

I'd rather see more than six weeks—and some of us sometimes see early work that leads to becoming a strip—but the more the better. As I said, the big concern now is whether they're going to be with us a while, or after two months are they going to turn out to be some really silly thing.

RON PATEL, THE PHILADELPHIA INQUIRER

I would just like to get right down to the strip, and I'll tell you whether I like it or not.

SUE SMITH, DALLAS MORNING NEWS

I look at the strips. That's it. The folder is nice because it sits on a desk, and it's easily identifiable. I look at the bio. Background is useful, if we buy the strip and want to write a story introducing it at the starting point.

There's lots of hype in promotions with various people saying, "It's the greatest thing since sliced bread," but none of that means anything to me.

JOSEPH "CHIP" VISCI, DETROIT FREE PRESS

THE RELEASE DATE AND THE LAUNCH

While smaller comic feature syndicates may release only one new feature a year, the larger syndicates try to launch two or three new features a year.

The larger syndicates sell new features spaced throughout the year so their sales efforts don't collide.

We have three sales meetings a year. We would talk to the cartoonist and say, "Can we be ready for this one, or do we want to wait a while?"

LEE SALEM, UNIVERSAL PRESS SYNDICATE

We were actually too afraid to express much input.

"You want us to release in January? Great! You really want to wait until January? Great! Is that good?"

We kept asking them, "Is that a good thing? Is that a bad thing? I don't know."

They assured us, "Well, it's too late to release it for the fall sales push. That would start in October."

JERRY SCOTT, BABY BLUES AND NANCY

You don't really want to be out selling a new product in August, because it's very difficult to find editors who are not on vacation. And you don't want to be out doing a big sales campaign during the the whole month of December either, because of the holidays. The timing is important, because you want to have as many papers on board on the launch date as you can.

STEVE CHRISTENSEN, LOS ANGELES TIMES SYNDICATE

We try to take out three a year. We look at how well the preceding strips are selling, and whether we're finished.

A strip has a natural cycle that all strips go through, in the initial selling. You go to an editor, and you say, "Do you want to buy this?"

They have three choices. Yes, no, maybe. You get very few "yes's" to begin with, because there are very few people who have the authority to give you a "yes" on the spot. You get some "no's." But then you get 50 percent "maybe's," and then you have to go back. You have to force them to get you an answer. Then you get some more "yes's" and some more "no's," and you keep going back, until they give you a definitive "yes" or "no."

If they say, "no," you're polite about it. You don't throw it in their face again for a year, at which time you can say, "Look, it's improved. You should take a look at it again."

If they say "yes," you have accomplished your goal.

So when you're down to a point where there aren't too many "maybe's" left, then you know that you can take on a new feature.

JAY KENNEDY, KING FEATURES

You don't want to have features being too close together in sales. When syndicates begin selling your feature, you are the focus of their

---

sales for about a three-month period, and they're out there getting as many people as they can for the launch.

After that, you're pretty much on your own. It's up to you to do quality work to build a reputation.

It can really hurt if the syndicate is just releasing one strip one top of another. You have that initial sales cheer, and then basically they really forget you, as they're all concentrating on something else.

So the syndicate's job, to really do their best, is to release only a couple of features—we're talking about comic strips—so that they can have their initial sales, then have follow-up, and then release something new.

There should be good follow-up, and that's usually where syndicates really fall down. The most difficult time for any comic strip is the first year.

Fortunately, Non Sequitur *didn't have that problem. We went with a smaller syndicate, so we don't have a lot of features up there to take time and attention away from sales. The strip started so strong—I think the initial launch was something like eighty papers—and it kept growing very quickly. We're at over two hundred now, and the strip is three years old this February.*

WILEY MILLER, NON SEQUITUR

THE FIRST YEAR

In the first year of a new comic feature, there can be editorial growth or decline and sales growth or decline.

While it may take sales growth (or decline) a while to catch up to editorial growth (or decline), the growth (or decline) of one is often connected to the other. In other words, a great launch doesn't guarantee continued success without great work.

THE LIST AND THE SLOW START

While there's no way to anticipate all the factors that go into determining the success of the launch of a new feature, the fact remains that some features get off the ground faster than others, and some never get off the ground at all.

There have been a lot of unfortunate situations where a very talented person, through one reason or another, wound up working for about a handful of newspapers, doing as much work as he would if he had a thousand. And that is something to avoid.

It's not instant success at all. You're competing with all the other cartoonists for space. You're working in an environment that is slowly throttling down the amount of space available, therefore making it impossible to tell a story the way you'd like to, either graphically or in writ-

ing. So it's pretty discouraging, the way things are going in most of the papers today, and I hope it will change.

HANK KETCHAM, *DENNIS THE MENACE*

The biggest misconception is about the number of papers you can be in. People think when they become syndicated, that they just automatically go into a hundred papers. They see these figures connected to top cartoonists, and of course those are the greatest exceptions.

I think that's where the disappointments come, because each feature finds its level, and it may not be that impressive. It's something of a mystery where that level is going to be. More often, it's less than a hundred papers.

STUART DODDS, CHRONICLE FEATURES

This is one step at a time. It's like building a beautiful house. It's one brick at a time. It's not going to be fast. This is not a thirteen-week deal. We are talking about longevity. It takes time to get to the first hundred newspapers. In some cases, you can fly to it, but those are few and far between. It's a building process. It's not the quick fix. You have to build characters. You have to build a story line. You have to build an identity. And this takes time.

Today everything is so immediate. You turn on the TV, you get the immediacy of everything. And we have to impress on newcomers that it takes time.

You have something very special, and people are going to see it every day, color on Sunday. You will become part of that family, but they are not going to let a stranger in the door. It takes time to build that.

You have to have a mentality to say, "It's a tough market out there." It's tough, and you have to know that it does take time to get your message across to that reader.

JOHN MCMEEL, UNIVERSAL PRESS SYNDICATE

SALES GROWTH AND DECLINE

As a result of design or the promotional push that achieves liftoff, some rocket ships are going to reach outer space faster than other rocket ships. Meanwhile, some rocket ships are so poorly designed that they explode on liftoff or run out of promotional push far too soon and crash to the ground.

I think the initial sales are very important, and you want to just keep lighting the fire and keep it going.

MORT WALKER, *BEETLE BAILEY*

It becomes a matter of focusing everything on the development and introduction of that strip. That happens at a particular point in time, when the most energy is concentrated on selling a strip.

After that, some have legs and some don't, and the good, effective syndicate is the syndicate that can harness the ones that get legs and turn them into features that appear in two thousand newspapers. Or sometimes they get legs and they get into three hundred to four hundred papers.

DAVID HENDIN, LITERARY AGENT

I think the initial sales had a great deal to do with the growth of Non Sequitur, especially when selling to somebody in the major markets.

The editors in the secondary market are all sitting around, using the judgment of other editors to base their decisions on. All of them. They see that it appears in all these papers, so it must be good. It's such an asinine way to do things, but there are so many noncompeting markets and so very few papers per town, that most of these newspapers won't change their comics package unless they are forced to.

That's the nice thing about The Far Side retiring. It forced editors to change their comics. Just look at their comics pages. It's amazing. So many of them had the same comic page for years. It's just awful to break into the secondary markets, unless something happens. They sit around and wait for something to die out, before they do anything.

WILEY MILLER, NON SEQUITUR

The hardest part about a new strip is getting it off the ground. That's where the heavy lifting is. Getting those first two hundred papers is always the biggest challenge. If you can do that, and it's a good, consistent strip, then getting the next two hundred is a lot easier.

Things in motion tend to stay in motion. An airplane flying from New York to Los Angeles uses half its fuel to take off and the other half for the remainder of the trip. It's the heavy lifting to get it off the ground that's the hard part. Once you get it going, it's easy. It's like someone going on a diet. Those first weeks are torture, but once you get into the program, it becomes habit.

RICHARD NEWCOMBE, CREATORS SYNDICATE

There's no set way in which strips start and continue. But generally speaking, the first six months can pretty much tell you how well it's going to do in the future. Now, there are some features that have a very slow start and build gradually, but I think more often than not one can tell from the beginning.

STUART DODDS, CHRONICLE FEATURES

It just grows like a weed.

SCOTT ADAMS, DILBERT

I used to think that the syndicate would actually do more for you. Usually the pattern I've seen is that they take on a strip, they'll give it a push for the first couple of months, and then it's up to you for the rest of your life to make that thing salable. Very often they are so interested in the next strip that they're working on that they forget all about you, and I've found that a little bit frustrating.

MORT WALKER, *BEETLE BAILEY*

I think the most important time in the life of a comic strip is its first few months. The way it is launched can do more to hurt it, sometimes, than to help it, especially if you've cut corners on the brochure, you haven't done all the travel, you haven't done all the mailing and all the follow-up. You can hurt it. You can really damage it, because nothing sells like something new.

The second most important period of a comic strip is after six months. After it's been in six months, editors have a sense of it, and readers have talked about it.

ALAN SHEARER, WASHINGTON POST WRITERS GROUP

A strip could hit a plateau for no explicable reason and then suddenly take off.

I try to explain that there are no hard, fast routes to success. Each strip is really a whole new marketing effort, and what preceded it is not necessarily what happens to you.

Usually within a year, year and a half, we're in a better position to say, "You've got a career here."

LEE SALEM, UNIVERSAL PRESS SYNDICATE

Some sucessful strips come out of the chute very quickly and get picked up by many newspapers very quickly. On the other hand, a lot of successful strips didn't have very successful launches, because they were either ahead of the curve or because the quality of the strip got better as the cartoonist continued to do it.

STEVE CHRISTENSEN, LOS ANGELES TIMES SYNDICATE

Now there's a question. How is it a strip is good enough to get into three hundred to four hundred papers but can't get into six hundred? I don't know the answer. Some get to fifty, and they never get to sixty. Some get to one hundred, and they never get to 110.

You would think by the time a strip gets into three hundred to four hundred, the sky should be the limit, but it just doesn't seem to work that way.

It is true that syndicates get busy. The syndicates have a lot in their briefcases. They're not able to take things out all the time. As somebody that represents talent I am acutely aware of that, and one of the jobs I have is to stay in touch with the syndicate and continue to encourage them to promote.

But it is a very interesting phenomenon. Why do some strips have life potential and some strips don't? I don't know.

What about the strip that can make $100,000 a year in licensing revenue? Now, why can't that make a million dollars a year in licensing revenue? Why can't the strip that makes a million a year make thirty million a year? I don't know.

There's only one Peanuts, one Garfield, one Far Side, and there's only one Calvin and Hobbes. After that there's a precipitous drop, a dramatic drop in the next level of strip. And I find that very interesting, although in every field there are superstars.

In baseball, you can tell what the difference between a superstar and a good ballplayer is. In any sport you can. In cartoons, I guess the difference is also very clear, but from an analytical, creative standpoint.

It's very hard to predict something might become a superstar. If you have a ballplayer that plays in a certain way, you can predict what he is going to do, but you can't do that with a comic strip or a column or a book. That's what creative properties are all about, and I often say to people, "Listen, it's a big world out there, and different ideas are what make the world go round. This particular idea is not for me but don't stop trying to sell it, because it has some merit to it."

DAVID HENDIN, LITERARY AGENT

THE EDITORIAL CHALLENGE

Working on a daily comic feature is an infinitely different process than working on a comic feature sample.

You are no longer selling. You're producing.

Your work can no longer simply show "the promise" of great things to come. The great things have to happen now, and you're on a deadline that doesn't allow for a lot of noodling.

Basically, you're no longer hanging out at your gym, standing at the line and practicing free throws. The NBA season has started, Shaq is in your face, and if you don't start swishing net, then you're going to get cut from the team.

My other fear was what happens when I run out of ideas—of course, my girlfriend said I've already done them all—then what do I do? But you don't run out. It's the opposite. You get better at it.

SCOTT ADAMS, DILBERT

I'm having a great time now, but in those early days, what you're trying to do is get acquainted with the characters. You don't know them. You start off with a kid, and you don't even know his name or what his mother and father look like. And you say, "Gee whiz, what kind of a house does he live in? Does he have any friends? Who are they, and what about a dog and a cat?"

What you're doing is you're casting a show. You're making these decisions as to how you want this show to run and who are going to be the stars. It's very much R&D [research and development] time the first couple of years, and it's exciting. You are creating something that is being read by an awful lot of people.

And then, as the years progress, you get to know them better, and it's much easier to write for characters that you know. It's much easier for the readers to understand the humor, if they know who is saying the words. Humor is not what is done so much or what is said. It's who says it, and I think that's important.

So over the first few years, you're building up your cast of characters. You just have those creative juices running all the time, and sometimes you run down a blind alley, and you have to retreat and go somewhere else. It's very exciting. It keeps you on the edge of your seat for sure.

HANK KETCHAM, *DENNIS THE MENACE*

I always tell people that the first five hundred are the easiest, because that's the first year that you've ever had a crack at doing anything, the first time that your characters have gone Christmas shopping. It isn't as though you have done two to three laps. Then it starts to get a little bit harder to do. If anything, the first year was the easiest, because you've never done one before. There is no possibility of repeating yourself, and what a great thing that is.

BRUCE BEATTIE, *BEATTIE BLVD.*

I think I started out using felt-tip pens for everything, and sometimes the printed strip would be invisible. People didn't want to say that to me, but some people would say, "You know, I couldn't read it today."

So I experimented on my own and finally found Rapidographs, something I hadn't known existed.

In fact, early on, this is how I met two people that are still my closest friends today. I looked up in the Yellow Pages to find calligraphers. This is how goofy I was. I wasn't looking for letterers; I was looking for calligraphers. There was one guy in the Yellow Pages, and he he told me about a calligraphers' collective. I got the names of ten people. One of them answered her phone, and she and I became very close friends.

For a while, in the beginning, she did the lettering, and I hated the way she wrote the lines. I had no idea this was important to me. Jean said you can do it, and you will do it, because I'm not doing it anymore. And so I did.

I was very self-conscious. I noticed in the newspaper that people wrote different than I did, and then I began to understand the way I wrote the words was the way I grew, and that was okay.

NICOLE HOLLANDER, *SYLVIA*

GIVING THE NEW FEATURE A CHANCE

Traditionally, when editors put new comic features in their papers, they know it's going to take those new features a while to find an audience.

I think a strip ought to have started perking along by six months. Things take time to gel, but I think you can pretty much tell if it's improving by six months.

SUE SMITH, *DALLAS MORNING NEWS*

If we take something in we'll leave it for a while, unless it's just so horribly unfunny or unless I start having a lot of other problems, like it's late or has bad words in it.

JANE AMARI, *THE KANSAS CITY STAR*

In the beginning, the feedback from editors—by way of sales—is very important. Now, we are a relatively small syndicate, and feedback is almost instant.

I handle a large part of our sales, and I'm also involved in the new feature departments, so the feedback I get from editors finds its way back to the author/cartoonist very quickly and in a discreet way. Obviously, I don't pass on damaging criticism or anything that may not be constructive.

I think in the early weeks and early months, when the feature is first being sold, that feedback is valuable, because that's the greatest growing period. There is a lot of big excitement, and everyone is so motivated.

The importance of getting a newspaper's feedback to the syndicate editor is critical. Newspaper editors are extremely helpful, and they can be extremely perceptive. Of course, their decisions are critical to syndicates.

STUART DODDS, CHRONICLE FEATURES

Well, some strips are real clunkers from the start. We don't have a rule of thumb for that.

If a strip shows some promise you're gonna live with it quite a while, because you realize that sometimes it can take a while for something to catch on.

But there are times when you start getting complaints right off the bat. Since you hardly ever put something in without taking something out, people who liked the thing you took out are really going to look at

---

the new strip critically. They're going to let you know how they feel about it. You get lots of negatives right off, and you're not getting any positives at all. You ask around the office, and no one seems to think it's anything terrific.

I think people can be wrong. I don't know about this, but I'll bet you anything that when people started running The Far Side *there was just lots and lots and lots of negative feedback, because people just weren't used to that wild, crazy, dark humor. And so, if you immediately caved in to that, you would have maybe made a bad judgment, because it turned out to be one of the really great comic panels.*

JAY AMBROSE, *ROCKY MOUNTAIN NEWS*

THE DROP IN QUALITY OF A NEW FEATURE

Don't panic. This is not inevitable.
Just don't let it happen to you.

It's not uncommon to see a strip decline in quality after four to eight months.

I think the first thing you have to do is determine why you think there has been a decline in quality. Is it that the cartoonist spent two years coming up with three months' worth of writing that was really good, but then has trouble producing that same level of quality week in and week out? Has the cartoonist lost a level of enthusiasm for the project? Depending on what the problem is, you have a candid conversation with the cartoonist.

The cartoonist is the producer of the work and has to be the one that maintains the quality. And they can do it, or they can't.

STEVE CHRISTENSEN, LOS ANGELES TIMES SYNDICATE

When they bring out a new feature, it seems to work at least for a while, and if it drops off, it drops off after a couple of years.

I think that probably is because when something first comes out, there is a heavy sales push and everyone at the syndicate is very conscious of what is happening with that strip. There is a lot of thought given to that strip. A lot of attention.

After something has been out for a while, they're worrying about the new push for the next campaign and sometimes they forget what's going on.

JANE AMARI, *THE KANSAS CITY STAR*

I've had it happen to me that what you ultimately get isn't as good as the samples that you looked at. That's happened a few times, I wouldn't say it happens often.

JAY AMBROSE, *ROCKY MOUNTAIN NEWS*

Certainly, that happens to some, and so I keep an eye on them. I watch to see if they pick up again. If not, then they go on my list for possible cancellation.

SUE SMITH, *DALLAS MORNING NEWS*

UNFULFILLED EXPECTATIONS IN A NEW FEATURE

After delivering a terrific promotion with great samples, sometimes the new ongoing feature just can not achieve the standards established in its promotion or it simply fails to fulfill the expectations editors have for it. It's like paying to see a film that's advertised to be the greatest film ever made. If it's not better than *Citizen Kane*, you want your money back.

I remember very clearly an instance in which a panel was brought out by people who were in the greeting-card industry, and they had been doing it for a very long time.

The first six weeks looked really good. It was supposed to be a family panel, but after the first six weeks—the next phase—we could almost watch, week by week, their anxiety growing as they realized that they had to do this every day. They had to come up with these panels, being funny every day.

Over time, the strip sort of degenerated into something a little more bawdy than you ever would have expected from the first six weeks, so we dropped it.

RON PATEL, *THE PHILADELPHIA INQUIRER*

I think editors are unnerved by features that don't quite live up to their original promise, when features are something different than what they were thought to be about.

STUART DODDS, CHRONICLE FEATURES

THE CONTINUING PROMOTION

Traditionally, there is very little continuing promotion for a comic feature after the launch.

The syndicate continues to mail strip samples to papers that have not signed up.

The occasional news article about a strip or the strong showing in a readers' poll may merit a flyer.

There is some trade advertising support, not much.

New brochures are few and far between.

Basically, after the initial launch, it's up to the continued work of the cartoonist, a book publishing program, a licensing program and the sales personnel to gain additional papers.

A new promotion keeps your name out there.

PETER KOHLSAAT, *SINGLE SLICES* AND *THE NOOZ*

Anytime you get a success story—if it's an important one—I think the syndicate should promote it.

RICHARD NEWCOMBE, CREATORS SYNDICATE

New promotions help keep the profile public, and I think that's an important ingredient for selling a feature. So we do some advertising in E & P [Editor and Publisher] periodically, and we do direct mail, but the best form of promotion we have found is through affiliation with Andrews and McMeel. Once we come out with a collection by a cartoonist, the book features certain strengths that a promotion might not have.

LEE SALEM, UNIVERSAL PRESS SYNDICATE

You produce a brochure, you produce a mailing piece on a particular strip, and it gets on the desk of a particular editor. He may or may not look at it. If he looks at it, there is a chance that it will trigger an idea in his mind, remind him of something that's out there.

It is not something we do on a routine and regular basis, because it's expensive, and we like to think we can do better with our salesmen visiting the newspaper.

JOSEPH D'ANGELO, KING FEATURES

I probably don't pay attention. You get one chance around here.

ROSALIE MULLER WRIGHT, SAN FRANCISCO CHRONICLE

I think repromotion is becoming important again, because syndicates don't have as many road people as they used to. They do a lot of it by phone and mail. Good promotions are more important than ever. But I'm not sure how productive they are. I don't think there is any substitute for a guy sitting on the editor's desk saying, "Buy this, or I'm never leaving."

MELL LAZARUS, MISS PEACH AND MOMMA

If, at the launch of a feature, you only had a few newspapers on board, then after a year you had many newspapers—including prestigious newspapers—that's an opportunity to promote it to editors and say this thing is really catching on. Or, if you feel the quality of the strip or panel is substantially better than it was at launch, that's an opportunity you could take advantage of to repromote. If merchandising started to come on board, that's an opportunity to repromote. But I think there needs to be a reason to do it.

STEVE CHRISTENSEN, LOS ANGELES TIMES SYNDICATE

They might say, "We've taken it back and worked on it some more," and sometimes they actually have. Or they might say, "I know you didn't buy it last time, but now it is in umpity-ump more papers. You might want to take a second look."

SUE SMITH, DALLAS MORNING NEWS

It would pretty much have to be the Second Coming. Unless you could tell me that it's got a new writer or artist, or unless it has changed syndicates and been redeveloped.

If you get something out on the market and it's not ready, I think that's real hard to come back from.

I'll look at most anything, but I have looked at a lot of things over and over, and I just don't like them. This is a real subjective business. Sometimes I don't like the concept at all. I just think it's stupid, or it doesn't happen to strike my wit, and that's not saying I am the wittiest person alive. But since it is subjective, it's hard to buy a strip that you don't think is funny on the assumption that you think someone else will.

When push comes to shove and someone comes to you and says, "Why'd you put that in the paper?" I think to say, "Well, I hoped you'd like it" is a stupid reason.

JANE AMARI, THE KANSAS CITY STAR

LICENSING AND STRIP EXPANSION

Sometimes a product sells itself.

With licensing and publishing programs, a strip simply sells itself using other venues.

How do you expand an original concept and create income and popularity? By combining talent with professional guidance.

TONI MENDEZ, LITERARY REPRESENTATIVE

When I started a comic strip, I really hadn't ever thought of merchandising. It was kind of like German, a foreign language, and I didn't really know anything about it. I was too busy to really do anything about it, because I was doing two professions. I thought, "Boy, all I need now is a third profession. I can't do this."

First of all, I had gotten syndicated into about 150 newspapers, something like that, and then maybe 180, and then we stopped gaining any newspapers. I started my perfunctory whiner calls to the syndicate saying, "God, can't we do something to get in more newspapers?"

This one guy said, "You're level right here. It will vary a little bit, now and again, and we will try to do another push."

So I was kind of depressed. Meanwhile, I had done about five or six ideas that were just standing on that precipice and looking over into the black void of good taste. The syndicate did not want to send out these

cartoons to the public. They thought it would outrage them in such a way that I would lose papers, so I was upset.

Then these two crazy guys came to me and said, "Gee, we would sure like to do some T-shirts with Grimm on it."

I said, "Well, only if I can pick out the five or six that we use." They said okay, so I gave them all the dirty ideas.

They were selling pretty well, and then I found out that cities the T-shirts were being sold in eventually picked up my comic strip.

This T-shirt and merchandising arm was helping me pick up newspapers, so I jumped into it with both feet. I stick mainly to T-shirts and greeting cards. I don't do a lot of stuff, but I'm able to use ideas that I would not necessarily put into the comic strip. And so, I've got an outlet for these ideas that are just on the line for good taste. That's exciting to me. Very exciting.

MIKE PETERS, MOTHER GOOSE & GRIMM

I think what has helped me is that I have books out and also other products, greeting cards, so that people see my work in more than one place or more than one venue.

NICOLE HOLLANDER, SYLVIA

THE CONTINUING CAREER

Once a strip gets past ten years, if the cartoonist stays healthy, I think he has a job for the rest of his life. This doesn't mean that the thing is going to be good.

CHARLES SCHULZ, PEANUTS

After doing it for so many years, I still don't feel confident. Really, I feel that if I don't have the strip done by Wednesday—because there has to be that reading process and correcting—I'm in a very foul mood, because I'm worried. I'm very worried, and I can't think about anything else.

So if the strips are done, then I'm in a good mood.

I think it's awful, but if they're not done, then I'm not in a good mood.

You'd think that at some point in your life, you would relax and say, "Well, I've done this fifteen years now. Surely, I will continue to do it." But I don't believe it.

NICOLE HOLLANDER, SYLVIA

I don't think I have a job. I honestly don't think I work, even though I spend a lot of hours doing what I'm doing. People say, "Well, that's a good job," and I say, "It's not really a job." In two weeks, I'm heading down to Mexico for three months, and I'm taking all my stuff with me.

PETER KOHLSAAT, SINGLE SLICES AND THE NOOZ

THE EVOLUTION OF THE CARTOONIST

Over a period of time, the work is not the only thing that changes. As the cartoonist settles into the rhythm of producing a daily feature, he finds new ideas to express as well as new ways to express them.

One of the things I discovered a long, long time ago is: When you are going along and you're improving, you're trying to better yourself—in other words, trying to reach a new plateau in your career or ability—there comes a time of depression—just before you reach that plateau—where nothing seems to work. The old stuff isn't working anymore, and the new stuff is not coming through right, and nobody knows that you are personally reaching for a new plateau. There is this period of real mediocre material, so when I see that, I know this guy is moving to a new plateau. He is going to come out of the clouds now, and we're going to see some new, good stuff. A rekindling is taking place.

People come to me, and they say, "Do you ever get writer's block?" They say, "I've been in this period for so long, I think I'm losing it."

I say, "Are you trying hard?"

And he says, "Yes, I'm trying to write better than I ever wrote, and I'm trying to achieve this new thing."

And I say, "That's what it is. During this interim period, until you reach that new plateau, until you come out of the clouds and know what you're doing, you're going to have this mediocre thing." There is struggle in metamorphosis.

So whenever that begins to happen to you, I think you should take solace in the fact that you're improving and say, "Oh, boy this is good. I'm doing mediocre stuff. [laugh] I'm going to be great." (I think I just did Mike Peters.)

When I first started drawing, I had a period like that. I could not get down on paper what I saw in my mind. It's not like somebody hit my arm with Novocain or anything, I began to get real frustrated and angry, but then suddenly I was doing what I wanted to do. Things were coming out, and I'd say, "All right! That's a nice line right there. Just what I wanted to do."

JOHNNY HART, *B.C. AND THE WIZARD OF ID*

I'm sure the writing has evolved the same way I've evolved. I'm seven years older than I was when I began the strip, and I'm a father now. The strip's probably a little less silly than it was. Jason is less dry than he used to be. For the longest time Jason never smiled. He would deliver his punch lines with a straight face. I find I'm a little more free to give him that added facial expression. I can do a few more things with him.

I'm sure the strip also sort of drifts all over the place, and I think that's one of the problems you run into with a strip. But I think it's good for a strip to have a kind of organic flow, to where it isn't suddenly changing with time.

BILL AMEND, *FOXTROT*

Gary Larson is amazing. He quits at the height of his popularity. Who's done that? Somebody must have done it sometime, but I don't know who. That's right, Michael Jordan did it.

JOSEPH "CHIP" VISCI, *DETROIT FREE PRESS*

I think one of the most frightening things is the idea that you've used up all of your life's experiences, that you have no more life experiences to draw upon, and you keep rehashing these variations.

Fortunately, I have a cast of characters and lots of variations that I can fiddle with. I'm just amazed, when I think of another dog dish idea or another Linus blanket idea, after all these years, and I wonder, "Why didn't I think of that twenty years ago?"

CHARLES SCHULZ, *PEANUTS*

I just think there is something in human nature, at least American human nature, that everybody arrives at some degree of comfort. And when you get successful . . . well, this is what works, and this is where your reinforcement comes from. So why would you change it?

Believe me, cartoonists get their strokes from how many papers they're in, and they get their strokes from the people who buy their books. So where's the incentive to push themselves out of that comfort zone? If a bunch of papers start dropping their strip, then perhaps they'll say, "Maybe I ought to do something different. Maybe I better change it somehow."

JOSEPH "CHIP" VISCI, DETROIT FREE PRESS

THE EVOLUTION OF THE FEATURE

Since the comic feature is an extention of the cartoonist, it's perfectly natural for the feature to change along with the cartoonist.

As a feature keeps pace with the times, we tend to notice these changes less and less. However, when a strip is out of sync with the times, its changes become more obvious and noticeable.

Over a short period of time, these changes usually are subtle and imperceptible. They occur as a maturing of the drawing style, in the choices of characters added to the feature, in the type of ideas a cartoonist expresses and in the personality alterations the feature's characters go through.

The characters have to be developed a little bit at a time to know who they are, how they would react.

I think Lee [Salem] and I figured it takes about three years before people intuitively know a character—for example, that you would intuitively know that Lucy Van Pelt is going to be a grouch, or that Linus is going to be an intellectual or that Charlie Brown will be a loser. It takes the average reader about three years, because they only take maybe thirty seconds a day—if that—to read your stuff. So you have to consider that for at least three years, you're working on establishing a relationship as much as you are establishing that your work is worthy of their spending another thirty seconds tomorrow.

LYNN JOHNSTON, FOR BETTER OR FOR WORSE

One thing I've noticed is that characters tend to get softer. It's as if the cartoonists want to make them more lovable or something.

RICHARD NEWCOMBE, CREATORS SYNDICATE

YOUR CAREER IN THE COMICS

Herb & Jamaal *may not be the most accessible strip on the market, but I think the characters play very, very well off each other.*

I think the characters have become closer to one another. Let's put it this way. You make a friend, and you don't know what kind of friend you have until you have time to sit with them, and I think that is how the characters in my cartoon have begun to evolve. They started out as friends. They spent time together, and now they know each other as friends. I think they have a commitment to one another that probably was not there in the beginning.

STEPHEN BENTLEY, *HERB & JAMAAL*

The one thing that strikes me when I go over the old stuff is that the characters in both strips seem to have gotten a lot smarter.

When I started both strips . . . for instance, the kids in Miss Peach *seemed very young, always an indeterminate age, but I would have guessed at that point the second grade. Maybe they're still in second grade, but they sure have gotten smarter. They talk about everything. I think the same thing has happened in* Momma. *I mean, Francis is pretty dumb, but sometimes, he'll actually have a thought. It may be specious, but it's a thought. If anything, I guess it reflects my own impatience in working with dumb characters for so long I don't think they're funny. I used to think they were funny. I think there was a time when dumb characters were considered funny. Dumb, dumber and dumbest. I mean there is a kind of innocence that is charming.*

MELL LAZARUS, *MISS PEACH* AND *MOMMA*

I hope that in the heart and soul of Cathy *it is the same thing. It was probably a little more innocent in the beginning. In terms of the things that I wrote, I think there is a real freshness and innocence to it that is harder to capture now that I am older and not so innocent.*

I did a lot of strips that were a lot simpler, in the beginning. On the other hand, I feel like I am a more confident creator now than I was.

CATHY GUISEWITE, *CATHY*

Beattie Blvd. *has come away from what I thought originally it would be. There was something very appealing to me about* The Far Side *and the whole "off" nature of it, the popularity and the availability of that sensibility. It was something that I knew that I could do. As my strip has evolved, I think it has evolved more toward who I am. I don't really do* Far Side–*type gags anymore. I don't do the anthropomorphic humor. The stuff has just evolved as much as possible from who I am, and it's about things I'm concerned about and thinking about or that formulate my personality.*

BRUCE BEATTIE, *BEATTIE BLVD.*

You can certainly look back thirty years—even fifteen to twenty years—and physically see the changes, the differences in the characters. You can also see a period where I'm discarding old-fashioned things that we don't use and picking up on the new models. Like push-button phones. We don't have the rotary phones anymore, and we don't have milk delivered at your back door anymore.

When I was living abroad, I had the Sears Roebuck catalog sent to me every year, so that I would know the change in toys and toilets in America and keep abreast of developments.

I would not have any of my characters go on an airplane for the first twenty years, because in those days only 15 percent of the population had ever been up on an airplane. I didn't want Dennis to go up on an airplane and have Wilson wonder how old Mitchell got the money for it. Then group travel came in and everybody was traveling, and for two weeks I featured them on the airline. But that's how sensitive I was to the credibility factor. It's like making sure they only had one television set and one car that was always probably three years old. Alice did her housework, and she was there when Henry came home.

I build the world that I like, that I feel comfortable in, and if they misbehave I just erase them.

HANK KETCHAM, *DENNIS THE MENACE*

Two or three years ago I switched to dialogue balloons on Sundays. Originally I did pointers and found it was really limiting the backgrounds I could use. So I decided, "Okay, January first, just make the change," and I'm glad I did. It works fine.

BILL AMEND, *FOXTROT*

The topics have gotten different. At first Sylvia *was a totally feminist strip, and I think it has broadened. When I talk about politics it doesn't necessarily have to do with women, although there still is a very strong emphasis on women.*

NICOLE HOLLANDER, *SYLVIA*

Sparky Schulz asked me when I saw him last, "What are you doing? Are you doing anything new?" Baby Blues *had been around about four years at that time.*

I said, "Yeah, Wanda's going to have another baby."

He said, "Good. You need to introduce new stuff to keep trying new stuff out."

JERRY SCOTT, *BABY BLUES* AND *NANCY*

When the characters started to change, started to grow up a little bit, that's when there was some real concern.

A couple people at the syndicate said, "This shouldn't happen. We don't want this to happen, because we don't think the characters would be merchandisable," or "We don't think it would be a good idea as far as the concept of the strip goes to have the characters grow."

It was Lee [Salem] who said: "Wait a minute, it's working. Let's not rock the boat. Let's just see where this thing goes."

LYNN JOHNSTON, *FOR BETTER OR FOR WORSE*

Surprise is the essence of humor, so the challenge of writing a comic strip is to surprise yourself. The longer you work, the more effort it takes to jump tracks and go in new directions. Working with the same characters in similar situations year after year, it's inevitable that you fall into predictable formulas. When the characters are new, everything they do is fresh and surprising. Later, that's much less the case, so the cartoonist has to find ways to reinvent the strip's world. He has to find new subjects to address, new ways to approach things, or develop deeper and more subtle qualities of the strip. Sustaining that level of energy over decades is extraordinarily difficult, and I'm glad to see a few cartoonists acknowledging this and quitting their strips before they get stale.

BILL WATTERSON, *CALVIN AND HOBBES*

ADJUSTING TO REDUCED SIZES

As the printed size of comic features has been reduced over the years, cartoonists have made continual adjustments to accommodate the new sizes.

Physically, of course, it speaks for itself. I've reduced the size of my originals now, to about thirteen to fourteen inches. They're really tiny.

MELL LAZARUS, *MISS PEACH AND MOMMA*

The adjustment happens automatically. You don't mean to do it but there are a lot more close-ups. I've gone to three panels, and it's been almost naturally. I almost think that way when I'm doing my dailies, and the majority end up being two panels with a close-up in the middle. I think that's probably a subconscious response to the smaller size.

I think if you brought back the old Pogo and ran it today, he would be run off the page, because they'd say, "Your printing's too small."

JEFF MACNELLY, *SHOE AND PLUGGERS*

I'm using fewer words and simpler drawings. I used to put in a lot of shading, and now I don't use Benday [half-tone shading] on the uniforms, although I wish I could. I found that when they ran the strips smaller, it all blackened in.

MORT WALKER, *BEETLE BAILEY*

How Far Ahead Do Syndicates Want Delivery?

Oh, months. But that never happens.

LEE SALEM, UNIVERSAL PRESS SYNDICATE

Generally, syndicates prefer to receive dailies six weeks ahead of publication and Sundays eight weeks ahead of publication.

The discrepancy between the two is accounted for by the additional time it takes to create the color separations for the Sunday strips and distribute them so the newspapers can print them the previous week.

Time Management

Since newspaper comics are an extremely personalized art form, it should come as no surprise that the time-management processes used to make the deadline is just as personalized.

Just do it.

I think it takes an organized, orderly, disciplined mind, as well as a very creative mind, just to be able to produce the work constantly.

JERRY VAN AMERONGEN, *BALLARD STREET*

After eighteen years, there should be a system, and there just doesn't seem to be one.

CATHY GUISEWITE, *CATHY*

I don't do a Sunday page, so I'm generally thirty-six cartoons (six weeks) ahead of publication. Some guys work much, much further out than that, and I really can't. There just isn't any way I'm going to be able to do Christmas cartoons in July. It's tough enough in November.

BRUCE BEATTIE, *BEATTIE BLVD.*

I think I'm about five to six weeks ahead. It's pretty good on the cartoonist side. It's terrifying on the syndicate's side. They'd like to have us all about sixteen months ahead, so if we die no one will find out about it.

JEFF MACNELLY, *SHOE* AND *PLUGGERS*

As far as managing their deadlines—I hate to say this—but I think the majority of cartoonists have not been that good at managing their deadlines. They tend to push them off as far as possible.

ANONYMOUS SYNDICATE EXECUTIVE

I'm three to four weeks ahead of publication. I'm one of those borderline guys.

JOHNNY HART, *B.C. AND THE WIZARD OF ID*

Many cartoonists are very late, and very few of us are early. It frus-

trates the syndicate people and rightly so. I think they have every right to say, "If you don't get this on time, we will fine you or use some other means to motivate you to be here on time."

LYNN JOHNSTON, FOR BETTER OR FOR WORSE

If you don't dearly love cartooning, you'll never meet a deadline. You better make sure this is what you want to do. In this kind of work, it's not that the deadlines are so immediate, it's that they are inaccessible. They are always going to be there, seven days a week, fifty-two weeks a year. It's very hard work.

WILEY MILLER, NON SEQUITUR

I've always been three months ahead. I've never fallen behind on it. They told me if you fall behind, you spend the rest of your life catching up. So I've always done a week's worth every week, and if I go on vacation or anything like that, I do my work before I go, not when I come back.

MORT WALKER, BEETLE BAILEY

When I send Ballard Street to the syndicate, it is a month ahead of when the papers need it. That gives the syndicate time to print it up, make proof sheets and ship them out.

I keep the strips here for a month, and I send off a full month's worth. Once a month. My deadline is day to day, but I keep a month ahead of that, so basically I'm two months ahead. As we talked earlier, this allows me to keep it around here. It allows me to look at these things more than once. I feel comfortable with it.

JERRY VAN AMERONGEN, BALLARD STREET

BEING THE FIRST TO SHOW UP AT THE CONVENTION, LENNY WAS CHOSEN TODAY AS THE PRESIDENTIAL NOMINEE FOR THE NATIONAL PROCRASTINATORS PARTY

I jog in the morning, I hit the studio here about nine o'clock, and I'll work on whatever needs to be done. Sometimes it's roughing out gags, penciling in dailies, penciling in Sundays.

I like to get the Sunday page out of the way as soon as I can, because that's the most work. The dailies are sort of fun to do. I turn on the television. I have a CD player and I like jazz music. I usually have jazz or Dixieland music playing in the studio while I'm working.

Answering the mail takes a lot of time these days, but I'm truly thankful for the volume of fan mail I receive.

BIL KEANE, *THE FAMILY CIRCUS*

Monday I write gags. For both strips, dailies. I manage, by the end of Tuesday, to have a week of each drawn. Then on Thursdays, I start writing for Sunday. I finish it on Friday. I'm always finished ahead of time.

MELL LAZARUS, *MISS PEACH* AND *MOMMA*

I think United wants strips about six weeks ahead of publication on the daily and about ten on the Sunday. I've been working hard lately, and I think I'm fifteen weeks ahead of publication date on the Sunday. In other words, right now, if I wanted to, I could quit for a month, and I would still be all right as far as getting work into the syndicate.

Most of the time, unless there is something going on, I am always two or three weeks ahead of the syndicate deadline.

The furthest I've ever been ahead was three months because I was about to have heart surgery, and I wanted to get ahead so that I would have some slack time.

CHARLES SCHULZ, *PEANUTS*

I usually do most of my work in the evening. It's quiet. No phone calls. No interruptions. A lot of the writing occurs then. I can do the drawing anytime during the day. There is no fast rule. There are times when I work weekends, work nights. Not too much or I piss my wife off. Having an office in the home is another problem. I don't know what the rest of the house looks like.

STEPHEN BENTLEY, *HERB & JAMAAL*

I start in the morning. Eight-thirty at the office. I read the paper, and work on the editorial stuff until about three-thirty.

Then I start working on Beattie Blvd., *thinking up ideas, coming home and drawing until about nine o'clock. Yeah, it's a long day, but what else would I be doing? Sitting around watching sitcoms? I work that way Monday and Tuesday. Wednesday night I take off. Thursday and Friday nights I work. Then I usually work a little bit on Saturday and a little bit on Sunday, maybe a hour and a half to three hours.*

I find that I go very cold very quickly if I don't do anything. It's like the old thing about practicing the piano. If I don't practice one day, I notice it. If I don't practice two days, my agent notices it. If I don't practise three days, the audience notices it. I am always doing it, and when I go on vacation and come back, I have a hard time even recognizing stuff I did three weeks ago.

BRUCE BEATTIE, *BEATTIE BLVD.*

I try so hard to keep my nose to the grindstone and work hard, but things happen.

I am at home, and I do cook the meals and brush the dog. It seems to me a female in the family generally has the lion's share of the stuff to do, whether it's Christmas cards and wrapping at Christmastime, or grocery shopping and making the meals during the week, or all those other time-consuming things that females tend to do.

LYNN JOHNSTON, *FOR BETTER OR FOR WORSE*

I work every day. I do most of my creative work in the morning. The creative work is the writing, the ideas, getting the composition down of writing and drawing. You need to do that when your brain is fresh—in the morning—before it gets all cluttered up with the crap of the day-to-day living. Free associate, just really let it flow.

Then you end up getting the ideas down, drawing them out. Produce the cartoon. I try to get two complete cartoons done a day, or one Sunday. That's my goal. Sometimes I get more, sometimes I get less, but my absolute minimum is getting one cartoon done—that's just to maintain what I already have—then if I get two cartoons done a day and I get ahead, then I can take a day off once in a while and do real-life stuff.

WILEY MILLER, *NON SEQUITUR*

I come over here to the studio about—I don't know, sometimes four o'clock in the morning, sometimes nine o'clock in the morning.

I usually work through to about seven o'clock at night, every day of the week, and it takes me about two and a half to three hours to do a week's work, and it takes me about forty-five minutes to do a Sunday. That's three hours and forty-five minutes. Right?

Now what happens to all the rest of that time [laugh] I have never figured out. There is no structure. There are always things that are coming up, things that I have to do, and actually, I find myself without time to do all these things.

JOHNNY HART, B.C. AND THE WIZARD OF ID

KEEPING THE CREATIVE GAS TANK FILLED

There are a variety of motivating factors that keep cartoonists producing new ideas.

Fear kept my gas tank filled.

JERRY VAN AMERONGEN, BALLARD STREET

Panic.

CATHY GUISEWITE, CATHY

Just terror. Terror is more like it. Cathy's just being nice.

JEFF MACNELLY, SHOE AND PLUGGERS

I just worked at it constantly. I know now—I have been in it long enough, as I'm sure you have—that if you are constantly having to produce things, you're going to have rise and fall. You're going to be in the valley, and you're going to be on the mountaintop.

I always used to comment that there are times where you just figure that the last idea you're ever going to have happened a day and a half ago. But if it's what you're working on, if that's what you're doing all day, sooner or later you have these little blocks, and then it bursts out. You just have to be ready to start writing down stuff.

You are driven by that fear. That's the reality of the situation. You've got this deadline. I think a practical solution to trying to rejuvenate oneself is, if you're pressing real hard and nothing is happening, press as hard as you can, until you wear yourself out to some degree and then you let it go. Get up and go do something different. Get out of your environment and go to another one. Go hang out in a used bookstore, someplace or something. Then I've noticed the ideas suddenly come rushing in at you when you're not thinking about them.

JERRY VAN AMERONGEN, BALLARD STREET

That's the other thing. That's why I say you should do a bunch of strips at first. A lot of kids will send me comic strip ideas. They'll say, "Here's three strips. I've spent the last two months developing these three strips."

And I say, "Gee, you know, we don't have that kind of time here. You have to comfortably do a week's worth every week." So that's something that people starting out don't really understand. Once you sign on, it is relentless. And you've got to figure that out fast.

JEFF MACNELLY, SHOE AND PLUGGERS

I think it's harder now than it was then, because I had so many ideas, and I was experimenting with different characters and how they would speak to each other. And now, I try to create new characters every once in a while so that the voice is slightly different.

NICOLE HOLLANDER, *SYLVIA*

We have eight grandchildren I follow around for ideas now. I was doing things about Tinkertoys when I began, then they played with Nintendo games, then it got to be the Ninja Turtles, and now it's Power Rangers.

As long as you have the cartoons fresh and contemporary, people know that it's not just a 1960s family, its a 1990s family, and it reflects what goes on in homes across America today.

BIL KEANE, *THE FAMILY CIRCUS*

Bill Watterson seems to be on a pattern of taking sabbaticals regularly. That's an interesting way to rejuvenate.

JOSEPH "CHIP" VISCI, *DETROIT FREE PRESS*

I think it is a good idea for cartoonists to take leave, for them to recharge the batteries, but I don't like to pay the same thing for reruns. That does bother me.

ROSALIE MULLER WRIGHT, *SAN FRANCISCO CHRONICLE*

Things tend to take my time, so I'm forcing myself to really write. The writing part is the hardest part, the part that I fear the most, because there are days when nothing happens, and I say, "Well, maybe I ate too many radishes, and its gone. I will never think another good thought in my life."

Then I know I have to get out. I have to exercise. I have to go out and walk. In fact, I like to walk around the house. I like to walk downtown. It's not so much that I'm a shopper, as that I am an observer. I just love to be downtown, to walk into a coffee shop, sit down and walk out again. I need to get out of the house. I miss people, and people is what I write about. So if I don't get out and see people, I get pretty sad.

LYNN JOHNSTON, *FOR BETTER OR FOR WORSE*

I devised a way of writing that I think is foolproof. I love it. I don't panic anymore.

I asked a cartoonist to come play golf with me yesterday, and he said, "I can't. I just can't get any ideas. I've been to the library. I'm sitting here—I got one idea yesterday—and I'm about to fall behind in my work."

I don't want to tell him how I do it, but I just have a kind of stream of consciousness way of writing. I don't wait for an idea, I just start writing.

Sarge says something to Beetle, and Beetle says something back. Then they have a conflict, and then there's a solution in the third panel.

I find I write myself right into a corner, and I can always come up with a funny solution. You don't know where it's going, when you start, and it works real well. I can sit down and do thirty ideas a day, without any trouble at all. They're not all good. Usually, I write all those down, and then I draw up about ten. The better ones.

MORT WALKER, BEETLE BAILEY

WHAT HAPPENS WHEN THE MUSE GOES AWAY?

There is only one in the valley, but she's never been to my house.

MELL LAZARUS, MISS PEACH AND MOMMA

My muse can't go away, because the source of the muse is your imagination and you can't shut your imagination off. If nothing else, it would imagine bad things. You cannot not have ideas, unless you're into one of those transitional periods. But that's not like you can't function— you're just not sharp. It's because you're moving on to something better.

JOHNNY HART, B.C. AND THE WIZARD OF ID

It hasn't gone away yet. It's always with me. In fact, when we go to Hawaii, my wife likes to read, but I sit down and work on gags. That's what I would rather be doing than anything else. I read the newspaper and say, "Oh, yeah, that's something I could do." It's fun. It gives me such a comfort to know that I have a pocket full of these little pieces of paper that have gags I've scribbled on them.

BIL KEANE, THE FAMILY CIRCUS

I have a file cabinet filled with various beginnings of ideas. I always turn to that. It's done by subject matter, and the first half of the file cabinet is just miscellaneous. I flip through those and try to put something to work.

When I get really stuck, sometimes I read magazines. The problem is when I get really stuck I am really up against a deadline, so there isn't that kind of wandering-around-looking-for-inspiration time.

CATHY GUISEWITE, CATHY

I get out of the house, get away from what I'm doing. Literally, get away from it and try not to think about it.

I go to the bookstore, or read the newspaper, or go for a walk or exercise. Anything that's away from what I'm doing. I carry a pen and notepad, and I write on scraps of paper, napkins or whatever is closest. When I get home, I pull out all these scraps of paper and decipher them.

STEPHEN BENTLEY, HERB & JAMAAL

I sit here and wait for the muse to come back. I wish I had the confidence to say, "It's not a good day for writing. Let's go to the movies or go take a walk." It just scares me to death to leave the studio when I can't think of anything. I'll get crazy and want to come back. I just stay here.

Sometimes I'll go through books. Rhythm is such a part of me. I'll look at old gags I've done to get that rhythm going again. That helps, but of course Rick is being the editor, so I can't get away with repeating gags. He catches me in a minute.

JERRY SCOTT, BABY BLUES AND NANCY

CREATING ADDITIONAL FEATURES

It would be a Herculean task for most cartoonists to produce a second or even a third feature. Still, many cartoonists have found the resources and creative energy to accomplish just such a task.

Some people have tremendous talent. It just spills over, and just doing one thing isn't sufficient for them.

TONI MENDEZ, LITERARY REPRESENTATIVE

I would prefer the cartoonist concentrate on the one feature. Sometimes that's economically unfeasible. If they add another feature, I would just concern myself with the feature that they are doing for me. What they do with their own time is really up to them, but I have to watch very carefully to see that the quality is maintained.

I think doing a seven-day comic strip is more than a full-time job. I'm sure that some people can do two comic strips, and more power to them, but it's got to be a grind. I'm not opposed to it, but we all do our best work when we concentrate on one project. Are there exceptions? Certainly. But generally, it's just a case that we do one thing best.

ALAN SHEARER, WASHINGTON POST WRITERS GROUP

I'm astounded that anybody would have both the physical time and the mental energy to take on a whole second feature. I find doing just the one is so completely life-consuming. This is so completely it in terms of my sense of humor and point of view for the comic pages, but it's hard for me to imagine that someone else could have two whole unique strips in them.

CATHY GUISEWITE, CATHY

I think if it's different, if it's a new kind of project, something that allows you to stretch a little more and do different drawing. That's the great thing about Pluggers. I can draw anything. I'm not held down to two characters sitting around a kitchen table.

JEFF MACNELLY, SHOE AND PLUGGERS

Why would an oil painter want to paint in watercolor? Why would an editoial cartoonist like Paul Conrad want to sculpt? A cartoon is a piece of their work. It's not all their work. They have many other ideas and many other projects that they would like to bring forward, as all artists and writers do. So I would imagine that all of them at one time or another would like to try other things.

STEVE CHRISTENSEN, LOS ANGELES TIMES SYNDICATE

A lot of times, you may have a feature that does not accommodate itself to all of your thinking, so maybe you'll think the answer is to develop a new feature. But, in the long run, I think it is a mistake. I think the better direction is to expand your strip so that it will accommodate every idea you can think of. This is what Peanuts *does for me. It doesn't matter what I think of, whether it's silly or stupid or funny or—I hope— profound, I can fit it in someplace. I think that's more important than to try to think of another strip which really, in the long run, dilutes your work.*

CHARLES SCHULZ, PEANUTS

Most cartoonists have a full-time job in one strip, and that's reality. So that would be my initial and main concern about a cartoonist taking on a second strip. How can you take a full-time job, then double it? That's with keeping your sanity and private life. There are some who can do it, and do it well, but I think there is a small number of them.

LEE SALEM, UNIVERSAL PRESS SYNDICATE

Life is in some ways very unpredictable. You don't know what kind of a person you are going to be in ten years, after you have had all types of life experiences you don't currently have. One of the ideas that I am playing around with is the idea of doing a character-based strip, and in a way, I think you are in the situation where the cartoon feature that you are capable of doing today—that you understand how to do today—is not necessarily the one that you are capable of doing in five to ten years. Why do two? Well, for me it's the excitement of exploring new and different forms of the art.

BRUCE BEATTIE, BEATTIE BLVD.

I think if you can be happy, and if you can make a living doing one, great. I remember when I just used to do Single Slices, *and it was great. I would get two months ahead, go to the Caribbean, hang out for two months and turn my brain off.*

PETER KOHLSAAT, SINGLE SLICES AND THE NOOZ

I tell you, my wife says, "Oh, God, not another idea."
I've got all kinds of things out there I'm working on. A novel. I'm

working on a musical stage show. I've got three or four children's books in the works. I've got the museum. I've got an invention out there that's being patented right now.

I'm a creative artist. A creative person. It's something—it's a plague, because I don't know what I'm supposed to be working on from day to day.

MORT WALKER, *BEETLE BAILEY*

Pluggers think all scales are inaccurate.

As the saying goes, sometimes the spirit is willing but the flesh is weak. Just because cartoonists have the inspiration and the inclination to work on additional features, where do they find the time?

The biggest concern I'd have about a cartoonist adding to his workload would be, "Is he or she going to be able to take on that additional responsibility, and still maintain the quality and the deadline pressures of the feature he or she is already doing?"

STEVE CHRISTENSEN, LOS ANGELES TIMES SYNDICATE

It's funny. You know the old Murphy's Law? The time expands to take care of the workload.

MORT WALKER, *BEETLE BAILEY*

I have no idea, to tell you the truth. I'm plugging away. But it's enjoyable. I really enjoy it. A couple of things kind of had to go on hold for a while to get Pluggers started. I just wanted to see how it would go.

JEFF MACNELLY, *SHOE* AND *PLUGGERS*

Cartoonist Highlights

Cathy Guisewite, cartoonist
CATHY

My parents are the kind of people who go around telling you to be grateful for everything that goes wrong in your life. Every big crisis has

a purpose, they say. Every little disappointment, a bright and wonderful side.

Having grown up being forced to look for the good side of the worst moments of my life, I found that *Cathy* came about in a very natural way.

Instead of wallowing in the misery of waiting for phone calls that never came a few years ago, I was compelled to draw a picture of me waiting . . .

Instead of agonizing over where love had gone, I couldn't resist putting my questions down on paper . . .

And when I was filled with the drive to make radical changes in the way I was living, I couldn't help visualizing my determination . . .

Although I never suspected I was creating a comic strip, *Cathy* was in drawings just like these. They became a great release for my frustrations, and by sending them home, I discovered a great way to let my family know how I was doing without writing letters.

Anxious to have me do even better, my parents researched comic strip syndicates, sought advice from Tom Wilson, the creator of *Ziggy,* and, finally, threatened to send my work to Universal Press Syndicate if I didn't.

Just as Cathy began as a kind of self-therapy for my problems, she continues to be a voice for the questions I can never quite answer, and the things I can never quite say. Because our lives are linked so closely, she's affected by almost everyone I know and everything I do.

Through Cathy, I've learned that my little daily struggles are a lot like everyone else's little daily struggles. The feelings I always thought that only I had are ones that everyone shares. But maybe just as important, writing Cathy has taught me one of the even greater lessons of life: Anything is possible if you listen to your mother.

—Cathy Guisewite

Johnny Hart, cartoonist
B.C. and The Wizard of Id

Grace Ann and Irwin James Hart are two of the most beautiful people I have ever known. They no longer walk the thid planet with me, for

they have gone and I miss them deeply.

I met them in the predawn hours of February 18th in 1931, in a small town on the southern border of New York State. Not too many people have ever heard of Endicott, New York. I, in fact, had never heard of it myself before that morning.

We adjusted well, the three of us, there were good times and much love. Two squalling infants named James and Susan later enrolled in the clan and the fun increased. As a family we were far from well-to-do but never poor. At least if we were, Irwin and Grace never let on.

As far back as I care to remember, I drew funny pictures, which got me in or out of trouble depending on the circumstances. A certain amount of prominence and popularity resulted, which I guess is what I was after all the time.

My formal education ended abruptly when I graduated from Union-Endicott High School. School was different in those days. They taught softly but carried a big strap. Nowadays you can bad-mouth the teachers. In my day you resorted to placing reptiles in their drawers, which was pretty risky when they were wearing them.

Soon after I had reached the age of nineteen, a young cartoonist named Brant Parker became a prime influence in my life. In one quick evening we met, became great friends and began a relationship which would one day culminate in a joint effort called *The Wizard of Id*. Brant imparted to me, with remarkable insight and perception, the essence of all that he had observed from the practical application and study of his craft.

To this point in my life, I had never really considered cartooning as a *profession*, but in the years to follow it became a driving force, seemingly etched in my subconscious from that first meeting with Brant Parker.

In the latter part of that same year I joined the air force, which took me to Texas, Georgia and Korea. While in Georgia, I met and married an alluring lass named Bobby, who has stood by me through those years when I would labor far into the night over kitchen tables, drawing boards, card tables and the like, working toward the day when I would join that fraternity of cartoonists whom I had idolized over the years.

My application for enrollment in the fraternity arrived in April of 1954, on a small farm in Georgia, when Bobby came screaming from the mailbox with a sale from the *Saturday Evening Post.* We danced and sang and gorged ourselves on a chocolate cake that Bobby's mother whomped up for the occasion. Many magazine sales followed, but not with the frequency essential to sustain life.

Two years in an art department with General Electric returned Bobby and me to a more substantial diet. I continued my submissions to the magazines, working once more during those quiet hours when normal people slumber.

Caveman gags, for reasons which I still cannot explain, were an obsession in those days. Although I must reluctantly confess that I have not sold a caveman gag to a magazine, to this date. During my two years with G.E., I began to read, with astonishment, a comic strip called *Peanuts* by Charles M. Schulz. His sense of humor and my own seemed remarkably similar, which inspired me to attempt a comic strip.

"I shall repair to my domicile this evening and create a nationally famous comic strip," I announced to my cronies. "Why don't you make it a caveman strip? . . ." said one wag. "You can't seem to sell them anywhere else!"

I took it as a mandate.

B.C. was rejected by five major syndicates before it was accepted by the New York Herald Tribune Syndicate.

My wife Bobby enjoys reminding me on occasion of a prophetic moment in the early days, when in the throes of artistic frustration, I hurled drawing materials about the room, kicked over a card table, and declared fitfully that before I reached the age of twenty-seven, I would have a nationally syndicated feature. Although I never remember saying it, *B.C.* appeared nationally on the eve of my twenty-seventh birthday. To the best of my recollection it was the last time that I preempted a deadline.

Two year after *B.C.* began, I created *The Wizard of Id*, which lay dormant for several years thereafter. In 1963 I mentioned it to Brant Parker, and asked him if he would be willing to take on the job of illustrating it, and to my delight he consented. Brant and I threw *The Wizard* together during three wild days and nights in a small, dank New York hotel room, taping the finished drawings to the walls as we completed them. When the walls were filled, we called the syndicate and asked them if they would like to see a new strip. They said they would. The men from the syndicate arrived earlier than we had anticipated, finding Brant barefoot and shirtless and me in my shorts shaving off a three-day beard. Ignoring us, they edged their way around the walls, scuffing away an occasional beer bottle as they went.

When they had finished they seated themselves about the room amidst the rubble and eyed us carefully. "We think you're disgusting but the strip is great," they said. "We'll take it."

The Wizard appeared on November 9, 1964, with Brant Parker as its artist.

An interesting sidelight to this whole saga is that many of the characters in the strips are patterned after true, real-life friends.

That wasn't too smart.

—JOHNNY HART

P.S. Bobby and I have two daughters named Patti and Perri who have asked to remain anonymous.

LYNN JOHNSTON, CARTOONIST
FOR BETTER OR FOR WORSE

It was a hot and sultry night. Jim Davis (creator of *Garfield*), Mike Peters (creator of *Mother Goose & Grimm*) and I sat at a banquet table, invitees to a benefit dinner for the Sarasota Hospital. We were well into our second bottle of wine, when a *Garfield* fan sat down next to Jim and said, "Mr. Davis, I've always wondered; where *do* you get your ideas!?" Without missing a beat, Jim replied, "Schenectady." Satisfied, the inquiring mind wandered off. "That must be the question we're most often asked," I ruminated. Mike voted for: How far ahead of the deadline do you have to be? and Jim agreed.

In fact, he had considered having a T-shirt made with "six weeks, dailies" on the front and "eight weeks, Sundays" on the back. Then, when someone posed the chestnut opener, he would simply open his jacket and expose the appropriate response. This, of course, led to the proposal that we design the "benefit suit," imprinted everywhere with answers to all the questions a syndicated cartoonist is asked most often.

Oddly enough, the questions our readers most often ask us are the questions we ask each other and the toughest ones to answer. The toughest question has always been, "How do you get your ideas?"

How do you answer that? It's like asking runners how they run, or singers how they sing. They just do it!

We are all born with wonderful gifts. We use these gifts to express ourselves, to amuse, to strengthen, and to communicate. We begin as children to explore and develop our talents, often unaware that we are unique, that not everyone can do what we're doing!

I loved to draw funny pictures. If they got me into trouble, it was worth it. If they made people laugh, I was high. By the time I was in my teens, I knew I would be a cartoonist. I never imagined, however, that I would, someday, have the great fortune (and awesome responsibility) of producing a comic feature that would be read daily by millions of people worldwide.

Jim and Mike and I—and all of the people I know in this business—have all been overwhelmed by this "work" we do. We have heard Charles Schulz say, "Can you believe we really do this for a living?" Looking back on forty-five years of drawing *Peanuts,* he has said on several occasions, "How do we think of all of those things, anyway?!!!"

Where do the ideas come from?

For most of us, drawing comes easily—but, without ideas, there are no drawings! Truly, in this business, it's the thought that counts!

You begin with a blank page. When you have a deadline, a blank page is both a threat and a challenge! How do you create something from nothing? Somehow, we do it—and we love what we do.

Our methods vary. Some of us doodle, some of us sit, some of us work with writers. All of us know that the process can be difficult and we have to prepare in advance for those times when, no matter how hard we try, nothing comes, nothing works . . . and the blank page scores against us.

Because I still consider it something of a riddle, I wanted to try and describe what happens during those creative times when the writing is done—at least how it's done for *For Better or For Worse.*

On a lazy Saturday morning when you're lying in bed, drifting in and out of sleep, there is a space where fantasy and reality become one.

Are you awake, or are you dreaming? You see people and things, some are familiar, some are strange. You talk, you feel, but you move without walking; you fly without wings. Your mind and your body exist, but on separate planes. Time stands still. For me, this is the feeling I have when ideas come.

There is a small sunroom off our bedroom that overlooks a thick stand of birch trees. In this room, I keep a beach chair, an old carved table, some plants, a telephone, and a large wooden flamingo. This is my "writing place." It is here that I go to await inspiration! I wait and I wait and . . . I wait.

Like starting an old chain saw that's hard to start, you often have to apply every trick of the trade before work can begin! One idea-generator is the matching together of random things, let's say: a sock, a banana, and a typewriter, for example. I can then see April, one sock off, one sock on, kneeling on a chair, mashing a banana into her mother's typewriter. Aha—a daily!

If this doesn't work, I pace the floor, I go through material I have just sent in . . . I think about the characters and whose turn it is to be heard from next. I flick through the channels of my imagination, hoping to find something good, something I can build on, something funny!

Sometimes, there are voices without pictures. Sometime there are pictures without words. I observe my cartoon family by hovering above them like a visiting spirit.

Sometimes I become the characters themselves. I think their thoughts and feel what they feel. Always, I wait for things to happen. I wait for them to speak, to be spoken to.

I cannot always predict what the characters will say or how their world will evolve around them. I am often surprised by their conversations. There are times when they seem to take charge; take the stories where they want them to go!

Still, the director's chair is mine, and when a clash of wills happens and the writing stops . . . it's time to get up, get out, and break away from it all. (I usually raid the fridge, which is one of the hazards of working at home.)

Each cast member in *For Better or For Worse* is based on someone I know well. Elizabeth, for example, responds to situations the way my daughter Katie might respond. Her school is Kate's school, her body language and speech patterns are similar. Elizabeth Patterson, however, is also *me*. She has my childhood memories, my private thoughts, my passions, goals, and fears. She is me, she is my daughter, she is an imaginary girl of thirteen who has, believe it or not . . . a very definite mind of her own.

I am every character (even the dog) and, yet, every character is an entity unto itself. This concept, although complex and confusing to others, is part of the routine. No wonder cartoonists need an understanding family! Our minds are always "somewhere else"!!

A cartoonist is a writer, an actor, a director and an artist. We write, act and direct every scene. Even the camera work is important! The drawing is the final stage of the production and the time, for me, when I can touch these imaginary images, feel them, bring them to life!

Penciling my thoughts first, frame by frame, expression by expression, I act out every movement. I picture every scene and project that image onto the page—in pencil. When the panels are completed, the inking is done. Inking the drawings is an experience I always look forward to. It's like having a ghost in front of me, and by reaching out, moving my pen around its form, touching it, pressing against its face, its body, feeling it, I make it real. This part of my job is pure pleasure! After all these years, I still think of it as a kind of "magic," and I wonder how and why this magic was entrusted to me!

Knowing the other people in this industry with whom I share so much has been one of my greatest joys. We are what we do. I have admired some of these people for years. Some are contemporaries, some just coming through the door! All are open and giving. All of us reveal more of ourselves in the work that we do than our readers will ever know.

These small hand-drawn characters are projections of ourselves. The part that none of us can ever quite explain, however, is the wit and the wisdom. Where does it come from? The sarcasm, the laughter, the wry turn of phrase! Do we tap into a mental reservoir? Is there a spiritual connection to cartoonists from the past who'll say, "Psst—try this one!!!" If so—where are they when we need them the most?

—LYNN JOHNSTON

BIL KEANE, CARTOONIST
THE FAMILY CIRCUS

I was born in Philidelphia. Well, I wasn't exactly born, I was discovered there by Benjamin Franklin (October 5, 1922). I grew up in that city with a Penn by my side—William Penn! When asked who cracked the Liberty Bell I replied, "Not me!"—my first association with that invisible gremlin who showed up in *The Family Circus* many years later.

Taught myself to draw, so I can't blame anyone but me. Started cartooning in high school which I attended when I grew too tall for low school. Spent three years in the U.S. Army during World War II, but we won anyway. While stationed in Australia I met a cute koala bear named Thel Carne who was trying futilely to throw away a boomerang.

I, too, returned—five years later, and we were married in Brisbane. In Roslyn, Pennsylvania, we started our real-life family circus. They pro-

vided the inspiration for my cartoons; I provided the perspiration.

I worked at the *Philidelphia Bulletin* for fifteen years, where I was a staff artist. I drew staffs. I launched *Channel Chuckles* in 1954, a syndicated cartoon about TV. The TV repairman was at our house so much I thought he was part of the family. In fact, later I named one of my cartoon characters after him: Barfy. I drew freelance cartoons for the major magazines and a Sunday comic for the *Bulletin* called *Silly Philly.* In 1959, I decided to work

from my home and we moved the whole family, lock, stock and barrel to Arizona. We managed the lock and stock okay, but had trouble with the barrel. We still live in the same house near Phoenix and love the state. Even its canyons are grand.

The Family Circus bowed in 1960 and I've been going around in circles ever since. It now appears in well over 1,500 newpapers whose editors have excellent taste in comics. Readership polls place *The Family Circus* at the top regularly. And it's a very nice view from atop a poll.

The Family Circus has appeared on TV in holiday specials and is being published regularly by Fawcett Gold Medal Books in paperback collections. There are over fourteen million *The Family Circus* books in print. If you can't find a copy in your bookstore, come over to my house, I have thirteen and a half million of them.

In 1983, I was named Cartoonist of the Year by the National Cartoonists Society and at the awards dinner I was given a sitting ovation.

We now have six grandchildren who I like to follow around for grand ideas.

Thel is my editor and consultant. Bud Warner inks in my cartoons. Youngest son Jeff helps me with special projects, the mail, etc. The syndicate does the selling. Come to think of it, what do I do? I keep in shape (I'm not sure what the shape is) by playing tennis and jogging.

If asked when I will retire I say, "Probably about eleven o'clock tonight. But, hopefully, I'll be back at the ol' drawing board in the morning and happy to be there!"

Love to all!

—Bɪʟ Keane

Hank Ketcham, cartoonist
Dennis the Menace

Ketcham was born March 14, 1920, in Seattle, Washington. He became interested in drawing at the age of seven when a local art di-

rector, a friend of the family, doodled cartoon sketches to amuse him. The bug bit and Ketcham practiced cartooning in every spare moment of his school years.

He entered the University of Washington in 1937 as an art major, but after a year the cartooning urge lured him to Hollywood and the Walter *Woody Woodpecker* Lantz animation studio. Moving to the Walt Disney studios, he worked on *Pinocchio, Fantasia,* and other Disney productions for two and a half years—until December 7, 1941, and the bombing of Pearl Harbor.

He enlisted in the U.S. Navy and, as chief photographer specialist, spent the World War II years in Washington, D.C., developing cartoons, magazines, posters and animated film spots to promote the sale of war bonds. To supplement his serviceman's pay, Ketcham began drawing and selling gag cartoons to magazines, including a weekly panel that appeared in the *Saturday Evening Post.*

After the war, he plunged full-time into the highly competitive freelance cartooning market. He quickly became one of the country's most successful and prolific cartoonists, selling his work regularly to *Colliers,* the *Saturday Evening Post, Ladies' Home Journal, Liberty,* and the *New Yorker* as well as to advertising agencies. By this time Ketcham was also married and the father of a boy named Dennis.

In answer to the question, "How did you get the idea for *Dennis the Menace,*" one day Mrs. Ketcham came into the studio after Dennis had made a mess in the house and said, "Your son is a menace!" Mr. Ketcham looked up from his drawing board and said, "Dennis? . . . a menace?!"

With a constant flow of new projects and the demands of a daily newspaper panel, Ketcham arrives at his Pebble Beach, California, studio every morning at 8:30. He puts in eight-hour days on the panel, working at least ten weeks in advance of the publication schedule. Today he is aided by his secretary and two artists who work on the panel.

"People wonder how a little five-year-old kid keeps a grown man busy every day of the week!" says Ketcham. "I don't know, but he does—and I'm still smiling."

MELL LAZARUS, CARTOONIST
MISS PEACH AND MOMMA

BAKE YOUR FAVORITE COMIC STRIP A CAKE

You know that comic strip characters are among the best-known fictional figures in modern literature. But how much do you know about

the legal relationship of these marvelous characters to the people who actually created them?

The fact is, most comic strip characters are not owned by the talented people who created and produce them every day, but rather by the companies—the syndicates—who distribute them.

During the past several years a growing consciousness of cartoonists' rights has moved some syndicates to begin granting ownership to some comic strip artists. These artists complain, however, that it's merely ownership of a sort, because the syndicates also insist on contracts of such length that it makes ownership almost meaningless. The cartoonists can't exercise any proprietary rights until, as one of them put it, "We're too old to hold the pencil."

What's more, many of these contracts (as well as the "standard" ones) periodically renew themselves, based on the syndicate's performance; if a strip's income stays above a preestablished level, often modest, it can easily become a lifetime deal with never a clear opportunity for the cartoonist to improve the terms. It's worth noting that even in Hollywood (the home of unconscionable contracts) performance agreements don't run for more than seven years.

Moreover, there are comic strips extant, whose creators have long since died, that are still owned by their syndicates and have been continuously produced by a series of hired successors with no financial consideration for the original creators' families.

What about that word "syndicate"? Properly defined, it means a consortium of entrepreneurs, in this case newspapers, who band together for the purpose of sharing the costs of features such as comic strips and columns. A good idea and a good definition when, around the

---

turn of the century, William Randolph Hearst syndicated certain cartoon strips among the newspapers in his chain.

The way the business has been practiced since then, however, "syndicate" is a misnomer. Nowadays, newspaper feature syndicates are independent companies who distribute features to individual newspapers in much the same way that a manufacturer's representative sells ladies' blouses. There's no connection among the buyers, so the term "syndicate" doesn't apply. A better word is "agency."

Which makes the average cartoonist-creator's situation even more peculiar because an agency (again, not even in Hollywood) is not supposed to own its clients' creations.

As rickety as it sounds, this situation has obtained in the comic strip business all these years, and with no compelling rationale ever having been offered.

Besides owning the comic strips, the agencies, as we will now refer to them, usually take 50 percent of the receipts. In any other creative field, 50 percent is an unacceptably high agency commission, and we're talking here about 50 percent of the *net* receipts, which means the agency first deducts production expenses before they send the cartoonist his or her share.

The cartoonist, on the other hand, is not expected to deduct his or her own expenses from the mix, expenses that are often considerable, including things like studio rent, art supplies, copying, shipping costs, secretarial and art assistance, and so forth. All of which, plus writing and drawing time (which can mean ten hours a day) is at least as significant a capital investment as the agency makes. The comic strip artists, therefore, are in the unique position of helping to subsidize the entrepreneurs, large corporations whose avowed happy privilege it is to sell the features into newspapers.

You might wonder why cartoonists, reasonably sophisticated people, enter into such agreements. The fact is that most do so early in their careers, when the lure of newspaper syndication, the greenest pasture of their profession, is very heady. When you're hungry it's almost impossible to resist signing any contract that's slid across a desk in your direction.

I'm not comparing comic strip syndication to life in the Gulag. On the contrary, syndication can be a remarkably pleasant and rewarding way to earn a living. And should their contracts ever run out, cartoonists are certainly free to leave their agencies. But they must do so without the characters they invented from whole cloth and which have become part of their lives and psyches as well as the public consciousness. These characters, in their every past and current usage—the accumulated product of the cartoonists' careers—remain with their erstwhile agents, who are then free to replace the departed creators with hired hands. So, yes, the cartoonists can leave, but their characters must stay.

If, after leaving the agency, a cartoonist wishes to stay on in the business, he or she must then invent a different set of characters with as much artistic merit, reader identification and commercial impact as the ones they left behind. Which is often impossible.

In the early 1940s the late dean of comic strip artists, Milton Caniff, had grown increasingly resentful of the fact that he had no vested estate interest in his classic adventure strip, *Terry and the Pirates,* which was owned by his syndicate. Caniff finally found an opportunity to quit Terry in midcareer and make a selfownership deal with another organization to do a new strip, *Steve Canyon.* Canyon was certainly successful, by anyone's lights, but never quite found the devoted audience that Terry had.

I don't want to spoil your fun, but the next time you read your favorites on the comic page, take a little pity on them. Most of them, the best-known fictional characters in modern literature, are very much the hostages of the syndicate/agencies who represent them. Bake them a cake. With a file in it.

How To Be Happy Though Syndicated

When that contract is offered to you, bear in mind that this industry does not recognize a "standard agreement." Everything in a deal is negotiable and subject to the give-and-take tradeoff system between any two parties of good faith.

If you're prepared to say "no" and walk away, here's what you should try for:

1. Continuous ownership, by you and your heirs, of all your rights, title and interest in and to the feature.

2. The shortest possible contract. Five, six or seven years seems fair.

3. No obligation on your part to give them "first look" at any new features you might decide to create. You should have the right to do business freely.

4. An unconditional termination to the contract, one that does not provide for an automatic, unilateral renewal on any basis whatsoever, including performance. If at that time you feel you've been happy with the syndicate, its people and the way they've been handling your property, you'll have no problem sitting down with them and renegotiating a new agreement that could include refinements you feel are reasonable. Such as an increase in your precentage of the take.

—MELL LAZARUS

Mike Peters, cartoonist
Mother Goose and Grimm

My mother and father both had eighth-grade educations, and they did fabulous things. She had a TV show in St. Louis for about twenty-five years, and my dad was a fabulous salesman, but they never pushed me as far as school was concerned.

In grade school and high school, I never had to worry about homework. We always got to watch TV and things like that, so I was a terrible student. I was always going to summer school, and I never knew that if I got good grades I wouldn't have to go to summer school. I just assumed that this was my life.

I had a terrible stutter as a real young kid, so the only way I could really communicate—the only way I could control the way people reacted about things I did—was through drawings. and so I drew. I drew all the time.

When I went all through grade school and all through high school, I was always in trouble because I was never doing any work. I was always making the students laugh with my drawings, and I was always doing my little drawings in the margin of books. I used to do posters and cartoons for my school newspapers and I was always very prolific, but I did no homework or schoolwork at all.

When I got out of school, I just kept drawing, and then I got my jobs. Then I eventually got some sort of a name, and then my high school asked me to come back.

I thought this was really ironic because I had not changed at all, so I was trying to figure out what to do when I went back because some of my teachers were still there. Finally, since I got into so much trouble drawing their caricatures in the school papers, I decided I'd relearn how to draw their caricatures. Then I'd stand up and say, "Oh, yeah, this is how I drew Brother Peter," and all the different teachers that I had.

So I went back to my mom's house in St. Louis. I got up in the attic and looked at my yearbooks, which I hadn't looked at for fifteen to twenty years. I started looking through them and I was fascinated by reading a lot of the stuff that the kids had written at graduation. You know, "Roses are red, violets are blue, and you suck." Stuff like that.

And so, I was going through my yearbooks, and I found this picture of Mr. Morgan, my senior English teacher. Mr. Morgan—just like anyone else at that school—did not see any justification for me being at that school, had no use for me, and did not like me very much—even though I was adorable. I just didn't do any work, so he put me in the last row of his class.

He called that row his vegetable garden. These were all the kids who were brain-dead and hooked up to machines and stuff like that. Some of us were drooling, and I'd be back there doing my cartoons. He put us in that row, because it was closest to the window.

He said, "If you get nothing else out of this class, you'll get sunlight. And so, maybe through the process of osmosis, you'll grow and you'll flourish."

Well, I found his picture and he had written something underneath it on graduation day.

Now, you have to understand, tonight I'm going to my school to get this award because they think I'm hot stuff, and here, under Mr. Morgan's picture, he wrote, "Dear Mr. Peters—You had better start growing up real soon, because remember, you can't always draw cartoons."

Boy, that's the whole story of my life. Isn't that a hoot? Of course you can always draw cartoons. You can always do the stuff you love.

—MIKE PETERS

CHARLES SCHULZ, CARTOONIST
PEANUTS

We comic strip artists frequently feel that our profession is not regarded very highly on the artistic totem pole. When I first started

drawing the *Peanuts* comic strip in 1950, I was given a very small space in which to work. *Peanuts* was sold as a space-saving comic strip, and each panel was drawn so it would fit neatly into one newspaper column. In other words, the strip could be printed horizontally, with each panel taking up one column, or it could be printed vertically, with the entire strip running down one column, or it could be printed two panels beneath the other two panels, forming a square. All of this was used as a sales gimmick for a feature in which, looking back, I believe the people at the syndicate really didn't have much confidence.

Not long after that, they came out with a couple of other features that were drawn to the full size that most comic strips were printed. This bothered me for a long time and, little by little, I have tried to increase the size of *Peanuts* in both the daily strip and the Sunday pages. Unfortunately, these sizes seem to be shrinking. But I came across a marvelous quote by S.J. Perelman: "To me, the muralist is not more valid than the miniature painter. In this very large country where size is all and where Thomas Wolfe outranks Robert Benchley, I am content to stitch away at my embroidery hoop." This was a most reassuring statement from that great humorist, and has helped to make me content to draw my tiny little comic strip every day.

I am always amazed at some of the things people say when they first discover what it is that I do for a living. "Oh," some of them exclaim, "are you still drawing the strip?" This is probably one of the most insulting things they could say. I am tempted to ask them, "Who do you think has been drawing it lately? Do you really think that the syndicate can go out and find just anyone to draw the strip?" But I suppose most people are under the impression that everyone who draws a comic strip has two or three people helping him or her.

Another question that continues to baffle me is, "Do you ever draw anything in your strip that has social meaning?" I have always felt that down through the years my strip has been filled with little tidbits of social meaning. I like to think that many of them are not obvious, but that I have had some important things to say.

In the August 24, 1992, edition of *Publishers Weekly,* I saw this quote: "This is a book with the intellectual depth of a cartoon strip." That's the kind of sentence that gets your day off to a bad start.

One evening recently, I was rereading a biography of James Thurber which I have next to my drawing board, and I came across the most wonderful quote. Thurber apparently had been accused of drawing cartoons which some critics felt did not have enough social criticism in them, and he replied, "Art does not rush to the barricades."

I have read of authors who have outlined the personality and the history of a character in a novel in order for them better to understand the character when they begin to write about him or her. While much of the information about this character may never be written, it helps the author better to understand what this character is like and how he or she may think or act under certain circumstances.

The same is true in a minor way with cartoon characters. I feel I know each one of these little personalities quite well and many of their attributes are known to me, even if in a vague way, which helps me to direct their actions when they are called upon to perform. If I happen to think of an idea, I can always turn to my repertory company and choose just the right character to act out this idea.

Many cartoons, of course, come from the personality of the characters themselves. The longer I live with the characters, the better I get to know them, and the more ideas they seem to provide.

If a character, by the very nature of the personality I have given him or her, provides me with ideas, then that character remains in the strip. If the character has attributes which are too distinct, such as the little boy, Pigpen, then he will not appear very often, because his appearance in the beginning of the cartoon will mislead the reader into thinking the idea is going to be something about the fact that he is dusty and dirty all of the time. In other words, Pigpen does not make a good straight man for any ideas.

It is also absolutely essential that the readers build up their own ideas as to what the personalities are in these characters. This obviously means that I always have to very careful to make sure that no one ever acts out of character.

—CHARLES SCHULZ

MORT WALKER, CARTOONIST
BEETLE BAILEY

Cartoons have been my life, almost my religion, since I was born and my father read the comics to me. He read and we both laughed. I had to know what those pictures were about so I learned how to read before

I went to school. I also began drawing cartoons as soon as I could guide a pencil. Throughout school I was always known as *The Cartoonist.* It was my identity and later was my salvation from a life of poverty.

I had worked since I was three, selling magazines, fudge, washing windows, mowing lawns, delivering stuff at ten cents an hour until I was eleven years old and sold my first cartoon for $1.00! At last I knew where the real money was! I dropped out of school and began mailing cartoons to magazines all over the country for as much as $7.50. (I returned to school in the meantime after six months.) By the time I was fifteen I had sold over three hundred cartoons and had my own comic strip in the *Kansas City Journal.* The die was cast, there was no turning back.

For those so dedicated, cartooning is a wonderful career. It gives you the right to work on your own time and express yourself in your own way. I don't know of any other career that gives you such complete creative control of your own ideas and feelings. You can make a lot of money, become famous, and laugh all day while working in your old comfortable clothes wherever you feel like working.

Working consists of getting an idea while stretched out on a lounge chair staring at the ceiling and taking a snooze in between ideas. I write my ideas down on a piece of typing paper, six to a page. I usually don't wait for an idea to jell before I start to write. I just begin writing whatever comes to my mind, like Beetle and Sarge are walking along and Sarge sees some trash on the walk. He tells Beetle to pick it up. Then I write whatever I think Beetle would say like, "Why me? I didn't drop it there." Then I imagine what Sarge would answer and I write myself back into a corner where I have to come up with a punch line. I always do. It's not always a great punch line but it's *something!* Better than scratching your head all morning waiting for great ideas that never come.

After I get a bunch of ideas I sit down and sketch out the better ones on typing paper, one to a page. Several other people contribute ideas to *Beetle Bailey.* Jerry Dumas has been working with me about forty years, Bud Jones, twenty-five, and three of my sons, Greg, Brian and Morgan are learning the business. We get together about once a month and read each others ideas, vote on them and offer suggestions for improvement. We reject about 30 percent of the ideas. Then I take them, store them in fireproof boxes until I am ready to draw. I sort them out into batches of twenty-five weeks and reject another 20 percent in the sorting process. I staple each week together and am ready to produce comic strips.

I get my drawing paper cut by the art store to the size I need. I use three-ply Strathmore with an eggshell finish. Within each sheet I leave about half-an-inch border. I have a template that I use to line out the actual strip size so I don't have to resort to rulers.

I look at the idea sketch and see if I can improve on it. I act it out as if I were on stage . . . How is Sarge sitting when Beetle enters, what are the expressions on their faces, how can I make it realistic, how can I make it funnier . . . the original gag sketch is constantly improved on, always looking for the best way to do it. This is a very competitive business with young people emerging every year trying to knock you out so that they can get in. So, instead of lying back and enjoying my success, I find I have to work harder just to stay alive and pay my bills.

I start my drawing with the lettering so I can see how much room I have for the drawing. I keep trying to boil down the lettering to the least number of words because people are always in a hurry and won't read the strip if it's wordy. I sketch in the balloons and block out the figures to get the best composition. I want to make everything easy to see and understand. If anything is difficult to read or see, the readers will pass you by for some strip that's more open. After I block everything in I begin to draw in earnest. I like to make a careful line rather than sketch and erase, sketch and erase. I like to try and do it right the first time. Of course, if you do it right the first time it saves a lot of time. When I feel I've got it right, I give it to my son, Greg, who then goes over my lines in ink. Then Bill Janocha, my assistant, checks both of us for quality and accuracy, then makes copies and sends them to King Features for distribution.

I have always stayed fifteen weeks ahead of my publication date because my first editor told me, "If you ever fall behind you'll spend the rest of your life trying to catch up." That scared me. I never go on a vacation without doing my work in advance and I've never fallen behind my fifteen weeks' deadline. Working so hard to build the International Museum of Cartoon Art has cut into my schedule in a tremendous way. Fund-raising, organizing, speeches, interviews, constant meetings, creating floor plans and galleries, so many things to think about and people to talk to has pushed my job to the back burner, so to speak. I almost feel guilty sneaking off to make my deadlines, but I've still kept up somehow.

I love cartooning and I love cartoonists. They both are the essence of life, dealing with our basic experiences and emotions. Most of the cartoonists I know still have the joy and excitement that children enjoy. They see things in an elemental way and help people come back to the reality of everyday living. They serve a very important function of reminding people who they really are.

—MORT WALKER

A COMIC STRIP FROM START TO FINISH

In **Figures 1–6** of *Beetle Bailey* by Mort Walker you can see the evolution of a daily comic strip. While there are many different processes for taking an idea from start to finish, it's important to note that each stage of the evolution involves a re-examination and refining of the concept.

Sgt - who took any cookies?
B - oh, you're always
      blaming me for everything?
(otto licking B's hand)
Sgt - otto helped!

Figure 1

Figure 2

Figure 3

Figure 4

Figure 5

Figure 6

Appendix I

Biographical Information of Contributors

Scott Adams, cartoonist
DILBERT
Scott Adams wears many hats and most of them fit. A resident of Dublin, California, he is the first cartoonist to put his strip on the Internet. Now available in more than 450 newspapers and four book collections, his strip *Dilbert* has been syndicated by United Feature Syndicate since 1989.

Jane Amari, managing editor of design and features
THE KANSAS CITY STAR
Jane Amari has been managing editor for design and features at the *Kansas City Star* since February 1993. Prior to that, she was managing editor of the *Daily News* of Los Angeles and the *Rockford Register Star*. Earlier in her career she held management positions at the *Philidelphia Daily News*, the *Miami Herald* and the *Detroit Free Press*. She was editor of the Los Angeles Times Syndicate.

Jane received a B.S. in communications from the University of Illinois and an M.B.A. from California State University. She teaches journalism at the University of Missouri, Kansas City, and she is second vice president on the board of directors of the Newspaper Features Council.

Jay Ambrose, editor
ROCKY MOUNTAIN NEWS
Morris (Jay) Ambrose has been the editor of the *Rocky Mountain News* since 1989. His affiliation with this paper began in 1977 when he started as a reporter. Since then, he has been an assistant city editor and editorial page editor. Jay left the *News* in 1983 to become managing editor, then editor, of the *El Paso Herald-Post*, and he returned to the *News* in 1988 as executive editor. Prior to 1977, Jay had worked for the *Winchester Sun,* the *Clay City Times* and the *Knickerbockers News.*

In 1989, Jay was elected to a three-year term as a member of the board of the American Society of Newspaper Editors, and currently he is chairman of the ASNE History Committee. Jay is a member of the

Inter-American Press Association, has been a Pulitzer Prize juror, has served on the Newspaper in Education Committee of the American Newspaper Publishers Association Foundation, and he is on the board of directors of the Newspaper Features Council.

BILL AMEND, CARTOONIST
FOXTROT

Bill Amend was born in Northampton, Massachusetts, in 1962. His childhood years were spent reading *Iron Man* comic books, watching countless episodes of *The Wild, Wild West,* and abusing his younger brothers and sister. When comic books soared to the exorbitant price of forty cents per issue, Amend began drawing his own, featuring the invincible Super Monster and his arch-enemy, the dreaded Six Gun Toad.

During this time, his family moved from state to state, finally settling in Burlingame, California. There, in high school, Amend contributed artwork to various school publications and made a number of short films, including the epic *Trek Wars,* a *Star Trek* meets *Star Wars* spoof. These projects crippled his grade point average but earned him "Most Creative" status in his senior class poll.

Amend attended Amherst College, where he absorbed himself in the school newspaper, doing among other things two editorial cartoons a week. Knowing that this would leave him little time to study, Amend decided to major in something easy. Physics seemed a good choice. Somehow he graduated with honors.

After college, Amend returned to California, where he pursued filmmaking, first as an animator and then as operations manager of a motion picture studio in San Francisco. Throughout this, he continued drawing cartoons, hoping that a syndicate would be wise enough to sign him up.

FoxTrot is syndicated by Universal Press Syndicate, and Amend currently resides nearby in a Kansas City suburb.

BRUCE BEATTIE, CARTOONIST
BEATTIE BLVD.

Bruce Beattie began his career as an editorial cartoonist while a senior at the University of Pennsylvania, cartooning for the school newspaper. He then attended the Art Center College of Design in Los Angeles, where he was formally trained in the art of cartooning. Not long after that, he became the staff editorial cartoonist for the *Daytona Beach News-Journal,* where he still works today. Many programs and periodicals feature his cartoons, including NBC's "Meet the Press," the *Washington Times,* the *New York Times,* and *Newsweek.*

While Beattie enjoyed his editorial cartooning success, he also wanted to diversify his cartooning talents, and in 1986 the Newspaper Enterprise Association launched *SNAFU,* which later became *Beattie Blvd.*

Beattie is a member of the Association of American Editorial Cartoonists, the Newspaper Features Council, and he is president of the National Cartoonists Society.

STEPHEN BENTLEY, CARTOONIST
HERB & JAMAAL

Stephen Bentley, creator of *Herb & Jamaal,* first became interested in cartooning in grade school.

"The kid who sat next to me in class drew cartoons and was very popular with the other kids," he explains. "So I begain drawing cartoons, too. Later on, I thought I might be able to do something with my cartoons besides make friends."

During a tour of duty in the navy, Bentley illustrated stories and drew comic strips for a hospital base newspaper. After the service, Bentley attended Pasadena City College, where he majored in commerical illustration and minored in English.

For the past several years, Bentley has worked in advertising and as a freelance artist, drawing cartoons and illustrations for clients such as the Los Angeles Dodgers, Wham-O Toys and *Skateboard World* magazine. He also illustrates a regular feature for *Swimming World* magazine. Bentley is a past president of the Comic Art Professional Society, a southern California–based cartoonists' organization. *Herb & Jamaal* is distributed by Tribune Media Services.

Born and raised in Los Angeles, Bentley currently lives in southern California with his wife and daughter.

STEVE CHRISTENSEN, VICE PRESIDENT AND GENERAL MANAGER
LOS ANGELES TIMES SYNDICATE

Steve Christensen is the vice president and general manager of domestic operations for the Los Angeles Times Syndicate. Prior to his appointment as general manager in 1993, he served as the syndicate's executive editor and managing editor.

Christensen joined the syndicate in 1985 following six years of work for United Press International. His UPI assignments included stints as the Pacific division news editor, based in San Francisco; Idaho state editor; and reporting for the Salt Lake City bureau.

Christensen is the secretary/treasurer for the Newspaper Features Council. He has served on the NFC board since 1992, and he talked me into writing this book.

JOSEPH D'ANGELO, PRESIDENT AND CEO
KING FEATURES SYNDICATE

Joeseph F. D'Angelo is president and chief executive officer of King Features Syndicate, a division of the Hearst Corporation.

D'Angelo joined King in 1965 and rose to the position of president in 1973. He is credited with the steady growth of the organization, which included the acquisition of two major newspaper syndicates, Cowles Syndicate and News America Syndicate. During the same period, he expanded the company's long-time ventures in television and film productions.

D'Angelo's membership in professional associations underscores his devotion and intense interest in the newspaper business. He was named to the International Museum of Cartoon Art's board of trustees. D'Angelo is president and has been a major supporter of the museum since it opened in Rye Brook, New York, in 1974. In 1989, the National Cartoonists Society named him Member of the Year, honoring his twenty-five years of service to the newspaper industry. He also serves on the board of directors of the Newspaper Features Council.

STUART DODDS, EDITOR/GENERAL MANAGER
CHRONICLE FEATURES

Since joining Chronicle Features (an affiliate of the *San Francisco Chronicle*) in 1962, Stuart Dodds has worked in all phases of newspaper syndication from stuffing envelopes to ghost-writing advice columns for a psychiatrist undergoing an attack of writer's block. Over the years, he has helped to transform a syndicate focused almost exclusively on the staff columnists of its parent newspaper into one with a more national character and a broad range of features, comics and editorial commentary.

British-born and educated, Dodds says he has always been drawn to offbeat American humor. As sales manager and more recently as editor/general manager of Chronicle Features, he has worked with some of the most innovative cartoonists of our day and given them their start in syndication.

In his spare time, Dodds enjoys cooking and writing verse in Scots dialect.

CATHY GUISEWITE, CARTOONIST
CATHY

Born in Dayton, Ohio, Cathy Guisewite left a successful career in advertising for an even more successful career in comic strip syndication.

Since its launch in 1976 from Universal Press Syndicate, Guisewite's strip *Cathy* has grown to a distribution of more than 1,200 newspapers.

In addition to her B.A. in English from the University of Michigan, Guisewite has honorary doctorates from Russell Sage College, Eastern Michigan University and Rhode Island College. She was the 1982 Los Angeles Advertising Women's Outstanding Communicator of the Year, and she received the Eleanor Roosevelt Humanities Award in 1988.

Guisewite is a member of the National Cartoonists Society and the National Organization for Women.

JOHNNY HART, CARTOONIST
B.C. AND THE WIZARD OF ID

Born in Endicott, New York, Johnny Hart leaped feet-first into syndication with *B.C.* in 1958 then *The Wizard of Id* in 1964 with Brant Parker.

Since then Hart has won the 1968 Reuben Award for Cartoonist of the Year from the National Cartoonist Society. He has also won the NCS Best Humor award twice for *B.C.* and four times for *The Wizard of Id* with Brant Parker. Both strips are currently available from Creators Syndicate.

In 1970, Johnny received the Yellow Kid Award, which named him Best Cartoonist by the International Congress of Comics in Lucca, Italy. This was the first time an American cartoonist received this award. The next year he received France's highest award, Best Cartoonist of the Year.

DAVID HENDIN, LITERARY AGENT
LITERARY ENTERPRISES

As an independent literary agent, David Hendin specializes in literary and commercial fiction and nonfiction. Hendin also represents a number of nonbook areas, especially newspaper syndication for comic strips, columns, puzzles, greeting cards, and animation/licensing properties.

From 1970 to 1982, Hendin was with United Media in a variety of roles, including syndicated columnist, science editor, special projects editor, deputy editorial director, executive editor and vice president. In 1985, he assumed the role of chief operating officer of United Media and remained there until 1993.

A graduate from the University of Missouri with a B.S. in education/biology and an M.A. in journalism, Hendin has also been a teacher, professor, and lecturer. He's a frequent writer for monthly periodicals and has written or translated eleven books.

NICOLE HOLLANDER, CARTOONIST
SYLVIA

Nicole Hollander self-syndicates her strip *Sylvia,* which appears daily and weekly in over fifty newspapers.

Hollander received her bachelor of fine arts from the University of Illinois and her master of fine arts from Boston University. She has illustrated two children's books and numerous articles for the *New York Times Book Review,* the *New York Times* Leisure Arts section, *Washington Post* magazine, *Mother Jones* and *Chicago* magazine.

There are thirteen collections of Hollander's cartoons, and she has coauthored a musical comedy for the stage.

Lynn Johnston, cartoonist
For Better or For Worse

After three years at the Vancouver School of Art, Lynn Johnston worked as a cel painter for Canawest Films, then she became a freelance illustrator and staff graphic artist. Johnston's *For Better or For Worse* debuted from Universal Press Syndicate in 1979, and it now appears in over 1,600 newspapers.

For Better or For Worse was the NCS winner for Best Newspaper Comic Strip in 1991. A winner of the Reuben for Cartoonist of the Year, Johnston became the first woman to receive this award.

A resident of North Bay, Ontario, Canada, Johnston lives far enough north for her husband, Rod, to call it home, and far enough south for her to have a courier and junk food and *malls!*

Bil Keane, cartoonist
The Family Circus

Bil Keane writes and draws the internationally syndicated cartoon *The Family Circus,* which is distributed by King Features and appears in 1,500 newspapers. For more than thirty-five years the feature has ranked high in readership polls across the nation.

There are more than fourteen million books of *The Family Circus* in print, the latest titled *What Does This Say?*

The Family Circus started in 1960. The ideas and characters were based on Keane's own family. He was a staff artist on the *Philidelphia Bulletin* for fifteen years. In 1959, he and he wife Thel moved to Paradise Valley, Arizona, with their five children. Now eight grandchildren provide a whole new generation of inspiration for the artist.

Bil became president of the National Cartoonists Society in 1981. He has won many awards, including the 1983 Reuben for Cartoonist of the Year.

Jay Kennedy, Comics Editor
King Features

Jay Kennedy has been with the King Features Syndicate Group since 1988, and he succeeded Bill Yates as comics editor the following year.

Prior to King Features, Kennedy was cartoon editor at *Esquire* magazine for five years—while at the same time acting as cartoon consultant to *People* magazine and acquiring comic panels for the fledgling *Lear's* magazine. In addition, he was guest editor in 1985 for the "European Humor" issue released by *National Lampoon.*

Before getting a sociology degree from the University of Wisconsin–Madison, Kennedy studied sculpting and conceptual art at New York's School of Visual Arts.

HANK KETCHAM, CARTOONIST
DENNIS THE MENACE
Henry (Hank) Ketcham created *Dennis the Menace* in October 1950, and it was syndicated to eighteen newspapers the following March. Today *Dennis the Menace* is distributed to more than one thousand papers in forty-eight countries by North America Syndicate, a division of King Features.

Ketcham's success has enabled him to travel extensively. He lived in Switzerland for eighteen years, where he worked on *Dennis the Menace* from a penthouse studio overlooking Lake Geneva.

Ketcham received the Billy deBeck Trophy (now called the Reuben Award) from the National Cartoonists Society as the outstanding cartoonist of 1952.

PETER KOHLSAAT, CARTOONIST
SINGLE SLICES AND THE NOOZ
Peter Kohlsaat, a dentist turned professional cartoonist, began cartooning while at the University of Minnesota dental school. Since leaving his Duluth practice in 1983 to devote full attention to art, his work has appeared regularly in more than eighty papers in his home state.

Through the Los Angeles Times Syndicate, Kohlsaat's panels *Single Slices* and *The Nooz* appear in more than a hundred papers.

A longtime Twins fan ("and boy that's tough!") who was born in 1951 in St. Paul, Kohlsaat has become expert in budget traveling as a way to escape the infamous Minnesota winters.

MELL LAZARUS, CARTOONIST
MISS PEACH AND MOMMA
Mell Lazarus is the creator of *Miss Peach* (launched in 1957 by the old New York Herald Tribune Syndicate) and *Momma* (launched in 1970 by Publishers-Hall Syndicate). Currently distributed by Creators Syndicate, these features appear in more than seven hundred newspapers.

Momma is partly based on Mell's mother, Frances. When Lazarus first showed the comic strip to his mother, she replied, "You caught Aunt Helen to a tee!"

Lazarus has written two novels, *The Boss Is Crazy, Too* and *The Neighborhood Watch,* and five television specials based on *Miss Peach.* He writes occasional newspaper articles, including two for the *New York Times* magazine.

A native of Brooklyn, New York, Lazarus has lived in Los Angeles since the 1970s. He received the 1982 Reuben Award from the NCS for Outstanding Cartoonist of the Year.

Jeff MacNelly, cartoonist
Shoe and Pluggers

Jeff MacNelly graduated from Phillips Academy in Andover, Massachusetts, in 1965. While attending the University of North Carolina, he got his start with the *Daily Tar Heel*. He joined the *Richmond News Leader* in 1970 as an editorial cartoonist, and since 1977 he has been drawing the comic strip *Shoe*, which is distributed to more than one thousand papers by Tribune Media Services.

In his dual career as a syndicated political cartoonist and as the creator of the comic strips *Shoe* and *Pluggers*, Jeff MacNelly has earned top honors in both roles.

He has been paid journalism's highest compliment three times for his political cartoons, winning the Pulitzer in 1972, 1978 and 1985. He is also a two-time recipient of the NCS Reuben Award for Outstanding Cartoonist of the Year.

When he's not plugging away at his cartoons or illustrating Dave Barry's column, MacNelly paints, sculpts, and tries to keep his 1959 DeSoto running. He lives in the Blue Ridge Mountains of Virginia with his wife, Susie, next door to a hog farm.

John McMeel, president
Universal Press Syndicate

John P. McMeel was born in 1936 in South Bend, Indiana. In 1957, he graduated with a B.S. from the University of Notre Dame.

McMeel was sales director of the Hall Syndicate from 1960 to 1967 and assistant general manager and sales director of Publishers-Hall Syndicate from 1968 to 1970.

In 1970, McMeel cofounded, with James F. Andrews, Universal Press Syndicate. Since that time he has served as the company's president and chairman of the board. In 1973, he became chairman of the board of Andrews and McMeel, the publishing affiliate of Universal Press Syndicate.

John McMeel is the father of three daughters, and he lives with his wife, Susan, in Kansas City, Missouri.

Toni Mendez, literary representative
Toni Mendez, Inc.

Toni Mendez, a life member of the Newspaper Features Council Board (previously the Newspaper Comics Council) since its inception in 1955, has provided the initial impetus and concluded many projects that have benefited the Newspaper Features Council.

Toni Mendez, literary representative and president of Toni Mendez, Inc., received the council's prestigious Jester Award in 1972 "In recognition of her untiring efforts on behalf of newspaper comics," and she received it once again in 1984 "in appreciation for outstanding contributions to promote the work of the council and its members."

WILEY MILLER, CARTOONIST
NON SEQUITUR

Wiley Miller was born in Burbank, California, in 1951. He attended high school in McLean, Virginia, and his school bus went by Bobby Kennedy's house every morning. (He always wondered what it was like inside.)

Miller was an art major at Virginia Commonwealth University, and in 1976, he became a staff artist and editorial cartoonist in North Carolina at the *Greensboro Daily News.* In 1978, he became an editorial cartoonist for the *Santa Rosa Press Democrat,* and in 1980 Copley News Service began syndicating his editorial cartoons.

In 1982, Miller created his first comic strip, *Fenton,* for North America Syndicate. He became an editorial cartoonist for the *San Francisco Examiner* in 1986, and he won several awards, including the Robert F. Kennedy Journalism Award in 1991 (so he finally got to go inside Bobby Kennedy's house).

In 1992, Wiley created the comic strip *Non Sequitur,* and it became the first strip ever to receive the National Cartoonists Society Best Comic Strip award in its first year of publication.

RICHARD NEWCOMBE, PRESIDENT AND CEO
CREATORS SYNDICATE

Richard S. Newcombe accomplished what most industry analysts considered impossible: He founded the first successful independent newspaper syndication company in two decades—only the second major independent syndicate started since the 1930s.

Prior to founding Creators Syndicate, Newcombe served as president of News America Syndicate until its sale to King Features. Before that, Newcombe served as vice president and general manager of the Los Angeles Times Syndicate from 1978 to 1984.

A Phi Beta Kappa graduate of Georgetown University, Newcombe worked as a reporter and editor at UPI for four years. He also studied at the graduate business school of the University of Chicago.

Newcombe's primary hobby is keeping fit, and he coauthored the book *The Businessman's Minutes-a-Day Guide to Shaping Up* with Dr. Franco Columbu. Newcombe lives in Brentwood, California, with his wife, Carole, an attorney, and their two children.

LEE NORDLING, CARTOONIST, WRITER
DC COMICS

A third-generation San Franciscan, Lee Nordling was born in 1952, raised a little bit south of there in Palo Alto, graduated from college a little bit south of there at San Jose State University, and worked a little bit south of there in Los Angeles as a freelance comic art packager for Mattel Toys, the art director at the Los Angeles Times Syndicate, a comic strip, children's book and comic story writer, project supervisor

---

and designer for the Walt Disney Company, and comic story writer for
Disney Adventures and *Aladdin* for Marvel Comics. Nordling narrowly
averted a career move a little bit south of there in Baja, California,
when he went to New York in 1994 and joined DC Comics as group
editor/creative services.

Nordling is a past president, vice president and board member of
the Comic Art Professional Society, a Los Angeles–based southern California organization for print cartoonists. He currently lives in Stamford,
Connecticut, with his wife, Cheri, their two dogs, Pecos and Christmas,
and three cats, New Year, Modesty and Blaise.

RON PATEL, ASSOCIATE MANAGING EDITOR/FEATURES
THE PHILADELPHIA INQUIRER

Born in Detroit, Michigan, in 1947, Ron Patel attended Wayne
State University while working as a police reporter, township reporter,
education editor, real estate writer, TV columnist, rewriteman and assistant city editor for the *Daily Tribune.* From 1969 to 1970, Patel was a
news-summary writer, humor columnist, copy editor, wire-service editor, assistant news editor and photo editor for the *Detroit News.*

In 1970, Patel joined *Newsday,* as an assistant news editor and an
assistant on the paper's first Sunday editions. In 1973, Patel became the
news editor of the *Philadelphia Inquirer.* In 1975, he was given overall
responsibility of the Sunday edition, and in 1980 he was promoted to
assistant managing editor. In 1986, he moved into the weekday operations of the paper as the managing editor for all feature sections, both
daily and Sunday.

Patel was elected an officer of the American Association of Sunday
and Feature Editors in 1980, served as president in 1983 and continues
on the executive board of the association. He is the current president of
the Newspaper Features Council and America's oldest press club, the
Pen and Pencil Club of Philadelphia.

Patel shared in the 1980 Pulitzer Prize for General Local Reporting
as one of the *Inquirer* staff who were assigned to reporting or editing
coverage of the nuclear accident at Three Mile Island.

MIKE PETERS, CARTOONIST
MOTHER GOOSE & GRIMM

Born in 1943, Mike Peters was educated in his birthplace of St.
Louis, Missouri, where he graduated from Christian Brothers College
High School in 1961. In 1965, he graduated from Washington Univer-
sity with a Bachelor of Fine Arts.

Before and after two years of military service as an artist for the U.S.
Army, Peters worked on the art staff of the *Chicago Daily News.*
Through the recommendation of cartoonist Bill Mauldin, Peters joined

the *Dayton Daily News* in 1969. His editorial cartoons were syndicated by United Feature Syndicate in 1972.

In 1984, Peters began the comic strip *Mother Goose & Grimm,* which is syndicated by Tribune Media Services to over six hundred newspapers.

Peters received the Pulitzer Prize for editorial cartooning in 1981 and the Reuben Award for Outstanding Cartoonist of the Year in 1992.

ROBERT S. REED, CHAIRMAN AND CEO
REED BRENNAN MEDIA ASSOCIATES, INC.

Robert S. Reed, who served Tribune Media Services as president, chief executive officer and chairman for twenty years before retiring in 1993, was presented the Newspaper Features Council's Jester Award "in appreciation for his sound advice and unwavering dedication to the Newspaper Features Council."

LEE SALEM, VICE PRESIDENT AND EDITORIAL DIRECTOR
UNIVERSAL PRESS SYNDICATE

Lee Salem has been with the Kansas City–based Universal Press Syndicate since 1974, when he began as an assistant editor. He has helped with or actually overseen the development of such strips and panels as *Doonesbury, Herman, Ziggy, Cathy, For Better or For Worse, Calvin and Hobbes* and *The Far Side,* as well as a number of other comic features that both newspaper editors and Universal's salespeople would rather forget.

A master's degree in English fostered a love for the prose and characterizations of Charles Dickens. That was easily transferred to an appreciation for the eccentricities of cartoonists and their creations, though perhaps not quite the dark inventiveness of a Gary Larson. What better prepared him for the world of cartoon humor, he believes, are a wife who teaches college-level mathematics and two grown children, all of whom will acknowledge only that Salem "reads comics for a living."

CHARLES SCHULZ, CARTOONIST
PEANUTS

Charles M. Schulz is well known as the creator of the daily comic strip *Peanuts,* which is read by more than one hundred million people daily in over two thousand newspapers. An entire world has been built around the *Peanuts* family, which also appears in books, films, and on countless products.

For his creative efforts, Schulz has twice won comic art's highest honor, the Reuben Award—in 1955, and again in 1964. Snoopy and Charlie Brown went to the Moon as mascots of the *Apollo 10* astronauts in 1969. In 1987, the National Cartoonists Society presented Schulz with the Gold Brick Award as he was inducted into the Cartoonists Hall of Fame.

Schulz went to Paris in January 1990, for the opening of a *Peanuts* exhibit at the Louvre honoring the fortieth anniversary of his strip. At the opening, he was named commander in the Order of Arts and Letters, France's highest award for excellence in the arts. Two years later, he received a similar award from the Italian government.

A native of Minnesota, Schulz now lives in northern California with his wife, Jeannie.

JERRY SCOTT, CARTOONIST
BABY BLUES AND *NANCY*

Jerry Scott writes and draws *Nancy*, the strip created by the late Ernie Bushmiller. *Nancy* is distributed by United Feature Syndicate.

Scott is also the writer of *Baby Blues,* a King Features–distributed strip that Scott created with his artist partner, Rick Kirkman.

Scott began drawing *Nancy* in 1983. With a diverse artistic background in cartooning, advertising and television, Scott has also drawn gag cartoons for many national magazines, including *Good Housekeeping* and the *Saturday Evening Post.*

Born in Indiana, Scott got his start in newspapers delivering the *South Bend Tribune.* He now lives in Phoenix, Arizona, with his wife.

ALAN SHEARER, GENERAL MANAGER/EDITORIAL DIRECTOR
THE WASHINGTON POST WRITERS GROUP

"My background is news," says Alan Shearer, general manager and editorial director of the Washington Post Writers Group. "I started at UPI out of college and worked there for fourteen years. I started as a copy boy and worked in six different states, going from reporter to editor to bureau chief and eventually vice president and general manager of a region."

Shearer left UPI in 1985 to become director of eastern operations for the Los Angeles Times Syndicate.

After six years, Shearer returned to his hometown to become only the second person to hold his present position at the Washington Post Writers Group.

SUE SMITH, ASSISTANT MANAGING EDITOR/LIFESTYLES
DALLAS MORNING NEWS

Sue F. Smith, currently responsible for lifestyles, joined the *Dallas Morning News* in 1991 as assistant managing editor for the Sunday paper.

Before that, she was associate editor of features at the *Denver Post* for eight years. She went to the *Post* from the *Dallas Times Herald,* where she was features editor.

Smith began her career at the Corpus Christi, Texas, *Caller-Times* in 1962 after being graduated from the University of Texas at Austin with a degree in journalism. In 1964, she went to the *Chicago Tribune,* where she spent twelve years as a writer and an editor.

She has a daughter, Jordan Meredith, who is a senior at the University of Maryland.

ANITA TOBIAS, EXECUTIVE VICE PRESIDENT
CREATORS SYNDICATE

Anita Tobias joined Creators Syndicate in February 1987—one month after the company's inception. She established and directed the company's editorial, production, sales and accounting departments. In 1989, she was promoted to the position of vice president and general manager, and in 1994 she advanced to her present position.

Prior to joining Creators Syndicate, Tobias started with Field Newspaper Syndicate in 1980, which was later sold to Rupert Murdoch and renamed News America Syndicate. At the time she left, Tobias served as manager of Select Features for News America Syndicate. In addition to negotiating the purchase of feature articles and book serializations for resale to newspapers, Tobias actively sold features to every major market in the country.

Tobias studied business administration and finance at California State University, Fullerton.

JERRY VAN AMERONGEN, CARTOONIST
BALLARD STREET

Jerry Van Amerongen, forty-six, started cartooning for his school newspaper while attending Ferris Institute in Michigan. Nearly twenty years later, he restarted with a cartoon panel for a community newspaper in Minneapolis, where he now lives. In between, he was a middle management member of corporate America, a great source for many of his ideas.

Prior to creating *Ballard Street,* which is distributed by Creators Syndicate, Van Amerongen wrote and drew *The Neighborhood,* a successful comic panel from News America Syndicate that ran in 130 newspapers.

Van Amerongen grew up in Grand Rapids, Michigan, his boyhood memories shaped by the ethnic influences in his Dutch and Polish heritage, images of roly-poly women in large print dresses and rotund men in baggy trousers. The characters in his strip are older, exaggerated versions of the people from this neighborhood.

In his spare time, Van Amerongen reads and runs and travels, catches all the movies and the art openings. But mostly, he just observes.

JOSEPH "CHIP" VISCI, DEPUTY MANAGING EDITOR/BUSINESS AND
FEATURES *DETROIT FREE PRESS*

"I'm forty-one," says Joseph "Chip" Visci, "and I wish I were thirty-nine. I have always loved comics. That was probably the first thing that got me involved in reading newspapers. I considered it a real privilege when I started at the *Free Press* and discovered I would pick them."

Visci grew up in Ohio, graduated with a degree in journalism from Ohio Wesleyan University, and continued with a masters degree in journalism from Ohio State University.

"I've been in Detroit for sixteen and a half years," says Visci, "and I love telling people I pick the comics."

Visci is on the board of directors of the Newspaper Features Council.

MORT WALKER, CARTOONIST
BEETLE BAILEY

Addison Morton Walker was born in Kansas in 1923, reared in Kansas City and graduated from the University of Missouri. In World War II he served with the U.S. Army in Italy as a first lieutenant.

Walker began selling cartoons to magazines at the age of twelve. At fifteen he was drawing a comic strip, *The Lime Juicers,* for the now defunct *Kansas City Journal.* As chief designer at the Hallmark Greeting Card Company, his earnings paid for his college education.

After the war and graduation from college, Walker moved to New York and concentrated on the magazine marketplace. Within a year he became one of the top ten magazine cartoonists in the country.

At the age of twenty-six, Walker created *Beetle Bailey* and sold it to King Features Syndicate. Three years later, he won the Reuben Award for Outstanding Cartoonist of the Year.

In 1954, Walker collaborated with cartoonist Dik Browne to produce *Hi and Lois.*

In 1961, Walker and his longtime assistant, Jerry Dumas, created *Sam's Strip,* which ran until 1963. Out of *Sam's Strip* evolved *Sam and Silo* in 1977, which is now being written and drawn by Jerry Dumas.

In 1968, Walker launched *Boner's Ark* under the pen name of Addison. It was his fifth feature for King Features, and it is now being drawn by Frank Johnson.

In 1982, Walker and Johnny Sajem created *The Evermores.*

In 1984, Walker put together Betty Boop and Felix the Cat in a strip entitled *Betty Boop.* This feature was produced by Mort's sons, Brian, Greg, Neal and Morgan.

In 1987, Walker launched another strip under the pen name of Addison for United Features Syndicate, *Gamin and Patches.*

In 1974, Mort Walker founded the Museum of Cartoon Art in Ryebrook, New York. It has been relocated to Boca Raton, Florida, and is now under construction as the International Museum of Cartoon Art.

Walker is the author of *Backstage at the Strips* and *The Lexicon of Comicana.* He has seven children children from a previous marriage, and he now lives in Stamford, Connecticut, with his wife, Catherine. His hobbies are writing, golf and photography.

BILL WATTERSON, CARTOONIST
CALVIN AND HOBBES

Bill Watterson is the two-time Reuben Award–winning cartoonist of *Calvin and Hobbes*

ROSALIE MULLER WRIGHT, ASSISTANT MANAGING EDITOR OF FEATURES *SAN FRANCISCO CHRONICLE*

Rosalie Muller Wright joined the *San Francisco Chronicle* in 1981 as feature and Sunday editor, and she was promoted to her current position in 1987. She is responsibile for producing more than ten sections of the newspaper, including the comics.

Wright was executive editor of *New West* magazine from 1977 to 1981. She began her career at *Suburban Life* magazine in Essex County, New Jersey, where she was a full-time managing editor at the age of seventeen while a full-time honors student at Montclair State College.

A graduate of Temple University, Wright was a writer, assistant managing editor and then managing editor of *Philadelphia* magazine from 1969 to 1973. In 1973, she became the founding editor of Billie Jean King's *Womensport* magazine.

Ms. Wright is a past president and current executive board member of the American Association of Feature and Sunday Editors.

Appendix II

Eight Major Newspaper Syndicate Guidelines

If you do not know a current syndicate representative who reviews blind (unsolicited) submissions, send your samples to: Comics Editor, c/o (*insert syndicate name, address*).

◆ ◆ ◆

CHRONICLE FEATURES
870 Market Street
San Francisco, California 94102
(415) 777-7212

Chronicle Features looks for ongoing features (of predetermined length and format) that will endure well into the future. We ask that your submission arrive accompanied by a stamped, self-addressed envelope of a size adequate for either the return of your materials and our response, or just our response, whichever you prefer. Please send *copies* of graphic materials, not originals. We try to get a response in the mail within thirty to forty days. We prefer that any communications regarding our response to your submission be tendered in writing.

While there are no restrictions as to subject, we already carry features in the following special-interest categories, and it is *unlikely* that we would take on new features that are similar:

Columns: Pacific Rim business, business travel, up-to-the-minute Wall Street news, home entertainment (video/audio) equipment, pet care, food and wines, singles' interests, sewing, aging.

Graphics: Editorial caricatures, business page cartoons.

Comic Strips and Panels: Please submit four weeks' worth (twenty-four strips or panels). The photocopies should show your strips or panels in standard newspaper comics page size.

◆ ◆ ◆

CREATORS SYNDICATE, INC.
5777 W. Century Blvd., Suite 700
Los Angeles, California 90045
(213) 337-7003

Thank you for considering Creators Syndicate.

Creators Syndicate distributes a great variety of continuing features (such as comics, columns and political cartoons), freelance articles, book excerpts and other materials. We are constantly on the lookout for quality features. The potential distribution for your work is enormous. It includes virtually every American newspaper that buys syndicated material, as well as other national and international publications.

We are happy to say that we receive a veritable sea of submissions every week. Because all of this must be reviewed and considered with care, please allow a *minimum* of six weeks for a response to your submission. Volume also makes it impossible to respond to every submission individually. We are therefore compelled to use rejection slips. They are, we understand, impersonal—and the last thing you want to get in the mail—but necessary to expedite the reviewing process.

Should your material be rejected, it does not necessarily mean that your work is not of adequate quality; it may simply be a matter of too much similar material already in distribution. In all, the quality of submitted material is very high. We therefore ask that you continue to submit new ideas to us. If we can possibly use the work, we will respond with all possible dispatch.

As we would like to develop a personal relationship with the artists and writers we syndicate, please include some information about yourself with your submission (résumés are fine). While having been published before is of course a great recommendation, good writing and cartooning stand on their own, and your material will be considered whether you have a cabinet full of clip or not.

Please include a stamped, self-addressed envelope with your submission, so that we may return your work to you.

If you have a cartoon or comic strip you would like us to consider, we will neeed to see at *least four (4) weeks* of samples, but *not more* than six (6) weeks of dailies and two Sundays. If you are submitting a comic strip, you should include a note about the characters in it and how they relate to each other.

As a general rule, drawings are most easily reproduced if clearly drawn in black ink on white paper, with shading executed in ink wash or Benday or other dot-transfer. However, we welcome any creative approach to a new comic strip or cartoon idea. Sundays should be colored with flat washes of gouache, keeping tone and value variances to a minimum. The fewer and bolder the colors, the better. Your name(s) and the title of the comic or cartoon should appear on every piece of artwork. If you are already syndicated elsewhere, or if someone else owns the copyright to the work, please indicate this.

Sizes for submissions vary. Most newspapers have a standard size to which they reduce work, and most syndicates circulate the work in a particular size and format. It's easiest for mailing and procession if the artwork is about standard sheet-size (8½ x 11 inches), three daily strips to a page, in the order in which they should appear. The page size, however, is not firm. Work in the size and format you are most comfortable with. But please remember, as we cannot accept responsibility for originals, work in a size you can photocopy easily and accurately.

◆ ◆ ◆

KING FEATURES SYNDICATE GROUP
235 East 45th Street
New York, New York 10017
(800) 526-KING and (212) 455-4000

King Features is always happy to look at new comic features for possible syndication. We believe in the art of cartooning and place great importance on looking at new material. Without exception, every comic strip or panel idea submitted to us is carefully considered.

In order to help you present your work in the best possible light and to help us respond to it more quickly, the editors have put together the following questions and answers.

How many cartoons should I submit?
Send twenty-four daily comic strips and four Sunday comics.
What size should I draw my comics?
Most cartoonists draw their daily comic strips 23 inches wide by 4 inches tall. They draw their Sunday comic strips in two rows one above the other, with the total area measuring 13 inches wide by 8¼ inches tall. You can draw larger or smaller than that, as long as your cartoons are in proportion to these sizes.
What format should I submit my cartoons in?
You should reduce your comics to fit onto standard 8½ x 11 inch sheets of paper. It is best to Xerox just one cartoon per page. Write your name, address, and phone number on each page. Do not send your original drawings! Send Xeroxes instead.
What else should I include in the package of cartoons that I send?
Your total submission package should include:
1) Twenty-four daily comics strips—on 8½ x 11 paper
2) Four Sunday comics strips—on 8½ x 11 paper
3) A cover letter—that briefly outlines the overall nature of your comic strip
4) A character sheet—that shows your major characters (if any) along with their names and a paragraph description of each
5) A return envelope with your name, address and postage on it— without a return envelope and postage we can't respond to your submission

6) A résumé, samples of previously published cartoons or other biographical information on your cartooning career would be helpful, but aren't strictly necessary.

What do you look for in a submission?

We are looking for comic features that will simultaneously appeal to the newspaper editors who buy comics and the newspaper readers whose interest the comic must sustain for years to follow. We don't have a formula for telling us which comics will do that, but we do look for some elements that we believe people respond to.

First, we look for a uniqueness that reflects the cartoonist's own individual slant on the world and humor. If we see that unique slant, we look to see if the cartoonist is turning his or her attention to events that other people can relate to.

Second, we very carefully study a cartoonist's writing ability. Good writing helps weak art, better than good art helps weak writing.

Good art is also important. It is what first attracts readers to a comic strip. We look to see that your art is drawn clearly and with visual impact. We want our comics to be noticed on a page.

Finally, we look for your ability to sustain a high level of quality material. We want comics that readers will enjoy for years and years.

Do I need to copyright my cartoons before sending them?

No, it's not necessary, but if you feel safer doing so, you can obtain copyright information by contacting the Copyright Office, Library of Congress, Washington, D.C. 20559 at (203) 557-8700.

What are my chances of getting syndicated by King Features?

King Features is the largest syndicate. It gets over six thousand submissions each year of which only two or three are chosen for syndication.

If I am a better writer than an artist (or vice versa), will the syndicate match me up with a partner?

If your work is far enough along that we think it would succeed if only it had a little better art or a little better writing, then the syndicate will attempt to find you a partner. In most cases, however, it is up to the cartoonist to find a partner.

How long should I expect to wait before receiving a reply?

We'll make every effort to respond quickly, but at times, it may take us as long as six weeks, due to the high volume of submissions we receive.

If my comic isn't accepted for syndication, can you still give me a critique of my work?

We receive well over six thousand submissions a year and as much as we would like to, it is impossible for us to critique all the work we see. Please understand that receiving a form rejection letter from us isn't a negative criticism of your work. It simply means that at the time we saw your work, we didn't feel that newspaper editors would buy your feature.

What are the terms of payment, if my work is accepted?

If your work is accepted for syndication, the proceeds are split fifty/fifty between the cartoonist and the syndicate. Cartoonists can make between twenty thousand and a million dollars a year. It all depends on how many newspapers subscribe to your comic strip and how many products are made from your characters. In general, syndicated cartoonists make about what any normal job would pay.

Can you give me any tips to improve my chances of success?

The single best way of improving your chances for success is to practice. Only by drawing and writing cartoons do you get better at it. Invariably, the cartoonists whose work we like best turn out to be the cartoonists who draw cartoons regularly, whether anyone sees their work or not. Another key to success is to read a lot. Humor is based on real life. The more you know about life, the more you have to write humorously about.

What are some of the common mistakes made by aspiring cartoonists?

They often place too much emphasis on coming up with a novel character or setting. A strip starring a giraffe won't get critical acclaim just because there's never been a giraffe strip before. Characterization and humor are more important.

In many cases, they develop too narrow a premise. Syndicated comics are meant to last for decades. A cartoon about a character who always falls asleep at the wrong time or talks about just one topic day after day, will quickly get repetitive and boring. Develop characters and situations that will allow you many avenues for humor in the future.

In general, aspiring cartoonists don't pay enough attention to their lettering. The words need to be lettered clear enough and large enough that readers can easily see them. There shouldn't be too much writing either. People prefer reading shorter, quicker-paced comics.

Many aspiring cartoonists don't use ink to finish their drawings. Pencil, ball point pens, and most felt-tip pens don't reproduce well enough for syndication. Aspiring cartoonists need to learn how to use pens and/or brushes and ink.

Finally, many aspiring cartoonists develop comics that are too similar to already-successful strips. A newspaper editor isn't going to duplicate a comic that he or she already prints.

Has King Features Syndicate merged with North America Syndicate?

Yes, King Features is made up of several previously independent syndicates. They include Cowles Syndicate and North America Syndicate, which was formerly called News America Syndicate.

Since your work is reviewed by the editors of all these syndicates, it is only necessary to send one copy of your proposed comic feature for consideration by King Features, Cowles and North America (News America) syndicates.

◆ ◆ ◆

LOS ANGELES TIMES SYNDICATE
218 S. Spring Street
Los Angeles, California 90012
(213) 237-5485

The Los Angeles Times Syndicate markets comics, feature articles and commentary to newspapers and magazines throughout the United States and in nearly one hundred other countries.

The syndicate is always on the lookout for new material. A committee of editors evaluates all submissions. Because our open-door policy generates thousands of submissions each year, editors do not have time to provide an individual critique of each feature found to be unsuitable. Instead, we return the submission with that unwelcome but necessary device, a rejection slip. Although the quality of submissions is quite high, a frequent cause of rejection is that the proposed feature is similar to one already on the market.

To submit your comic, *do not send original drawings.* Instead, send a cover letter and neat photocopies of twenty-four panels or strips.

If you want your material returned, enclose a stamped, self-addressed envelope. We cannot be responsible for submissions that are not accompanied by a SASE.

Send your submission to: Comics Review Committee, Los Angeles Times Syndicate, 218 S. Spring Street, Los Angeles, CA 90012.

◆ ◆ ◆

TRIBUNE MEDIA SERVICES
64 East Concord Street
Orlando, Florida 32801-1392
(800) 245-6536 and (407) 839-5600

Tribune Media Services, Inc., a wholly owned subsidiary of Tribune Company, Chicago, accepts new comic strip and panel submissions for national syndication throughout the year. For work to be considered, several guidelines are suggested.

A brief summary about the cartoon and its characters should be included with samples of the feature. The author/artist's résumé, including a list of published works, if any, is also recommended. Although a self-addressed, stamped envelope will ensure the return of a submission, it is suggested that copies, not originals, be sent.

New comic strip and panel submissions are evaluated in terms of current newspaper requirements, and candidates should allow several weeks for a reply.

◆ ◆ ◆

UNITED MEDIA
200 Park Avenue
New York, New York 10166
(800) 221-4816 and (212) 692-3700

We are looking for innovative comic features with interesting characters. There should be an idea behind your feature that allows it to be open-ended. Whatever the "staging," you need an ongoing narrative structure.

CHECKPOINTS

- Your feature must have a theme.
- Create innovative, interesting characters.
- Keep your drawings clear and easy to follow.

TECHNIQUE

Use India ink and pen or brush. Keep coverage even. Rough in lettering and balloons in nonreproducing blue pencil so that erasures will be unnecessary. Use a speedball pen for lettering. (Size of pen will depend on the size of the originals.)

Work in whatever size you find comfortable, but remember to keep your work in the right proportion for reducing to newspaper size.

MAILING YOUR SUBMISSIONS

We would like to see at least three weeks of samples so that we can judge the consistencey of your work. It is not necessary to send color Sundays with your first submission.

Do not send original artwork. Please send stats or photocopies. If we are interested in your work, we will ask you to submit more material, including originals.

Please put your name and address on the back of each piece of artwork you submit. *Include a stamped, self-addressed envelope* for the return of your material in the event that we cannot accept it. Submissions not accompanied by an SASE will *not* be returned. Do not send material that requires special handling. Please enclose an international money order if you are overseas.

Response time is two to six weeks. We regret that we cannot grant appointments prior to seeing your work.

Good luck, and we'll look forward to hearing from you.

◆ ◆ ◆

UNIVERSAL PRESS SYNDICATE
4900 Main Street
Kansas City, Missouri 64112
(800) 255-6734 and (816) 932-6600

Size requirements: Usually comic strips and panels are drawn twice the size that appears in your local newspaper. Any size is acceptable as long as it can be reduced proportionately. Strips should be reducible to 13 by 38.4 picas; panels to 24 by 19 picas.

Paper and ink cartoonists use: Some cartoonists use a quality bristol board and black India ink. Others use marker pens on chemically treated paper for their cartoons; but a consistent, *quality black line* drawing is necessary. Zipatone (or other shading sheets) is sometimes used for shading, although many cartoonists use freehand line shading. (Note that any shading tone used must be no finer than 65-line screen in the reduced size of the cartoon.)

How many cartoons should you submit? We prefer four to six weeks of samples of a proposed feature so that we can judge the quality and consistency of your work. As long as the material is clear and easy to read, it may be submitted in any form; copies or stats are preferable. Please keep your submission compact.

What compensation is paid for syndicated comic art features? It is impossible to quote specific rates paid for any feature. Rates depend on the popularity of the feature and the number and circulation of the newspapers that carry that particular feature. Generally, our contracts provide for an equal division of revenue with the creator, after deduction of production costs.

How far ahead of deadline do cartoonists work? Usually cartoonists work four weeks ahead of the release date for daily releases and eight weeks ahead of release date for Sunday releases.

What should be included with the comic strips/panels you submit? Please include a letter explaining the purpose and scope of your material. *A stamped, self-addressed envelope for the return of the material should be included.* Be sure to put your return address on both the letter you send and the submitted material.

◆ ◆ ◆

THE WASHINGTON POST WRITERS GROUP
1150 15th Street NW
Washington, D.C. 20071-9200
(800) 879-9794 and (202) 334-6375

The Washington Post Writers Group welcomes submissions from columnists, political cartoonists and comic strip artists. We review submissions on almost any topic and pay particular attention to originality. We receive upward of three thousand submissions annually and will syndicate perhaps one or two each year.

Here are some guidelines that can help you decide whether to submit your material to the Writers Group and some tips to help it get attention:

Cartoonists:

• The Writers Group is currently syndicating four comic strips and three editorial cartoonists. The market for editorial cartoonists and caricaturists is saturated as of this writing and shows no sign of opening up in the near future. Until the market changes, editorial cartoonists working for newspapers have the best chance of syndication.

• Comic strip artists should send twenty to twenty-four examples of their strip—*no original art please, photocopies are fine*—an introductory letter and a list of published credits. Enclose an SASE large enough to return all materials. Color copies are not necessary. The Writers Group looks closely at artists with experience and whose work shows polish.

• We see limited potential for new single-panel comics. Remember that a newspaper may publish anywhere from ten to fifty comic strips, but has space for only four to eight single-panel comics.

• We have little interest in games, puzzles or similar features.

You can expect a response to your submission within three weeks. If it takes longer, it may mean that your idea has passed the first screening and is getting closer scrutiny.

Appendix III

Color Indication and Sunday Format Guides

Most of the following appears courtesy of American Color.

Since the formation of Syndicate Service in 1973, American Color has continuously strived to develop better and more efficient methods for meeting the needs of their customers. They have developed new systems and equipment, and pioneered technological breakthroughs which enable them to provide both syndicates and artists with the quality which is so important to maintaining today's comic readership.

This appendix will provide you with an overview of their services, as well as descriptions and terminology used in reference to those services. Also in this appendix, you will find graphic examples relating to preparation of both art and color guides, as well as detailed descriptions for both.

Hopefully, the following information will provide you with the knowledge of how their systems work and will enhance your working relationship with them.

Glossary of Terminology

Color Chart: A numbered chart showing the exact percentages of color required to produce each color in the final printed result. By using these numbers, you indicate to American Color your choice of color for each specific area.

Color Guide: Coloring and numbering from the color chart on a photostatic copy of the keyline art. The colors are indicated in two ways: by numbering from the color chart, and by coloring with markers, pencils, dyes, or any medium comfortable to the artist. All panels should be colored and numbered. Any color guide not meeting these specifications will be completed by American Color and charged accordingly.

Color Separations: A process of creating, by computerized separations, the correct proportion of each color indicated on the color guide. These values of yellow, red (magenta) and blue (cyan) are combined with the black to create a four-color feature. The final color is viewed on color monitor (electronic proof) and compared to the color guide. To ensure the accuracy of this visual inspection, American Color cannot overly stress the importance of a clear, defined and complete color guide, eliminating interpretation by the separator. To avoid this, color guides must be *numbered and colored.*

Conversions: A realignment of the principal panels of a feature in order to achieve the various sizes required by client newspapers. This is a mechanical operation using existing separations.

Film Positives: The reverse image of a film negative that is used by certain printers, American Color included, to "build" newspaper pages according to the paper's layout. As with a negative, one is needed for each of the four colors.

Keyline Art: The original drawing, in line form, as the artist submits it for color separation. Original is preferred, however stats can be submitted providing they are clean and dark. Artists drawing with flair pens or markers should make sure they are fresh and dark. Originals produced with markers that are old lose line weight when shot on camera due to the grayness of the ink. If this occurs, additional work may be required to strengthen line weight in the black negative and will be charged accordingly.

Late Charges: Due to the amount of work that needs to be done on each strip, it is imperative that American Color receives art on time. Late charges are progressive in that the later you are the higher the charges mount. Late charges do not ensure that late art will print in all papers, it merely covers overtime costs to expedite the separations and conversions. Additional package, postage, and freight charges may be applied to expedite the feature to printers and newspapers.

Negatives: Sheets of film produced by various methods that break the color separations down into the four basic colors required: Black, Yellow, Magenta (Red), and Cyan (Blue).

Packing Slip: American Color generates a two part packaging slip. One is shipped with the proofs so the customer can check the accuracy of the order upon arrival. The other is kept for their records.

Red Keylines: Line work that is not to appear on the black plate, but used on the original art to indicate the bounds of a color fill. American Color advocates this only if the artist is very particular that the color fill is exactly to their specifications. Otherwise, color boundaries can be indicated on the color guide. At no time should red keylines intersect or touch regular black lines, as this makes it extremely difficult to eliminate these lines from the black negative, thus maintaining the integrity of the original art.

Reprint: A color proof printed on 70-pound matte finish stock using all four color plates. These are generally only made for promotional use, usually when a feature is first starting up, and is an additional cost item.

Repro Proof: Short for reproduction proof, these are proofs of each color plate, printed on black ink on a strong matte finish paper, and are shipped to newpaper clients or other printers to reproduce comics for sections they print in-house. These are shipped on a weekly basis.

Standing Order: An order to ship repro proofs to a client on a regular weekly basis.

Stop Order: An order given to American Color to discontinue shipping to a certain client on an effective issue date.

Special Order: An order given to American Color that will be used on a one-time-only basis and will only be shipped for the particular issue for which it is ordered.

FORMATS

The following formats depict available options for Sunday comic artwork. There are advantages and disadvantages to each format, and choosing the correct one for a strip depends on the size availability chosen by the syndicate, and the artistic and creative talents of the artist. Following is a recap of those formats.

Format A: Half standard—13 inches wide by 9 inches high. Converts to ½ tab, full tab, ⅓ and ¼ tab standard conversions without additional headings.

Note: Many newspapers eliminate panel one and panel two. Cartoonists often use a separate gag in this space that is not necessary to the rest of the cartoon.

Format B: Half standard—13 inches wide by 9 inches high. Converts to ½ tab, full tab, ⅓ and ¼ standard conversions. This format allows for papers to run the strip in a vertical format, allowing five features on a page instead of four. This opens up space on a page which may have been otherwise unavailable. There are two options for full tab and ¼ standard conversions.

Option 1: Drop either panel two or panel three and use title panel and remaining seven panels. This creates larger gutters between panels.

Option 2: Drop title panel and use additional header panels for full tab and ¼ standard conversions. Full tab head: One inch high by 8½ inches wide, ¼ standard head: 4¼ inches high by ¾ inches wide.

Format C: Half standard "splash"—13 inches wide by 9 inches high. Converts to ½ tab, ⅓ and ¼ standard only, no full tab. This format must be drawn so that the "gag" is in the bottom 4¼ inches of the strip, as anything above that will be cropped for the ⅓ and ¼ standards. This format requires a head measuring 4¼ inches high by ¾ inches wide for the ¼ standard. There should be ½ inch of copy on either the left or right of the strip that can be cropped to allow this title.

Format D: One-third standard—13 inches wide by 6¼ inches high. Title panel runs vertically on left of strip, ¾ inches wide by 6¼ inches high. Converts to ½ tab and ¼ standard formats with additional title panels: ½ tab—9¼ inches wide by 1¼ inches high. Quarter standard—3¾ inches wide by 4¼ inches high. This format allows total versatility of artwork as there are no panel restrictions for conversions. The entire body copy can be used as a "splash" or broken into panels at the artist's discretion.

Format E: One-third standard—13 inches wide by 5⅞ inches high. A title bar will be placed over the strip to extend height to 6¼ inches as in format D. Converts to ½ tab and ¼ standard. Half tab is converted by cropping two left-hand panels, so strip must be drawn to allow for this crop without detracting from the strip. Quarter standard is a paste-up panel, 3½ inches wide by 4¼ inches high. This format does allow the artist to have freedom within the panel(s) to the right of the cropped panels.

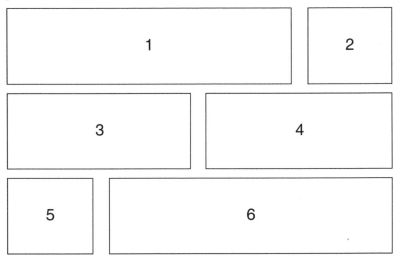

Format A: Half standard—13 inches wide by 9 inches high. Panel breaks must be positioned as shown, but individual panels can be broken into smaller panels as desired. This format allows for all conversions using existing panels.

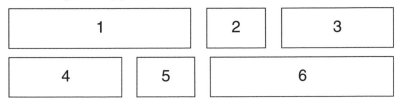

Format A: Quarter standard conversion—13 inches wide by 4¼ inches high, using all panels. Note how panel breaks allow three rows of panels to convert to two rows of panels.

Format A: Full tabloid conversion—9½ inches wide by 13 inches high. Panel breaks allow comic to be cut apart and stacked for tabloid newpapers.

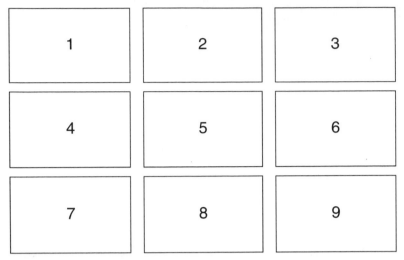

Format B: Half standard—13 inches wide by 9 inches high. Nine equal panels. Advantages: Converts easily to vertical format allowing newspapers to run five feature on a page as opposed to four.

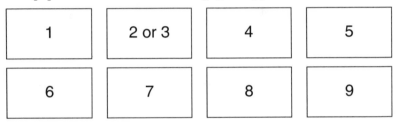

Format B: Quarter standard conversion, option 1—13 inches wide by 4¼ inches high. This creates larger gutters between panels.

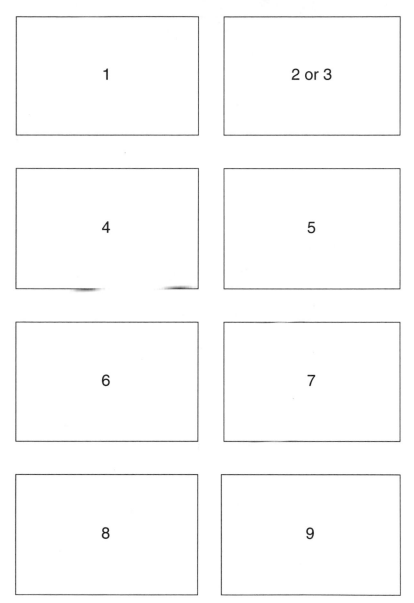

Format B: Full tabloid, option 1—8½ inches wide by 13 inches high. This creates larger gutters between panels.

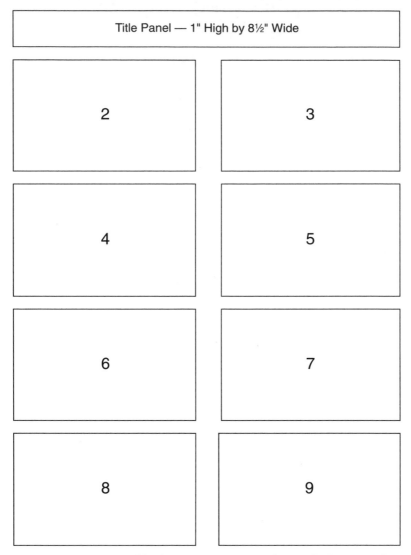

Title Panel — 1" High by 8½" Wide

2

3

4

5

6

7

8

9

Format B: Full tabloid, option 2—8½ inches wide by 13 inches high. Title panel from strip dropped and title header added. This eliminates large gutters between panels.

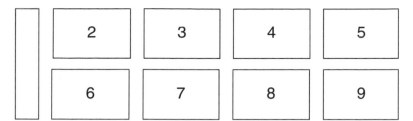

Format B: Quarter standard, option 2—13 inches wide by 4¼ inches high. Title panel is dropped and title header added: ¾ inches wide by 4¼ inches high. This eliminates large gutters between panels.

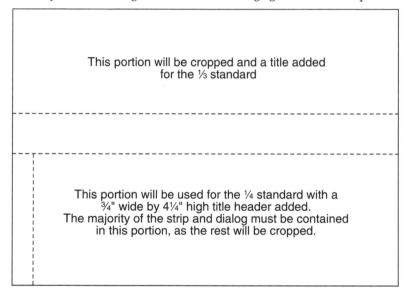

This portion will be cropped and a title added for the ⅓ standard

This portion will be used for the ¼ standard with a ¾" wide by 4¼" high title header added. The majority of the strip and dialog must be contained in this portion, as the rest will be cropped.

Format C: Half standard "splash"—13 inches wide by 9 inches high. Converts to ⅓ and ¼ standard and ½ tab. Note where strip will be cropped for these sizes.

Format D: One-third standard—13 inches wide by 6¼ inches high. Title panel applied by artist. With this format, body copy can be individual panels as shown, or one big panel. This format offers the artist the greatest amount of freedom within the strip. Title panel is ¾ inches wide by 6¼ inches high.

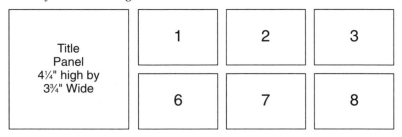

Format D: Quarter standard conversion—13 inches wide by 4¼ inches high. ⅓ standard reduced to a ⅓ tab with header panel added.

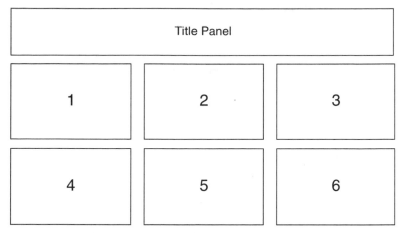

Format D: Half tabloid conversion—9¼ inches wide by 6¼ inches high. Title panel is supplied by artist and used weekly: 9¼ inches wide by 1¼ inches high.

These 2 panels will be cropped for the ½ tab

Title bar will be added to remainder of panels for ½ tabloid

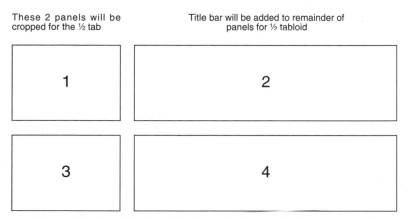

Format E: One-third standard—13 inches wide by 5⅞ inches high. A ¼ inch title bar will be added above the feature, so the depth must be shallower than format D. Panels one and three must be drawn keeping in mind that they will be cropped for the ½ tab format. Panels two and four can be drawn as a splash panel, or as any series of panels, this layout is for visual purposes only, but there has to be a break 3¾ inches from the left-hand side for the crop.

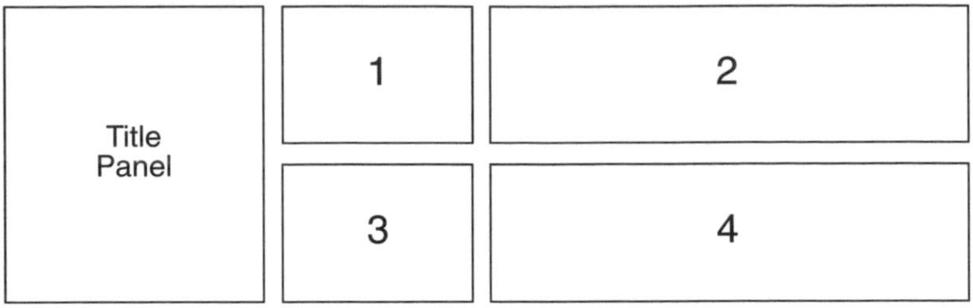

Format E: Quarter standard conversion—13 inches wide by 4¼ inches high. Title panel is provided by artist to be used weekly: 3½ inches wide by 4¼ inches high.

Size of Original Artwork

Art can be drawn at any size, provided it is proportional to the final reproduction size. If unsure as to what size to draw original art, we recommend one of the following methods:

Using the reproduction size, draw a diagonal line from corner to corner and continue outside the box. Using a square, blow up the borders to the desired size, and this will be proportionate to the final:

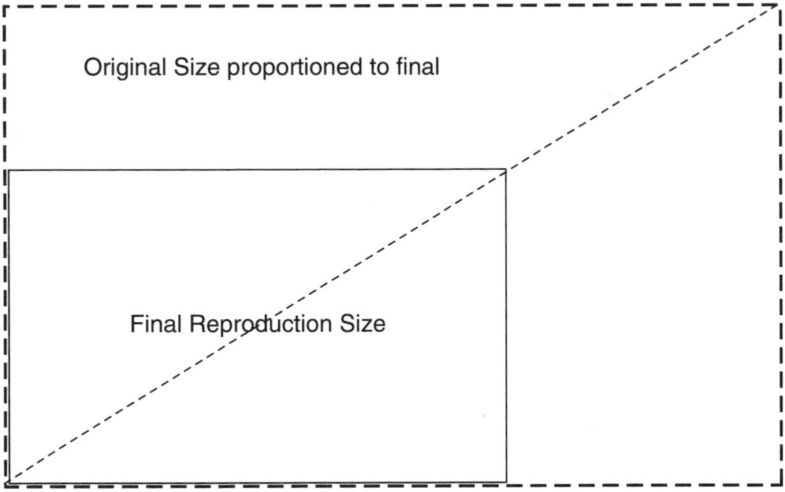

Another method is to use the following chart which is divided into half-inch increments for determining size of original.

% OF ORIGINAL	WIDTH	HEIGHT (1/2S)	HEIGHT (1/3S)	% OF ORIGINAL	WIDTH	HEIGHT (1/2S)	HEIGHT (1/3S)
100%	13"	9"	5⅞"	123%	16"	11"	7¼"
104%	13½"	9⅜"	6⅛"	127%	16½"	11⅜"	7⅜"
108%	14"	9¾"	6⅜"	130%	17"	11¾"	7⅝"
112%	14½"	10"	6 9/16"	134%	17½"	12⅛"	7⅞"
115%	15"	10⅜"	6¾"	138%	18"	12½"	8⅛"
119%	15½"	10¾"	7"	142%	18½"	12¾"	8¾"

APPENDIX IV

CARTOONIST ORGANIZATIONS

Please write to the organizations for further information about entry requirements.

Comic Art Professional Society (CAPS)
P.O. Box 1440
Burbank, California 91507

Entry requirements. Full membership—professional print cartoonist, living in southern California; Associate membership—professional print cartoonist, living outside southern California; Friends of CAPS— People in related fields or professions who are not print cartoonists.

Entry fee: Membership—$50; Friends of CAPS—$50; Associate membership (for people living outside the southern California area)—$35.

Meetings: Every second Tuesday of the month at 2006 Magnolia Boulevard, Burbank. Doors open at 7:30 P.M.; meeting begins at 8 P.M.

Membership privileges: Monthly newsletter; banquet in summer; holiday party in December.

◆ ◆ ◆

National Cartoonists Society
Regional Chapters:
Connecticut
Florida
Long Island
New England
New Jersey
New York Metro
Northern California
Ohio/Michigan
Philadelphia
Rocky Mountain
San Diego
South Central
Southeast

Southern California
Upstate New York
Washington, D.C.

For questions about membership, contact:
Wendy Little, Olson Management
4101 Lake Boone Trail, Suite 201
Raleigh, North Carolina 27607
(919) 787-5181

◆ ◆ ◆

Southern California Cartoonists Society
Jim Whiting, President
773 S. Nardo #M10
Solana Beach, California 92075
(619) 755-7449
Dick McIntire, Treasurer/Membership Director
5360 Oakleaf Pt.
San Diego, California 92124
(619) 560-6156

Entry requirements: SCCS welcomes membership to those working in the cartoon/advertising industry and who have an active interest in the cartooning field.

Dues for applicants living inside San Diego County—$20; Dues for applicants living outside San Diego County—$15.

Meetings: Second and fourth Tuesdays of each month.

Membership privileges: Monthly newsletter, *A Slice of Wry,* and periodic special events.

Appendix V

Sunday Comics Readers Survey

The following survey results appear courtesy of the Metropolitan Sunday Newspapers, Inc. Source: 1993 Belden Study, commissioned by Metropolitan Sunday Newspapers, Inc.

Methodology: Telephone interviews, based on a national, forty-eight–state, random probability sample design. Randomly selected telephone numbers included listed and unlisted telephone households.

Telephone interviews were weighted to balance properly for numbers of adults in the household as well as several known population characteristics.

There were 1,531 telephone interviews with adults. In the households where adults were initially interviewed, 284 children from 8 to 17 were also interviewed.

Interviewing was conducted between September 15 and October 16, 1992.

Adults who read the Sunday comics in the past four weeks (86,323,000)

Very Seriously Important Section for Newspapers:

- Nearly half (45 percent) of the comics readers say that the comics contribute very much to the enjoyment of the Sunday newspaper.
- Three-quarters of all comics readers say that reading comics is a good way to start people reading the newspaper.
- Close to nine out of ten comics readers (87 percent) agree that comics help children learn to read.

Top Ten List of Favorite Strips for all Adults:

Calvin & Hobbes	*Doonesbury*
Blondie	*For Better or For Worse*
Garfield	*Beetle Bailey*
The Far Side	*Family Circus*
Peanuts	*Cathy*

Lifetime Habits Begin Early:

Age Adults Started Reading the Comics	Percent Composition
Under 6 Years Old	16%
6 to 8 Years Old	38
9 to 11 Years Old	24
12 to 14 Years Old	13
15 to 17 Years Old	4
18 Years or Older	5

Demographics	Percent Composition
Age 18–24	17%
Age 25–34	25
Age 35–54	31
Age 55+	27
Any College Education	55
HHI $60,000+	21
HHI $50,000+	25
HHI $35,000+	50
Adults with Child in Household	33

Demographics	Percent Coverage (Rating)
Age 18-24	58%
Age 25-34	56
Age 55+	43
Any College Education	50
HHI $60,000+	47
HHI $50,000+	45
HHI $35,000+	46
Adults with Child in Household	42

Adults 18–34 who read the Sunday comics in the past four weeks (36,761,000)

Demographics	Percent Coverage (Rating)
Age 18–34/Child under 18	44%
Age 18–34/HHI $35,000+	49

Demographics	Percent Coverage (Rating)
Age 18–34/Child under 18	47%
Age 18–34/HHI $35,000+	57

Kids 8–17 who read the Sunday comics in the past four weeks (25,413,000)

Demographics	Percent Composition	Percent Coverage (Rating)
Boys	52%	75%
Girls	48	71
Age 8–11	44	78
Age 12–17	56	70
Age 9–14	67	73
HHI $35,000+	63	75

Thing of Value

Percent of Adults Who Agree with the Following Statements:

• "Comics help children read."	82%
• "Comics are a good way to get people to start reading the paper."	65
• "Color comics are an important part of the Sunday newspaper."	66

Top Ten List of Favorite Strips for Adults 18–34:

Garfield	*Family Circus*
Peanuts	*Marvin*
Calvin & Hobbes	*The Born Loser*
Dennis the Menace	*Cathy**
The Far Side	*Hi and Lois**
Blondie	* Tied

Ratings Winner:

Adults/Households with Children	Rating
Adults 18–35 with Kids in Household	42%
Women 18–34 with Kids in HH	47
Adults 18–24	48
Adults 25–54	58
Adults HHI $50M+	45
Adults 18–34 with HHI $35M+	57

Appendix VI

Books, Periodicals and Museums

The following bibliography comes from a variety of sources. While most of the books are still in print, many may not be and will need to be sought out at libraries and used bookstores.

Books

Becker, Stephen. *Comic Art in America.* 1959. Simon and Schuster, New York, N.Y.

Berger, Arthur Asa. *The Comic-Stripped American.* 1973. Walker & Co., New York, N.Y.

Blackbeard, Bill, and Martin Williams. *The Smithsonian Collection of Newspaper Comics.* 1977. Smithsonian Institution Press and Abrams, Washington, D.C.
   [Author's note: a book to remind a cartoonist that he's part of a great legacy.]

Borgman, Harry. *Drawing With Ink.* Watson-Guptill, New York, N.Y.

Bridgman, George B. *Book of One Hundred Hands.* 1972. Dover Books, New York, N.Y.

Bridgman, George B. *Constructive Anatomy.* 1973. Dover Books, New York, N.Y.

Bridgman, George B. *Heads, Features and Faces.* 1974. Dover Books, New York, N.Y.

Bridgman, George B. *The Human Machine: The Anatomical Structure and Mechanism of the Human Body.* 1972. Dover Books, New York, N.Y.

Card, Orson Scott. "The Finer Points of Characterization. Part I: Just How Important Are These People?" *Writers Digest.* October 1986, pp. 26–28.

Card, Orson Scott. "The Finer Points of Characterization. Part II: Creating Characters That Readers Care About." *Writers Digest.* November 1986, pp. 37–38.

Card, Orson Scott. "The Finer Points of Characterization. Part III: Making Your Characters Believable." *Writers Digest.* December 1986, pp. 32–36.

Carter, Judy. *Stand-Up Comedy: The Book.* 1989. Dell, New York, N.Y.
[*Author's note: This book contains useful guides to coining fresh gags, finding one's own comedic voice, refining and polishing gags, and so on.*]

Couperie, Pierre, et al. *A History of the Comic Strip.* 1968. Crown, New York, N.Y.

Egri, Lajos. *The Art of Dramatic Writing.* 1972. S&S Trade, New York, N.Y.

Eisner, Will. *Comics and Sequential Art.* Revised edition. 1991. Eclipse Books, Forestville, Calif.

Field, Syd. *Screenplay.* 1982. Dell Publishing/Delacourte Press, New York, N.Y.
[*Author's note: The book is good for developing a rudimentary understanding of story structure*].

Foster, Walter. *Cartoon Animation.* Walter Foster Publishing.

Fry, Phillip, and Ted Poulos. *Steranko: Graphic Narrative.* 1977. Winnipeg Art Gallery, Winnipeg, Canada.

Gill, Robert W. *Van Nostrand Reinhold Manual of Rendering With Pen and Ink.* 1974. D. Van Nostrand Co., New York, N.Y.

Giordano, Dick, with Frank McLaughlin, and John Romita. *The Illustrated Comic Art Workshop. Vol. I: The Basics.* 1982. Garco Systems, New York, N.Y.

Giordano, Dick, with Frank McLaughlin, and John Romita. *The Illustrated Comic Art Workshop. Vol. II: Penciling.* 1984. Skymarc Publications, New York, N.Y.

Glubok, Shirley. *The Art of the Comic Strip.* 1979. Macmillan, New York, N.Y.

Goulart, Ron. *The Encyclopedia of American Comics.* Promised Land/Facts On File, New York, N.Y.

Guptil, Arthur L. *Rendering in Pen and Ink.* 1976. Watson-Guptill, New York, N.Y.

Hamm, Jack. *Drawing the Head and Figure.* 1981. Grosset & Dunlap, New York, N.Y.

Hamm, Jack. *How to Draw Animals.* 1969. Grosset & Dunlap, New York, N.Y.

Hardy, Charles, and Gail Stern. *Ethnic Images in the Comics.* 1986. Balch Institute for Ethnic Studies. Philadelphia.

Harvey, Robert C. *The Art of the Funnies: an Aesthetic History.* 1994. University Press of Mississippi, Jackson, Miss.

Henning, Fritz. *Drawing & Painting with Ink.*

Hoff, Syd. *Learning To Cartoon.* 1966. Stravon Educational Press.

Hogarth, Burne. *Drawing Dynamic Hands.* 1988. Watson-Guptill, New York, N.Y.

Hogarth, Burne. *Drawing the Human Head.* 1989. Watson-Guptill, New York, N.Y.

Hogarth, Burne. *Dynamic Anatomy.* 1990. Watson-Guptill, New York, N.Y.

Hogarth, Burne. *Dynamic Figure Drawing.* 1970. Watson-Guptill, New York, N.Y.

Hogarth, Burne. *Dynamic Light and Shade.* 1991. Watson-Guptill, New York, N.Y.

Hogarth, Burne. *Dynamic Wrinkles and Drapery: Solutions for Drawing the Clothed Figure.* 1992. Watson-Guptill, New York, N.Y.

Horn, Maurice. *The World Encyclopedia of Cartoons.* 1980. Chelsea House, New York, N.Y.

Hultgren, Ken. *The Art of Animal Drawing.* 1950. McGraw-Hill Book Co., New York, N.Y.

Hurd, Jud. *To Cartooning 60 Years of Magic.* 1993. Profiles Press, Fairfield, Conn.

Inge, Thomas M. *Comics as Culture.* 1990. University Press of Mississippi, Jackson, Miss.

Loomis, Andrew. *Figure Drawing For All It's Worth.* 1982. Viking Press, New York, N.Y.

Mamet, David. *On Directing Film.* 1991. Viking Press, New York, N.Y. *[Author's note: This is a clear and concise volume on storytelling with imagery].*

McCloud, Scott. *Understanding Comics.* 1993. Tundra Publishing, Northampton, Mass.

Meglin, Nick. *The Art of Humorous Illustration.* 1973. Watson-Guptill, New York, N.Y.

Meredith, Scott. *Writing To Sell.* 1987. Harper & Row. New York, N.Y. 3rd edition.

Muybridge, Eadweard. *The Human Figure in Motion.* Dover Press, New York, N.Y.

Novak, William, and Moshe Waldoks. *The Big Book of New American Humor.* 1990. Harper Perennial, New York, N.Y. *[Author's note: This book offers a wide variety of subjects, styles, approaches and authors.]*

O'Neill, Dan, and Marian O'Neill, and Hugh D. O'Neill, Jr. *The Big Yellow Drawing Book.* 1974. Hugh O'Neill and Associates.

[Author's note: A step-by-step guide to the fundamentals for cartoonists. This book's lessons are easy to follow and absolutely essential.]

O'Sullivan, Judith. *The Great American Comic Strip: 100 Years of Cartoon Art.* 1990. Bullfinch Press: Little, Brown & Co., Boston, Mass.

Pearson, Carol S. *Awakening the Heroes Within.* 1991. HarperCollins, New York, N.Y. .

[Author's note: This book is important for understanding the protagonist.]

Reed, Walter. *The Figure: An Approach To Drawing and Construction.* 1994. Writer's Digest Books, Cincinnati, Ohio.

Richardson, John Adkins. *The Complete Book of Cartooning.* 1977. Prentice Hall.

[Author's note: A clear, detailed overview of the basics: caricature, panel layout, tools and techniques, the different kinds of strips, etc. A practical, no-nonsense guide, illustrated with strips and comic-book pages.]

Robbins, Trina, and Catherine Yronwode. *Women and the Comics.* 1985. Eclipse Books, Forestville, Calif.

Robinson, Jerry. *The Comics: An Illustrated History of the Comic Strip.* 1974. G.P. Putnam's Sons, New York, N.Y.

Society of Illustrators, The. *Humor.* Madison Square Press.

Swain, Dwight V. *Creating Characters: How To Build Story People.* 1990. Writer's Digest Books, Cincinnati, Ohio.

Thomson, Ross, and Bill Hewison. *How To Draw and Sell Cartoons.* 1985. North Light, United Kingdom.

Twain, Mark. *The Unabridged Mark Twain.* 1979. Running Press, Philadelphia, Pa.

[Author's note: The wellspring of American humor.]

Vogler, Christopher. *The Writer's Journey: Mythic Structure For Storytellers and Screenwriters.* 1992. Michael Wiese Productions, Studio City, Calif.

[Author's note: Based on the works of Joseph Campbell, this volume is vital to the understanding of mythic and character archtypes.]

Walker, Mort. *Backstage at the Strips.* 1975. Mason/Charter, New York, N.Y.

Walker, Mort, and Bill Janocha. *The National Cartoonists Society Album '88.* 1988. The National Cartoonists Society.

Waugh, Colton. *The Comics.* 1947. Macmillan, New York, N.Y.

[Author's note: With a fascinating insight into the birth of the comic strip form, this book views the origins of the comics as though it were yesterday, which it was in 1947.]

In addition to seeking out the collected works of those creators who are interviewed in this volume, please refer to the printed and cinematic works of:

Charles Addams, cartoonist
Woody Allen, comedian/humorist/filmmaker
Sergio Aragones, cartoonist
Tex Avery, animation director
Lucille Ball, comedian
Carl Barks, cartoonist
Erma Bombeck, humorist
Berkeley Breathed, cartoonist
Lenny Bruce, humorist/comedian
Carol Burnett, comedian
Al Capp, cartoonist
Milton Caniff, cartoonist
Charles Chaplin, comedian/filmmaker
John Clease, comedian/filmmaker
Roy Crane, cartoonist
Percy Crosby, cartoonist
Robert Crumb, cartoonist
Billy deBeck, cartoonist
Will Eisner, cartoonist
Jules Feiffer, cartoonist
W.C. Fields, comedian
Hal Foster, cartoonist
Friz Freleng, animation director
Rube Goldberg, cartoonist
Floyd Gottfredson, cartoonist
Chester Gould, cartoonist
Harold Gray, cartoonist
Milt Gross, cartoonist
George Herriman, cartoonist
Burne Hogarth, artist/cartoonist
Crockett Johnson, cartoonist
Chuck Jones, animation director
Buster Keaton, filmmaker
Walt Kelly, cartoonist
Harvey Kurtzman, cartoonist
Gary Larson, cartoonist
Harold Lloyd, comedian/filmmaker
The Marx Brothers, comedians
Don Martin, cartoonist
Winsor McCay, cartoonist

George McManus, cartoonist
Dan O'Neill, cartoonist
Alex Raymond, cartoonist
Will Rogers, humorist
E.C. Segar, cartoonist
Shel Silverstein, cartoonist
Cliff Sterrett, cartoonist
Garry Trudeau, cartoonist
Mark Twain, humorist
Billy Wilder, filmmaker
Gahan Wilson, cartoonist
Chic Young, cartoonist

PERIODICALS

CARTOONIST Profiles. A monthly magazine.
Jud Hurd, editor
P.O. Box 325, Fairfield, Connecticut 06430.
203-227-2542

Since 1969, this periodical has been the only major publication to concentrate solely on the contemporary creators of comic strips, comic panels and editorial cartoons. Its contents include a healthy mix of interviews, profiles and articles aimed at the professional cartoonist. A must for aspiring cartoonists.

The Comics Buyer's Guide. A weekly tabloid.
Maggie Thompson, editor
700 E. State Street, Iola, Wisconsin 54990-001
Subscription service 715-445-3775, ext. 257

While this weekly paper concentrates primarily on the activities of the comic book industry, it keeps in touch with the broad-based range of new and reprint material that sporadically includes comic strips, comic panels and editorial cartoons. This paper will open up a wonderful new world of activity to you.

The Comics Journal. A monthly magazine.
Gary Groth, editor
7563 Lake City Way NE, Seattle, Washington 98115
1-800-657-1100

The magazine of comics news and criticism. This periodical offers a wide variety of comics-related news, insights and information for the fan as well as the professional. While *The Comics Journal* focus primarily on the comic book market, it often covers stories and discusses issues that are important to all comic art forms.

Comics Relief. A monthly magazine.
Michael A. Kunz, editorial and production director
P.O. Box 6606, Eureka, California 95502
Credit card subscriptions: 1-800-298-COMIC

This periodical concentrates on reprinting recent comic strips and editorial cartoons. This may be a way to receive some of those features your local paper does not carry.

Editor and Publisher Directory of Syndicated Services.
212-675-4380.

This annual supplement to one of the July issues of *Editor and Publisher* includes a directory of all syndicated features, creators and syndicates. All the major syndicates advertise in this directory, and it presents an opportunity to see how they position themselves in the industry. Contact *Editor and Publisher* for how to order this Directory of Syndicated Services.

MUSEUMS

Cartoon Art Museum
814 Mission Street, San Francisco, California 94103
415-CAR-TOON

International Museum of Cartoon Art
201 Plaza Real, Boca Raton, Florida 33432

Ohio State University
Graphic and Photographic Arts and Research Library
Lucy Caswell, curator
Wexner Center, 27 W. 17th Avenue Mall,
Columbus, Ohio 43210-1393
614-292-0538 FAX 614-292-7859

Word and Pictures Museum of Fine Sequential Art
140 Main Street, Northampton, Massachusetts 01060